S0-AFE-914

# Guarding Your Gold II

Ronald J. Iverson

## A Consumer's Guide

*How to protect your assets and family money by insuring against the high costs of:*

*Long Term Care*

*Home Health Care*

*Medicare*

*AND understanding the contemporary problems of:*

*Retirement*

*Social Security*

*Medicare*

*Medicaid*

*Women's Issues*

*Senior Fraud and Elder Abuse*

Guarding Your Gold II
Second Edition, Copyright 2004 by Ronald J. Iverson
First Edition, Guarding Your Gold, Copyright 1999 by Ronald J. Iverson

This book is printed and published in The United States of America.

All rights reserved. No part of this book may be reproduced or transmitted in any form or by any means, electronic or mechanical, including photocopying, recording, or by any information and retrieval system, without permission in writing from the publisher, unless by a reviewer in print, or audio, who wishes to make brief reference or select quotations. Please address inquiries to the publisher, Attention: Permissions Department, MAS Marketing, 2513 Heritage, Helena, MT 59601.

Published by MAS Marketing, 2513 Heritage, Helena, MT 59601. Phone 406-442-4016

Credits:

Cover design by Jeff Lovely of Parriera Graphic Design, 1375 Mill Road, Helena, Mt. 59602
Front cover photo credit to John Reddy Photographic Design, 8 Comstock, Helena, Mt. 59601
Back cover photo credit to Frank Shone, 905 Dearborn, Helena, Mt. 59601
Page setting by Summer Kitchen Press, 314 Chaucer, Helena, Mt. 59601
Editing by Harry Smith, 419 Coventry Court, Helena, Mt. 59601

This publication is designed to provide accurate and authoritative information in regard to the subject matter covered. It is published with the understanding that the publisher and author are not engaged in rendering legal, accounting or other professional service. If legal advice or other professional advice, including financial, is required, the services of a competent professional person should be sought. -*From a Declaration of Principles, jointly adopted by a Committee of the American Bar Association and a Committee of Publishers.*

Quantity Purchases—Companies, Distributors, Professional Groups, Associations, Insurance entities and other organizations may qualify for special terms when ordering in quantity. For information, contact MAS Marketing as listed above or on our web site at http://www.guardingyourgold.com .

ISBN 0-9673193-1-5

# Guarding Your Gold II

# Contents

# CHAPTER 1
# FOREWORD

## *HOW TO USE "GUARDING YOUR GOLD II"*

A lot has happened since the original publication of "Guarding Your Gold." I have been blessed with a great deal of travel; presenting Long Term Care seminars, guest appearances, and public forums coast-to-coast and border-to-border. I have enjoyed seeing America, and have been particularly amazed at the growth, building, progress, and renewal in the cities I have visited. America and her citizens are on the move-but that move is accompanied by another factor fast appearing on the American landscape-**what to do about the demographics of an aging American public**.

As the past half-decade evolved, the need for new and vital **additional** information regarding this "old growth" public also evolved. These new perceptions have been retrieved, digested, and included in **"Guarding Your Gold II."** Much of what is written in the update centers on retirement, the extended longevity of our population, and the women's issues involving both. I have concentrated on including important statistics relative to what our nation faces as we pass into uncharted demographic waters. In a sentence-**We used to worry about dying too soon, and now we worry about living too long**. This is certain...we can throw out all the politics...we can ignore all the signs...but, **we are all in this together-young, old, middle aged...so, hang on to your hat as we approach the next three decades**.

You may want to refer only to select chapters, in order to identify with your needs for Long Term Care. There are studious people who will read the whole book, but for those of you who are just trying to familiarize yourselves (and your families) with the need for Long Term Care Insurance, and gain an understanding of the contemporary matters at hand, we can shorten the strokes. My suggestion is to get a feel for the book by **starting at the "Preface," and working your way into "The Q's and A's of LTC**." These two chapters will give you a foundation of Long Term Care in general, as well as expose you to some of the problems you (and our country) will be facing.

Since this book is really about you, **you will see yourself and your family in the next two chapters, "The Emotional Issues," and "The Inheritance and Family Money Issues," wherein you will find that if you haven't lived it yet, you will!**

The subsequent six chapters deal with **several social issues which have, and which will continue to demonstrate the need for people to protect themselves and their longevity with private insurance.** It's not very pleasant reading, but at least you will be exposed to what to expect from the real world. **"The Insurance Issues"** comprise the makeup of adequate Long Term Care Insurance policies. Please remember, there is no such thing as a "perfect purchase," but that you can do well for yourselves, by using the chapter as a platform. "***The Tax Issues***" chapter will show you how to utilize the tax benefits of LTCI, at least until further reform comes along.

"***The Financial Issues***" will give you some idea of where we were, where we are, and where we'll be going, for payment of the incredible amount of needed care about to visit us. The first of the next three chapters, "***The Caregivers Issue***" is dear to my heart, as we realize that the "Saints" and "Angels" we now have, and those we will need, ***are underpaid and under-appreciated in the tasks they perform-in less than perfect working conditions***. That chapter is followed by the unsettling, even disgusting, details found in the "***Elder Abuse***" and "***Senior Fraud***" chapters, wherein you will be alerted and enabled, to ***prepare a shield for yourself against some highly possible grief***, which can eventually descend on older people in one form or another.

Since Long Term Care may not be the solution for everyone, thankfully, there are alternatives. They can be found in the Chapters on "***The Case for Short Term Care***" and "***The Case for Home Care and Community Care***." If you are employed, you should visit with your employer and encourage them to make Group LTCI available at your worksite, as outlined in "***The Case For Group LTC Insurance***."

By all means, give yourself time to read the "***Overcoming Your Own Objections***" chapter. I'm sorry to say it, but ***delay and denial are your two worst foes***, and this chapter will help you realize the importance of acting as soon as possible to protect yourself against the problem of procrastination, ***and encourage you to "beat the clock" in these important financial and physical matters***. "***The Personal Inventory***" chapter will enable you to evaluate what you have at stake financially. I have included six pages of "***Where to Go***" for further information. You will be able to utilize these sources to further your education on current matters facing all of us.

Many people have asked me, "***Where can I find Long Term Care Insurance, and how do I find and choose a good agent?*** Use the information in "Guarding Your Gold II" as a springboard***, for your own edification, then ask a Long Term Care Insurance producer to compare products with those found in "The Short List of what to look for in Long Term Care Insurance," found at the end of "The Insurance Issues" chapter.

Above all, as you visit the book, remember its' purpose-to encourage you to look out for yourself and answer some significant questions. Like the old prospector, you found your fortune, now you'd like to keep it, and-since you can't take it with you, why not leave it for your family? You look forward to an easy retirement, but the chances are better if you are prepared for both the expected and the unexpected. And this all important item-As our nation gets older, and ***we wear out, rather than die***, we must all prepare to cope with the "blessings" of extended longevity.

***My best to you,***

***Ron Iverson***

# CHAPTER 2

# PREFACE

## *IMPORTANT TOPICS OF A GENERAL NATURE*

### DEDICATION:

This book is dedicated to *You, Mother Nature, and Father Time—In the hopes that both of them will treat You kindly.*

### TAKE THE OFFENSIVE TO PRESERVE WHAT IS YOURS:

*We have been alive in a great time. Normal, average, middle-American workers and their families have been able to create an asset base that warrants preservation for themselves and future generations.* In other words, like the old prospector, you stored your cache—make that "cash"—and now would like to protect it for your own enjoyment. *Congress has realized that "supersizing" Medicaid spending on nursing home and home health care is not possible.* That leaves you—and only you—to protect your own family money, for yourselves, and your future generations. *Just as you took measures to build your assets, you will now have to insure yourself to protect those assets.*

This book is designed to point out problems and reveal the available Long Term Care, Short Term Care, and Home Health/Community Care Insurance solutions. Which ones you choose are up to you and your family, with the assistance of your long term care insurance agent, financial planner, and accountant.

We've all heard, or said, *"My spouse or the kids will take care of me."* That's fine. *That works. For a short time.* The "sandwich generation," however, has some unsettling news for you. Nearly two-thirds of them feel they end up becoming clinically depressed.

### ON THE TITLE OF THIS BOOK:

My original thoughts centered around the theme *"Guarding Fort Knox"—because, as near as we think, that's where the gold is.* Anybody over 50 years of age can identify with Fort Knox. But then, who really knows? Think about the fact that *over SIX HUNDRED AND FIFTY BILLION dollars of the Social Security Trust Fund is supposedly safe in Treasury Bills....IOU's....in a little file cabinet in Parkersburg, West Virginia.*

### ON USING THIS BOOK AS A COMMON SENSE GUIDE:

*This book is not addressed to America's poor,* thank goodness we have a safety web already in place for those faced with care problems, and no assets or money to pay for the services. *The book is written for the average middle class American wage earner who has, or is building, a comfortable retirement and needs solutions to keep from becoming poor! You will not find endless pages of "legal boilerplate."* Long Term Care, Short Term Care, Home Health Care, Home Care and Medicare, *are not a "one size fits all" proposition.*

> *Isn't this a little bit like all of us—?*

> They asked the wealthy old gentleman how he had obtained his great fortune.

> *"By using good judgment,"* he responded.

> "How did you get good judgment?" they asked.

> *"From experience,"* he replied.

> "How did you get experience?" they asked.

> *"By using bad judgment,"* the old man replied.

## ON PROPER PLANNING AFTER PROPER BUILDING—IS THERE AN URGENCY? YES, THERE IS:

There comes a time in every American's life when a change in spending habits occurs. *While building, you probably bought what you wanted, not necessarily what you needed.*

*When preserving, you must do a "flip-flop" and buy what you need, not necessarily what you want.* With the change in spending habits, there is an item of need, which allows you a *choice in preserving what you have built—LTC insurance.* During your lifetime the "law and the lender" have seen to it that you insured your property—home, automobiles, toys, etc. How many total home losses did you incur—or total automobile losses? *The law and the lender will not be dropping by for a cup of coffee, to tell you that you must insure your assets—which could be in jeopardy of a large loss, if not a total one.* That is up to you and your family. An LTCI policy is the only alternative I know of which offers *peace of mind to both the parents and their future generations.*

When you pick up a newspaper and read of someone retiring or changing jobs, their first comment is, "I want to spend more time with my family."—spouse, children, grandchildren, etc. *Seems to me that the message is clear. Most Americans are dedicated to the welfare of their families. Why would preservation of family money and your own assets be any different?*

The old adage, *"He who hesitates is lost,"* takes on serious meaning in the world of asset preservation. *Those who may think they are going to "take it with them," or that they "will live forever," will lose more than money. What should have been family money can become a family disappointment.*

Why is it that so many people do the least, to protect that which is worth the most— their living assets? *Procrastination is the greatest excuse in the world.* People need to remember that *delay often turns into denial, due to either old age or poor health.* In short, *you can't plan your future in the future, you've got to plan it now.*

## PREPARE NOW FOR EXTENDED LONGEVITY:

Would you believe that extended longevity has taken America to a place *where four-generation families will soon outnumber two and three generation families?* Imagine the middle-aged worker and spouse who have two sets of parents and four sets of grandparents on Social Security and Medicare. Realistically that doesn't happen, but *a lot of upper end combinations already really do exist.* As a result, many people in our country find themselves with more parents than children. *Who will pay the bill for care for aging family members—an insurance company with plans available and ready—or you?* Here's a thought—if the parents or grandparents are paying their own long term care bills currently—in actuality, the children are paying them through future inheritance diminishment or total depletion. *LTCI policies, purchased by each generation, in perpetuity, can put an end to this erosion for all generations.*

## EXPLAINING LONG TERM CARE TO PROSPECTIVE CLIENTS:

Long Term Care—*The issue few people want to talk about, but to which everyone should listen—and do something about.*

Freedom. Freedom in America. We have it. We all talk about it. But what does it mean to those who are faced with the need for some type of care, perhaps for the rest of their lives? Well, the insurance industry has come up with solutions. *No longer do we have to say, "I had to put Mom in a nursing home." Modern policies allow for freedom—freedom of choice—the freedom of whether to receive needed care at home, in a community setting, or in a new assisted living facility.* So, with today's policy, the oft said *"I'm never going to a nursing home!"* can, in fact, be a reality.

We really have about three choices:

First, you can be *super rich (somebody recently said, a Millionaire isn't rich anymore, but I'd sure like to try it and see for myself),* in which case, several years of long term care costs wouldn't be a factor.

Second, you can be *poor,* in which case Medicaid will pay your nursing home care costs, *but only after you have spent down your assets and can prove impoverishment.*

Or third, you can be *an average middle-American and be insured during a time of long term care needs, and an insurance company will pay your care costs.* If the first two choices are not appropriate to your case, you still clearly have the option of the third choice.

## WHO PAYS THE NATION'S BILL FOR NURSING HOME CARE?:

First of all, *Medicare doesn't do the job.* Please accept that. *Medicare wasn't designed or ever intended as a care service, it provides for cure service payment.* True, Medicare is now picking up about 12-14 percent of nursing home bills, but they are *short stays (normally 20 days or less) and must be for "skilled care only."* How does that provide for what most Americans want and need—care at home or in an assisted living facility?

Forty-two percent of all nursing home costs are paid *out of pocket by the patient, or their adult children, or their long term care insurance policy.*

*Nearly fifty percent of nursing home costs are paid by Medicaid (welfare).* But patients must "Impoverish" themselves in order to qualify. *The indignity of becoming a pauper, in order to qualify for a government program, which is in constant jeopardy, may be more than you wish to endure.* And if you are discharged from the nursing home, *after having exhausted or transferred your resources to qualify for Medicaid, you could re-enter the outside world the same way you came into the world—with nothing.*

## THE INHERITANCE AND "NEW FAMILY MONEY" ISSUES:

*What is it about the word "inheritance" that seems to make some people regard it as a four letter word? Why would people spend a lifetime building assets and then ignore the fact that some day they will be passed on to someone, somewhere, under less than desirable circumstances? Why is this important financial aspect of some peoples' lives left undiscussed, and misunderstood, to the extent that those people, in effect, refuse to face reality?* Not talking about family money with family members, does not make important matters go away—it just delays the matters until a day when somebody outside the family finally has to make decisions which should have been taken care of previously—by family members—*and before crises control becomes the operative phrase.* The knowledge, answers and solutions to this "delay and denial" syndrome are available, but only a handful of Americans have gained an insight on how to sensibly protect themselves. *Consider this—"Inheritance" is not a four-letter word, but "lose" is.*

## THE EMOTIONAL ISSUES:

Someday, and soon, hopefully, Americans will learn to quit wrestling with attitudes about nursing homes. No. That's not a misprint. That's what I meant to say. I said *"learn to quit wrestling" with attitudes.*

In my line of work the most common statement made by people in a discussion of aging and nursing homes is, *"I'm never going to a nursing home!"* As one of my best senior agents pointed out, **that comprises about 100 percent of the people who occupy nursing homes.** We need to remember, however, that there are real people living there, real administrators struggling with logistical problems, real "saints and angels" providing care, and real dollars being spent to provide living conditions that are as comfortable as possible. **America does not need to apologize for its efforts to assist its elderly. We may, however, be apologizing for the system under which some nursing homes are forced to operate—that of "bare bones" Medicaid money and bureaucratic dependency.**

When the need for care arises, the **emotions involved affect everybody—the patient, the spouse, friends, and the family.** Everyone involved experiences a different outlook than the one that preceded it. **The emotional effect of the patient is paramount. But, not surprisingly, the emotions of the spouse and family are greatly affected,** as the questions begin—What should we do?—What is the right thing to do?—Who is going to pay for all this?—Where do we turn for help?—Could I have done things differently? **All the questions get asked, and eventually all are answered. But all emotions must be dealt with at the time.**

The LTC insurance industry can deliver some help. The companies have designed today's comprehensive policies to **allow you to stay at home for your care, or go to an assisted living facility** should you so desire—in addition to providing coverage for a nursing home, or a special care unit. There is more than only one choice.

If you haven't lived it, within your family yet, you will.

## THE LEGAL ISSUES:

The provisions of the law are in place, and are actually improving from decade to decade. **All people need to do is pay attention to them before either bad health or bad laws take over.** Between the insurance solutions, legal solutions, and **genuine tax considerations now available,** Americans have a fighting chance to maintain their assets and preserve them for their families. **Both federal and state legislators are improving the financial benefits of the purchase of LTC insurance, because they have come to realize that "government" cannot afford to take on more than what currently exists for the country's elderly long term care needs.**

## THE PROBLEMS OF EXTENDED LONGEVITY

The message is simple. **That was then, this is now—and now is twenty or thirty years longer.** Ask any elderly person what the difference between "then and now" is, and you'll get a one-word answer. "Slower." **We would like to think "slower" is the simple answer for all older people, but unfortunately, for many people, extended longevity creates a host of other problems. For example, coping with the routine of daily chores (activities of daily living), to the extent that help is needed, and suffering through cognitive problems**—the two main triggers for receiving benefits under a Long Term Care insurance policy.

## PREPARE TO PROTECT YOURSELF FROM SOME NATIONAL ATTITUDES:

During the 1990's, we saw college campus groups agitating youngsters to openly *announce that they were not going to pay for the expected demographic and economic calamity of seventy to eighty million Social Security and Medicare recipients.* However, the elderly population problem is not going to go away, it is real, the numbers don't lie, and individuals must begin now to protect themselves from the retirement and medical inflation problems *which will surface in the next decade...and the next...and the next.*

## MAKE SURE THAT YOU DON'T UNDERINSURE YOURSELF:

Americans interested in obtaining proper insurance for themselves against long term care costs must remember that *TODAY's base plan should be NO LESS than $120 per day. Please also remember that costs are considerably greater in many parts of the country, with coastal and sunbelt states running FIFTY TO ONE HUNDRED PERCENT higher.* An inflation rider should be considered necessary so that *benefits will be closer to actual charges when the policy is called upon to perform. Every reader should check the rates of nursing homes and home care in the areas in which they intend to retire.*

Strange how it is, that when I begin to get seriously interested in Long Term Care insurance, about twelve years ago, we thought of $50-60 per day of coverage as being sufficient. *Now, that figure has more than doubled for most of the country, and the demographics and inflation in health care costs indicate that 4 to 7% increases in all types of care will be the rule rather than the exception—in other words—commonplace.* No matter what measures all health care providers take, they will not be able to cope with the reality of extended longevity *compounded by a doubling of the over age 65 population.*

## THE WASTE AND FRAUD IN MEDICARE — WHY DOESN'T THE MEDIA CARE?

*"NOT ON MY WATCH"* seems to be a rather contemporary term uttered by people in positions of policy-making and control. *Why then, is it that NOBODY seems to be concerned about making hay over the waste in Medicare that has proliferated during the past decade? Moreover, why did this issue not become a major part of the new 2003 Medicare Modernization Act?*

When the Health Care Financing Administration (HCFA—now known as CMS—Centers for Medicare and Medicaid Services) announced that its auditors found *OVER FIFTY-FIVE BILLION dollars worth of fraud and overpayment in the years 1996, 1997, and 1998 in Medicare spending, the information was treated as umpteenth page news, not front-page headline news. WHAT'S GOING ON (OR RATHER WHAT'S NOT GOING ON) HERE?*

I normally buy and read three newspapers a day. When Secretary of Health and Human Services, Donna Shalala, announced on February 9, 1999, that Medicare had "IMPROVED" its improper overpayment problem to $12.1 billion in 1998, the only place I could find the information was relegated to an inside piece by a single reporter under the "Capitol Roundup" tidbit section of "USA Today". *I scoured other papers and could find no reference to this highly important matter anywhere. What gives?*

The Pentagon has certainly not been immune to criticism regarding its foolishness in fraud and overspending, nor has the Department of the Interior escaped criticism over fiscal matters. Other departments of government seem to be fair play for criticism of nearly all fiscal matters or oversights. *But Medicare overpayments, which may well have allowed a skewering of America's elderly (and American taxpayers) to the tune of $150 BILLION DURING THE LAST DECADE, seems to be off-limits to national media attention.*

When the first major recognition of overspending was announced for 1996, the $23 billion problem gained momentum in Congress, but as 1997 figures rolled around to a mere $20.3 billion, and the 1998 numbers "dwindled" to $12.3 billion, nobody in the national media even seemed to care. *And the amount of fraud and overspending doesn't seem to get any better. The General Accounting Office reported that in 2001, the Medicare overspending amount was $19 billion, "down" from the amount of $20 billion reported in 1999!*

Finally, a name was named in June of 2003, when it was actually announced that, *HCA, Inc., the nation's largest for-profit hospital chain,* had reached an agreement to settle claims in the *government's longest running Medicare fraud investigation.* Combined with previous settlements, *HCA agreed to pay a record $1.7 billion in civil and criminal penalties.* Okay, that's one—where are the rest?

I'm not saying that DHHS, CMS, or Medicare itself, has fallen asleep on this issue, *and even though they have dropped the ball, they appear to be picking it up. The Justice Department has initiated dozens of suits on Medicare money recovery, but countless lawsuits taking endless years to consummate could hinder the real process of ending this national embarrassment.*

*What aggravates me is that this money could have been used to provide prescription drug coverage to millions of retired Americans.* I have sat in the homes of Medicare aged people who can't decide whether to pay the power bill, cut back on the recommended dosage, or leave something else unpaid to pay for incredibly large prescription drug bills. *No amount of "immunization" to this peril has descended on my thinking yet.* Hopefully, (after twelve years of pressure) politicians will decide how to handle this issue *immediately after* some election, *since it always seems to be the rhetoric before an election.*

The "Medicare Issue" chapter of this book offers a call for action with some solutions as to how to combat the Medicare inefficiency, by using a simple numbers game. *A game* *that had better get played before America's baby boomers swell the Medicare numbers, and ten percent of an expected $500 billion per year program becomes a $50 billion per year problem!*

## SOMETHING THAT JUST SEEMS TO DRAG ON AND ON—THE MEDICARE DRUG DEBACLE:

Most Americans won't remember that *in 1989, and during that year only, Medicare paid for prescription drugs.* Somebody got rid of a program that truly aided and benefited the elderly. Why? *The one place where average Medicare beneficiaries could really use help is with their prescription drug needs.* But even after all the hullabaloo about helping retirees with their medication needs, through some form of Medicare assistance, early in 1999, and again in 2001, Congress and the administration, had not only dropped the ball by summer on this issue, but also refused to act on needed Social Security changes. The "window of opportunity" then, was officially closed to agreement on, and solutions to, these issues during election "off-years".

Then, in December, 2003, the *"2003 Medicare Modernization Act"* was passed, but in reality, it did little to solve the problems of prescription drug *costs for most recipients.* (See the "Medicare Issues" chapter for further details on the new medicare act.) With costs expected to be in an annual $40 billion range over a ten year period, no matter what plan is adopted, it will not solve Medicare's basic problems. *A total restructuring of Medicare will be required, because a prescription drug plan is not going to make the basic problem go away.* The basic problem, simply, is the *cost* of prescription drugs. *A national embarrassment doesn't seem to be important enough to have cured this problem for more than a decade.*

As retirees dipped further into their savings to combat $200-1,200 monthly prescription bills, the Justice Department, in late May of 1999, *fined several drug companies a combined $1.6 billion for price fixing in the area of vitamins alone. No big deal?* Well, just think about what a 25 year old would pay a year for vitamins and assorted needs *compared to what a 75 year old would spend for similar items.* Even with a price fixing fine, antitrust experts didn't foresee a drop in vitamin prices. What's going on here? Drug companies have rightfully been vilified for the last decade over the prices charged for prescriptions, which many retirees desperately need. In fact, according to USA Today, May 21, 1999, F. Hoffmann-Laroche, a Swiss firm, "was investigated and fined *$14 BILLION in March 1997 for participating in a citric acid (Vitamin C) cartel!"*

On July 24 of 2003, USA Today reported a story which started like this: "Abbott Laboratories pleaded guilty...to felony obstruction charges and agreed to pay *$600 million to settle criminal and civil charges stemming from the marketing of products used to tube-feed patients."* How much should "feeding tubes" cost normally? *Could overcharge of one item, or the "marketing of it" be an indicator of how much the American public is expected to overpay in all the areas of pharmaceutical products? Yet, no one in "the chairs" does anything to bring these prescription drug and related over-the-counter health care price problems under control. What kind of profit is being made that allows companies to pay*

*MULTI-BILLION DOLLAR FINES, and just stay in business as usual?* Do retirees have to start, let me use a phrase, *"grey wars,"* in order to make some legitimate complaints known? *It is far past the time when politicians should have solved this problem, and it's a shame that elderly Americans have to take it upon themselves to pressure their government for relief from this travesty.*

## ON MEDICAID—WHEN ARE WE GOING TO GET IT RIGHT— AND QUIT BLAMING THE NURSING HOMES?

*Let's just stop this foolishness.* I don't want to read or hear any more *"expose's"* on nursing home and home health inadequacies—*unless,* in the same article, the *journalist is willing to include the reasons for failing to give quality care.* We don't do national features on the *less-than-subsistence (minimum) wages* paid to waitresses, or hotel maids, or yard care workers, or janitors—why should we do so with nursing homes? *Didn't know about that? Read the chapters on the "Caregiver Issues" and the "Medicaid Issues" and you'll find some interesting stuff.*

## AN ITEM THAT YOU MAY OR MAY NOT AGREE WITH—BUT AT LEAST GIVE IT SOME THOUGHT

*Do not think about retirement until you are at least nearly debt free, and can continue to be so.* With the myriad problems of demographic imbalances, inflation, extended longevity, and long term health expenses surfacing, *the signs are already visible for America to be approaching the event horizon of a fiscal black hole.* Social Security, Medicare, Medicaid and pension problems, along with government overspending, are creating a budgetary crunch for the future of all Americans. *Preservation of your existing money, and your ability to deflect future financial grief, will be of utmost importance,* because social (government) dollars are going to be scarce and worse than hard-to-find.

*Retirement thoughts need serious evaluation, and "early" retirement, requires even greater "high octane," heavy-duty thinking.* Financial planners warn that expecting to drop the financial needs of your "lifestyle" to 70 percent on some magical day, is just not realistic. Also, remember that *in the scramble for retirement, you will be joined by about 76 million of your friends and neighbors, all hoping for the same fine results. Think about it.*

# CHAPTER 3

# THE Q'S AND A'S OF LTC

**Q.** **WHY SHOULD I WORRY ABOUT THE COSTS OF LONG TERM CARE— NURSING HOME, ASSISTED LIVING, AND HOME CARE?**

**A.** Like the song says: "The times, they are a'changin'." Time was when people simply went to the "old folks home", the county "rest home", or the county "poor farm." In more fortunate situations (and not so many years ago) the children moved a loved parent or grandparent in with them and everyone coped as well as they could.

*However, that may not be possible*. A simple inventory of where older parents and their children CURRENTLY LIVE will show that few older parents and their children live in the same town, let alone the same county, or even in the same state.

In addition, when we ask a "child" in her or his fifties, sixties or even their seventies to care for an older person with separate special and personal needs, *we may be asking too much*.

So, then, since America's demographics and the needs of retired people have changed, the *costs of long term care—at home, in an assisted living facility or in a nursing home—have skyrocketed,* as utilization has increased, and will double over the next three decades. *Costs*, which even ten years ago would not have financially ruined elderly people *are now a major concern of retirees and their children alike.* Those who are within fifteen or so years of retirement should also be concerned about purchasing LTC insurance while age and the likelihood of no pre-existing conditions are on their side. Another factor for the pre-retired set is the purchase of a solid base benefit amount with an inflationary rider which will mean that they will not have to shop for insurance at a time when the *costs of care will have doubled or tripled from what they are today.*

**Q.** **LONG TERM CARE INSURANCE— WHO NEEDS IT?**

**A.** *Only those who have something to lose.* If you have *"considerable" assets, (or will have), or stand to inherit such, you are a candidate for LTC insurance.* Also, those with an existing asset portfolio should consider the use of some of the interest income to protect those portfolios.

**Q.** **WHO DOESN'T NEED LTC?**

**A.** ***Those who do not have substantial assets to protect.*** Also, those who do not feel that an extended nursing home stay of at least the lowest current rate of $42,000 per year (with inflation running from 4% to 7% per year) would be a critical drain on their existing asset portfolios. A fairly good measure is $30-40,000 in eligible assets for a single adult and about twice that for marrieds. ***Short Term Care may be a better answer for those with smaller assets and is less expensive.***

Finally, LTC policies ***SHOULD NOT BE PURCHASED by people who cannot afford them.*** It is far more important to pay for basic necessities ***than to be made to feel like you should purchase LTC.*** This is the main reason for purchase at a younger and more affordable age.

**Q.** **WHY IS LONG TERM CARE SUCH A BIG ISSUE NOW? I HAVEN'T HEARD OF THIS BEING A PROBLEM IN THE PAST. DOES IT REALLY AFFECT ME?**

**A.** Current American demographics tell us that, as a nation, we are living longer. ***The simple truth is—we are not faced with the same problems we were faced with even twenty years ago.*** The numbers tell us that if you live to age 65, you will live to age 84.

In many cases***, we are seeing not only one generation on Social Security, but TWO generations.*** The likelihood of Grandma and Grandpa AND TWO sets of GREAT grandparents being retired, is already here. In other words, ***many people in this nation find themselves with more parents than children.*** Read that sentence again, it's not a misprint. ***It's a fact.*** Today's ***extended longevity,*** with even greater growth in the older population then, creates the problem.

***The greater the longevity, the greater the chances of a need for long term care, either at home or in a facility.*** As we said before, if you've assets to protect, today's LTC policies will be able to help preserve the "nest egg" for the family, rather than losing it to pay for the costs of a long term home care need or nursing home stay.

**Q.** **I HAVE HEARD THAT THE COST OF LONG TERM CARE IS EXPENSIVE. WHAT CAN I EXPECT TO PAY FOR AN ADEQUATE PLAN OF PROTECTION WITH LTC INSURANCE?**

**A.** In a manner of speaking, what you have heard was probably about right. ***Long Term Care ITSELF is expensive***, whether at home, in an assisted living facility, or in a nursing home. AND, what you have probably heard about **LTC INSUR-ANCE being expensive** was probably also right. The **reason** (for what you've heard) is that **until recently, only older people who were close to utilization of the benefits were the main purchasers of LTC insurance.**

However, that picture has changed a great deal in the last few years. Because of a number or factors, **pre-retirees**—the 50-65 market—**have recognized the economic and physical reasons for purchasing at a younger age.** And that's where we are today. Yes, the rates for the 70+ market are high, but stable, and the under 70 market is beginning to understand the total affordability of purchase at a younger age.

Long Term Care rates are much like life insurance. In other words, the **younger you are when you purchase the policy, the less the premium for the life of the insured.** To answer your question about "adequate" protection, you should first find out something about the Home Health and Home Care rates, the assisted living rates, and the nursing home rates are in your community, or one in which you intend to retire.

Because of the above considerations, we can only develop "ballpark" figures for you, but they would go something like this. With most companies, a base plan of $120 per day with a three year benefit period; for nursing home, assisted living, and 100% home health care; a ninety day elimination period (deductible); and a 5% compound inflation factor, **costs about $25-30 per month up to age 40.** The pre-retired purchaser must **remember that simple inflation will not be in their best interests, and must compare to a much more sensible 5% per year compounding inflation product.**

Pre-retireds should also consider that the $120 daily benefit (which may or may not be adequate today depending on the cost of care in your chosen location) will have little relevance in even five years and even less in ten, twenty, thirty or forty years (as the cost of care increases) unless you have chosen the value of a **compounding** inflation rider.

At age 40, the rate will be closer to $40 per month and at age 50 the insured will be looking at about $50-60 per month. (The consumer should look for a plan, which will include Home Health Care/Home and Community Care at 100% of the base benefit, and Assisted Living as well as Nursing Home Care.) A note: We have included the spousal discount, (which can run from 10-50%), but have not included group or association group discounts The rates are based on an individual rate.

Other examples are:

| | |
|---|---|
| Age 55 | $60-70 |
| Age 60 | $70-100 |
| Age 65 | $100-130 |
| Age 70 | $160-180 |
| Age 75 | $250-320 |

Age 80     $350-550
Age 85     $400-600

Remember, this amount of premium is buying you a ***"pool of money" plan*** with over $131,000 of protection for at least a three-year period, with the pool increasing either at a 5% simple or 5% compounding amount, depending on the needs of the age of the insured, which would grow to at least no less than $262,000 in twenty years. ***As you can see, the rates raise dramatically as utilization grows closer.***

Americans need to start SERIOUSLY thinking of purchasing nursing home and home health care coverage at a younger age.

**Q.     PREVIOUSLY, YOU REFERRED TO A "CONSIDERABLE AMOUNT OF ASSETS." WHAT DO YOU MEAN BY THAT?**

**A.**     Simply put, if your assets in your retirement years have appreciated (or will appreciate) to the ***$40,000 to $50,000+ range for single people, or the $80,000 to $100,000+ range for couples, you have a "considerable"*** amount of assets to protect.

**Q.     DOES THIS INCLUDE MY HOME?**

**A.**     ***Yes.***   Why would anyone who has a need for LTC insurance not include their residence as an asset?  In most cases, ***at least for those who are already retired, the paid-for home is THE principal asset.*** For pre-retirees, the retirement portfolio and expected inheritances may be considered assets, with the residence perhaps not yet paid for.  But assuming that one day it will be paid for, ***the home again becomes a huge asset when considering preservation of the entire asset portfolio.***

Before most of the states implemented Lien and Estate Recovery laws, as the result of federal legislation requiring a "tightening up" of Medicaid (Welfare) laws, ***we formerly thought of excluding the principal residence, personal property, and one automobile as "eligible" assets.***

In other words, those assets were considered "exempt" from the list of "eligible resources" which needed to be sold or "spentdown" to pay for an individual's long term care, until such time that the "eligible resources" were diminished to an amount that would make the person eligible for Medicaid assistance in paying nursing home costs.

***But that thinking changed with the Lien and Estate Recovery laws and in many cases makes no sense anymore, especially for people with assets to protect and who would be better served with an LTC policy.*** Even though the *primary residence,* personal property and an automobile are *technically exempt* from *QUALIFICATION* for Medicaid, the Lien and Estate Recovery laws can *very well turn Medicaid assistance into nothing more than a type of loan.*

As a matter of explanation, let's say that you qualify for Medicaid LEGALLY by "spending down" your ELIGIBLE assets. Then you utilize Medicaid, and receive $100,000 of Medicaid money over a two-year period. Then death pays you a visit. Depending on whether you had a "community" spouse at home, or not, *your lien may now become due and payable on the sale of the home, and recovery of Medicaid money may now be subject to a suit against your estate.* Remember that each state has it's own rules regarding Medicaid recovery.

For these reasons, *protection of the ENTIRE asset picture (including assets LEGALLY thought of as exempt), is of major importance* when considering a Long Term Care Insurance policy of long enough duration that qualification for Medicaid money is not even a factor.

Refer to the *"Personal Inventory Chapter"* and tally your Total Asset Inventory for a *true and complete picture of what you really should consider protecting.*

**Q.** **WE ARE IN OUR EARLY 50'S. WHY SHOULD WE BE THINKING ABOUT THE LONG TERM CARE PROBLEM WHEN WE ARE IN THE BUILDING STAGES OF OUR LIVES?**

**A.** The reasons are many. *The PREMIUM amounts are probably the most* important factor. However, HEALTH considerations are no less *important.* The younger you are, the less likely you are to have developed physical problems which could affect the underwriting and issuance of a policy.

*Consider the following problems as a sort of "Triple Whammy."*

*1)* The problem of *inflation in health care costs.* It is no secret that our nation has been inundated with rising health care costs for more than a decade. With the coming "Baby Boomer" generation appearing on the Senior horizon, doubling the needs of retired health care roles, is there any reason to feel that the inflation factor will not continue? *Not one.*

2) The problem of dealing with *new attained age.* LTC insurance rates are "attained age" rated. That's right, the older you are at purchase, the more you will pay than somebody younger. So, if you delay purchase, for say ten years, you now get hit with the second whammy—new attained age. *You will be looking for a greater amount of base benefit, due to inflation of care costs, at a ten year older attained age.* In other words, if the daily cost of care has doubled from $120 per day to $240 per day, you now need to purchase the larger base benefit *just to be where you could have been ten years earlier. It may look like you have only doubled the cost, but that's not true. The actual charge in ten years*

*will likely be about four times greater than by purchasing similar coverage today.* When you delay for twenty years, make that twelve to fifteen times more. Delay in its simplest form leads to a great deal of problems, of which *cost is the major consideration. Sorry about the bad news, but that's the way the first two "whammies" work.*

3)  The third whammy is the problem of *medical conditions manifesting themselves during the period you are procrastinating, delaying, and self-insuring. Self-insuring?* Yes, that's what people do when they fail to insure and "play the odds." In short, it's too late to insure the car when it's sitting at the bottom of the lake, or in the wrecking yard. It's too late to insure the house after the garage catches on fire. So, it's obviously *too late to insure the body after the stroke, or after somebody blows a stop sign and T-bones the car carrying the body, so that a two-year "stay-at-home and recover from a bad back" event is reality.* There is a phrase in the LTC industry, *"Delay often turns into denial." Procrastination and self-insuring are a very cavalier approach to something as important as family asset preservation.*

Another important factor is preparing yourself for *protection of an INHERITANCE. Isn't family money, which can be used to perpetuate the welfare and happiness of succeeding generations as important as today's needs and desires?* We will talk a lot about inheritance, from the standpoint of all generations, and it should not be taken lightly, when simple, logical, and affordable solutions such as LTC insurance are available. Remember *that "inheritance" is not a four letter word, but "lose" is. Not discussing the issue or not preparing for it should certainly not be in the family thinking in this day and age.*

**Q.  WHAT DO YOU MEAN BY THAT?**

**A.**  If you are in position to inherit a business, farm or ranch, stock portfolio, assets (liquid or non-liquid,) or any other accumulated assets, and your predecessors have not made adequate provisions for transfer or protection through an LTC policy, *you stand to lose a great deal of your birthright should they need nursing home care of a lengthy duration. THIS IS NOT AN UNREALISTIC SITUATION.* We have all heard examples of families who had to cope with the "spenddown" of their *parent's or grandparent's assets to satisfy the cost of today's nursing home stays.*

Sorry, but that's the real world.

**Q.  WHY DO WE HAVE TO PROTECT OUR ASSETS?**

**A.**  Nobody says you have to, but *after working a lifetime to accumulate a "nest egg" most people consider PRESERVATION OF THOSE ASSETS for their* *retirement and their family's benefit to be of paramount importance.*

There is more than one way to protect assets, but OBRA "93 (the tax and budget law of 1993,) and HIPAA '96 left LTC insurance as the simplest and most logical way to protect your property. A transfer to your heirs outside of a 36 month period, or to an irrevocable trust outside of a 60 month period, may qualify you for Medicaid, *but most people prefer their independence and have great concerns about giving up their property and a lifetime of savings before it is necessary.*

Another problem with transfer is that *you may not always get a choice in the transfer process.* Therefore, *an insurance policy, which protects your life earnings UNTIL TRANSFER IS LOGICAL AND POSSIBLE, provides the most sensible solution.*

**Q.    MUCH OF WHAT YOU HAVE SAID IS "SCARY." DO YOU THINK IT'S RIGHT TO ADDRESS THESE ISSUES IN SUCH A MANNER?**

A.    A fair question and one easily answered. *It depends on what you have to lose, as opposed to what you want—asset preservation, peace-of-mind—freedom of where to receive care—and protecting family money.* Since the first insurance policy was written hundreds of years ago to protect a sea-going vessel and its cargo, insurance agents have been accused of *"scare tactics." This label is normally applied by those who have nothing to lose in the first place, or who look to "the government" for solutions.*

Those WHO DO HAVE SOMETHING to lose welcome a way to protect it and are happy to have the information presented to them (and affordable solutions offered to them) for their own consideration.

In a free world where diligence and hard work are rewarded with an opportunity to enjoy some "Golden Years," *insurance protection against the hazards of outliving your good health and increased longevity is welcome.*

When *YOUR MONEY is at stake, and your family is a consideration, you deserve to be statistically informed* of the importance of protecting against unforeseen events just as you did with your property (autos, homes, etc.) in your building years. You'll find "Guarding Your Gold II" chock full of informative statistics.

For instance, you may be surprised to find that only 1 in 1,000 will suffer a total home loss. 10 in 1,000 will encounter an automobile "total." *But 400 in 1,000 will require long term care (either nursing or home care of some duration) and 700 of 1,000 will require short term nursing care.*

*"SCARY" INDEED!!!*

*So, my commitment to you is to offer the very best and latest information that I can in this volume; and let you decide for yourself* the best way to make the decisions regarding longevity, asset preservation, long term care, short term care, home health/ home and community care, Medicare, Medicaid, asset transfer, and above all, the insurance solutions to these problems.

# CHAPTER 4

# THE EMOTIONAL ISSUES

## *EVERYONE IS AFFECTED—NOT JUST THE PATIENT, EMOTIONAL PREPARATION FOR ALL IS PART OF THE SOLUTION*

## (AGING IS NATURAL—IT IS NOT A FAULT)

Someday, hopefully soon, Americans will learn to quit wrestling with attitudes about nursing homes and long term care needs. No. That's not a misprint. That's what I meant to say. I said **"learn" to quit wrestling with attitudes.** We've all been led to believe that the nursing home is the last place you go. Maybe go to recover or convalesce, or maybe just to go to and wait.

Neither of the above is quite true anymore. **Long term care includes several new and innovative options—staying at home, staying with a family member, living in an assisted living facility, utilizing adult day care, or living in a residential care community—and having the bill paid by the benefits of an insurance policy.** "Guarding Your Gold II" will identify, explore and recommend ways to achieve the economic peace-of-mind available with all these options. But, for the moment, let's talk emotional peace-of-mind.

In my line of work the most common statement made by people in a discussion of aging and nursing homes is, **"I'm never going to a nursing home!"** As one of my best senior agents pointed out, **that comprises about 100 percent of the people who occupy nursing homes.** Nobody is ever going to a nursing home. Period. At this point, then, I may as well just shut down the computer and forget this foolishness. If nobody's going to a nursing home, why write a book about it? Maybe because today's American **people don't have to go to a nursing home and can instead, utilize several of the available options.**

However, the real world tells us that there actually are such places as nursing homes. The need is there and always will be there. **In short, nursing homes do exist and they have real live people living in them**. Why then, do we have such a Neolithic attitude towards nursing homes and the reality of people being in them? Or that as a body ages—it may need assistance—at home, at the home of a child, or in a facility designed to provide such assistance?

Chapter 4

The answer can no doubt be found in many professional terminologies, in technical terms, which only confuse the average person. Let us investigate the background of this normal human misgiving in a simple, understandable fashion, as we begin to "wrestle" with changing the attitudes.

## 1) ACCEPT "CHANGE"—IT'S GOING TO HAPPEN ANYWAY

In a word, the first reason would be *"change." Alas, a word which we can do nearly nothing about.* "Change." A word which we all hate to accept, sometimes refuse to admit to, and to which we fight with all our might to adapt, or refuse to adapt. But, regardless, it's here—always has been—always will be.

What was once a cute, bright-eyed little child, became a full-grown human body with normal senses, intelligence, emotions, and physical abilities. That was change. That body developed its own personality, its own characteristics, its own attitudes, and its own capabilities. As the body grew (changed) all of those items "maxed out," or reached their full potential. *Then the body aged. Events occurred which we can credit to Father Time and Mother Nature.* Some bodies lived longer than others. Some lived so long that the personalities, characteristics, and capabilities of that body *continued* to change. Science, technology and medicine contributed to this extension of life, and the changes brought about by this life extension *contributed to additional* change. *"Change", and our ability to accept, or not accept it, then, becomes the first encounter with attitudes about "going to the nursing home."*

We've had it pretty good in America. Every decade of our existence has seen a significant growth in the life expectancy of our population. "Change." *What was then was then. What we have now is now. And "now" is twenty years longer—and is well on it's way to becoming thirty years longer!* With a different set of circumstances, we see life expectancy upon us in a different light. Can't help it. But what we haven't, to this point, been able to do is change our attitude about the extension of life expectancy. We all want longevity, but we are so accustomed to having things our way, physically and mentally, that change is not acceptable*. We want to live longer, but only on our terms, and those terms to which we are accustomed.* As human beings, we seem to be unwilling to accept the fact *that if we are going to live longer, lifestyles in the sunset years are going to change*. They have to.

Reality is the here and now, and change calls for a new awareness of understanding. Human nature hinders our ability to properly prepare our attitudes and emotions for the inevitable. *The inevitability is that if we are going to live longer, there must some changes*. That adorable little child became a strong physical specimen, then spent a "lifetime" at maximum capacity. Then we *extended that lifetime for millions of our citizens and now we refuse to accept the changes that accompany that extension.* When we have LEARNED to accept that change, we will be a mature society. The "attitude adjustment hour" is upon us.

So, then, what are the emotions, what are the problems, what are the adjustments, and what are the adaptations we will have to learn to accept as a solution to this problem?

*First, get over the attitude that the nursing home is a bad place to be. That's where we're going to be!* At least six out of ten of us will be there for some period of time, or perhaps be fortunate enough to *just require some home health care,* or choose help in an *assisted living facility.* The length of stay seems to be the real crux of the problem. *Nobody can tell somebody else how long they will be staying in a nursing home, or even if they will need home care.* If the patient is presented with a short recuperative stay following a broken bone or surgery, nobody in the family (except perhaps the patient) seems to mind, because it is only considered a temporary "skilled care" short term stay and will probably be paid for by Medicare. But this only occurs for a small percentage of long term nursing home needs. What I refer to are the *long term care needs of life-long family members who are unable to care for themselves* and, who in reality, will probably not be seeing better days ahead.

## 2)  EXPECT, <u>IDENTIFY</u>, AND DEFINE THE <u>EMOTIONS</u>—FOR <u>EVERYBODY</u> INVOLVED—AHEAD OF TIME

Second, identify and define the emotions, which precede, and accompany, nursing home confinement, or other long term care needs. With the exception of short nursing home stays, which follow medically necessary hospital confinement, several people will face an emotional involvement should the need for long term care rear its head. *Not only is the person who is facing nursing home admittance affected, but also, in all likelihood; the spouse, sons, daughters, siblings and in-laws of that person will be affected. The secret is to prepare for, and accept the emotional "heartbreak" of arriving at the decision. But do not let the decision become that of a "crisis" in development. Proper control and constant assessment are imperative.*

Third, *"reality" becomes the key word.* What are the realities of a forty, fifty, sixty, seventy or even eighty-year old caring for an aging person who has his or her own special needs? How does a spouse or a younger person cope with the ever increasing demands of the person in need? Who gets the job of caring for the loved one? *How many weeks, months, and perhaps, years pass, until the final day approaches when a decision must be made?*

Every now and then a truly gifted author appears on the scene with an excellent work on an important issue. One such person is Barbara Deane, who several years ago, after an eight-year personal experience with caregiving in her own family, made it a point to *prepare people for the emotional needs of those about to embark on a journey of personal caregiving.* Deane brings the issue of Christian concept into play with countless Biblical references, relating to real-life issues and problems. She became an expert in identifying, defining, admitting and weighing her own burdens to provide excellent paths for others to follow. Her religious convictions and concepts, used as logical explanations for the emotional problems of care-giving, relate to Divine direction, no matter what the religious affiliation. In short, Deane addresses the *changes in attitudes of all parties involved, including the impending frustrations, and helps to solve the problems of change, which accompany care-giving and care-receiving.*

One such example of personal caregiving is found in the term, *"The Sandwich generation."* The term has given simple identification to the very old *time-honored practice of intergenerational living.* Since the beginning of time, in every society in the world, parents, children and grandchildren have lived together in the same household. Nothing is unusual about that. People got married and became parents. Then older parents became grandparents and in many cases all three generations lived in the same dwelling. *In many societies this was, and is, THE way. Not always—but surely more than occasionally.*

*Americans changed that lifestyle, to a degree.* Manifest Destiny, Westward Expansion, and the settling of new frontiers all brought about a mobile society, which was different from a settled European, African, South American or Asiatic culture contained by geographic limitations. Then, industrial growth and agricultural advances in America saw families diversify even more. That period was followed by the growth of cities, spurred on by scientific and technological revolutions, which created an even greater need for people to "go where the jobs are." Terrific improvements in communication and transportation have spawned another surge in relocation, from urban areas to the "burbs," to new housing developments, even to the hinterlands.

Aging populations have chased the sun and sought an easier life in warmer climates. Recently a wave of immigration from dozens of other countries has further propelled relocation. In short then, all of these historical trends have contributed to a common factor—the breakup of intergenerational living. *Seldom does the aging parent live in the same house, let alone the same city, same county, or even the same state, as "the kids."* Think about it. Does this picture fit the generations of your family? Would a genealogical study of your heritage prove this out? Certainly. The snapshot is in place. *Geography and the trends of a mobile society seem to create havoc for aging, economics, and the traditional obligation of family "caring."*

"When Mother or Father, or Great-grandparents, are in need, who gets the call? The children. *And in about 75% of the cases, the daughter.* Now we see a family in one state taking in a loved one from another state either because of economic factors or *because of feeling responsible for elderly loved ones—the "caring" factor.* "Kids" who have their own children and jobs to contend with are caught in the middle—hence the *term "sandwich generation."*

So, how does the sandwich generation respond? After a certain amount of anxiety and concern, the "second generation" *decides to do the "right thing" and move the elderly person into their home.* Things go right—for a time. Everyone learns to cope. Everyone (with the possible exception of the toddler or teenager) understands. But above all, everyone is a part of the situation.

While the elder is able to contribute help with household chores, provide wisdom and love for the younger set, "add to the household income," and generally "pull his or her own weight," everything is copascetic. The "sandwich generation" goes on about their lives, tends to their jobs, provides income and makes arrangements for the upbringing of their own children as well as "finding things for Grandma or Grandpa to do." *Then things change. Aging is not "curable." Any number of things start to take place.*

Hearing fails, sight weakens; falling down may become frequent; short-term memory lapses occur; bathing, dressing, toileting, continence, and eating and sleeping can all become problems. *Please don't infer that I am saying all of these things take place. They won't. But individually, some of them start to show.* (Interestingly enough, experts say that these skills begin to leave the person in the reverse order in which they were learned.) The signs are there. And that's for the fortunate ones.

Everyone, all three generations, knows problems are at hand and questions arise. Now, *the second emotion surfaces—What to do? Obviously, "do the right thing".*

Doing the "right thing" is the most confusing of all the emotional factors involved in the process. A whole bunch of considerations enter the picture. That's why people need help with the definition. *The "right thing" for whom?* The right thing for the person in need of a new level of care? The right thing for those who are caught trying to figure out what to do? The right thing for the people who have been giving the care? The right thing for the people who cannot continue to give that care, either to the extent of having to quit their job or employ new caring techniques totally outside of their abilities—physical or financial? *The answer is—all of the above, and unfortunately, there is no standard answer.*

I must back up for a moment and include a much more prevalent group in this picture, *those not caught in the sandwich generation. Many more people are outside of the intergenerational living picture than are in it.* Most elderly do not live with their children for many of the reasons described above. By and large, the elderly do not want to live with their offspring. They cherish independence as much at an older age as they did when they were young. *Is it their fault that genetics and geriatrics play a part in this "game"? Of course not.* Most elderly prefer not to "be a burden" to their children or anybody. They live in their own homes, lead their own lives, "do their own thing" as long as possible. Why would we expect anything different? We don't.

For that reason, the *children of the elderly, who might be hundreds or even thousands of miles away seldom recognize the changes occurring as aging takes place.* This group is usually presented with a phone call from a spouse, family *friend or neighbor who alerts "the children" that "something has changed, something's going on, they're acting differently," or that an unfortunate event has occurred.* Then it's time for action. What do we do? What can we do? And as the question implies, what is the "right thing" to do?

The right thing usually starts with calling the siblings, if there are any. Then a meeting of the minds takes place. Then the arguments start. *After a cooling off period, everyone agrees on the "right thing."* The proper people must be contacted. Nursing homes—"What? There's a waiting list?" Medicare—"What? You mean they won't pay?" Medicaid—What? They have to 'spenddown' their assets? What do you mean

25

'Spenddown'? I've never heard of such a thing! They paid taxes all their lives! They should have something coming from the government!" The county. The state. Whover. On it goes.

***All the questions get asked. All the questions get answered. Most of the process involves unpleasant answers—from everyone.*** "Who's gonna pay for this? Why can't you take them in, you're not working (or retired)? Who's gonna do the paperwork? Who's gettin' ahold of the lawyer? Who's This? Who's that?" But after the war, after the bureaucratic maze, after all the soul searching and angst, one phrase covered it all— doing the "right thing." ***The basic drive to do the "right thing" was an emotion in action. An emotion that people must expect to encounter and accept. Nobody has ever said "We want to do the wrong thing!"*** For that reason, the right thing becomes attended to, but must be prepared for. Identification and definition of the "right thing" and accepting those responsibilities ***well in advance of them, through expectation and preparation are the keys to avoiding havoc and crises.***

The emotions can be strengths, if all the people involved are ***prepared to accept the inevitability of aging.*** Financial planning, through Long Term Care insurance policies and transfer methods are a part of the solution for those with assets to protect. ***Avoiding a battle with "family" over finances is well within the reach of every American.*** Logistical preparedness for the actual admission to a nursing home is a waiting game, which needs to be assessed, then laid aside. ***These preparations will lessen greatly the next emotion—guilt.***

## 3) GIVE IT YOUR BEST, THEN ELIMINATE "<u>GUILT</u>" WITHIN YOURSELF—AGING IS NATURAL— <u>IT</u> <u>IS</u> <u>NOT</u> A "<u>FAULT</u>"

Guilt—The third definition involved in the emotions of aging and nursing home admission consideration. The reader must remember that "guilt" is not a four-letter word. ***Guilt is a very genuine emotion***. It is all encompassing. We hear of "living with guilt," "accepting guilt," "the guilty party," "feeling guilty," "guilt feelings, " "transferring the guilt," on and on. They all mean pretty much the same thing. They are feelings, which the human nature of good people projects as conscience. ***Feeling bad or feeling "guilty" about something illustrates compassion, or sorrow, or begs for forgiveness for a deed done poorly.***

Without delving into gruesome definitions of legal or sinful guilt, suffice it to say that for our interests, guilt accompanies the actions of people who are left with no choice. ***Those who have to do something which is genuinely against their wishes, but who are powerless in the face of the alternatives. All the parties must face issues, which they find distasteful. But, by no means should the actions, which must be taken, be considered wrong. Just distasteful. Just hateful. Just miserable. But not wrong.***

When it comes to aging, the reader must keep in mind that guilt feelings abound. Remember when we said that most aging people don't want to be a burden to their children? ***Well, consider the feelings of those who have to ask for help.*** Do you suppose they feel good about being in a situation of that nature, through no wrongdoing of their own? Most elderly who must rely on their children for help, live with a guilt feeling from day one. They find it distasteful, perhaps even hateful, if the living is a problem. *But aging has nothing to do with wrongness.* It's a fact of life. The problem is that *older persons may perceive themselves as a burden and thereby develop a feeling of guilt. The caregiver may sense this emotion and should work to abate that feeling in the older person. It may take a major effort.*

Above all, the family must not entrap themselves in a feeling of "religious" or "social" guilt. More than one adult has been presented with an unknowing or ignorant friend, or congregation member, laying on the "How can you do that?" guilt trip when the quandary of "what to do with mom or dad" becomes a decision that "I've got to admit them to a nursing home."

On the other hand, many people who have provided caregiving to the elderly relate *that the recipient sometimes starts with reasonable expectations and becomes increasingly demanding.* This fosters an emotional issue for the caregiver and if not properly assessed and attended to, can "boil over" into a situation which may later cause an otherwise caring person to be saddled with additional guilt feelings. At this point the caregiver should read this predicament with occasional "gut checks" and seek some professional advice from a clergyman or counselor on coping with the all-too-common dilemma of "How far can this go—How long can things go on this way?"

*Imagine the consternation of the healthy spouse who sees change taking place in the person with whom he or she has lived a lifetime.* As the indicators start to surface, then slowly manifest themselves into problems, *the healthy spouse is caught up in a completely new way of life.* What was once routine and commonplace begins to require effort. As the physical changes occur, *the mobility and athleticism of the affected person signal deterioration and degeneration.* The "creaks and groans" of old age turn into debilities, and *the healthy spouse takes on a new role, that of caregiver.* That lasts until the caregiver finally has to sit down and call someone with the plaintive cry, "I just can't do it anymore! I'm at the end of my ability to help." *Therein lies the most crucial and heartbreaking conclusion. The emotions for both parties are rampant. Both spouses feel the anxiety, and each feels helpless. The reality of personal caregiving has reached its ultimate end.*

*Then guilt rears its ugly head.* "Could I have done things differently? Could I have been more caring? Could I have been more understanding?" The answer is very simple—"Probably not." No matter how hard one person tries to help another, there are limitations. People, through no fault of their own, begin to question themselves about their ability to continue with what becomes an unbearable situation. *The secret to kicking guilt out of one's thinking, in this regard, is to admit one's limitations.* Yes, you did the best you could have done. Yes, you worked hard to provide care and comfort. *But, no, it's not your fault. It's no one's fault. It's called aging. Acceptance of the situation, without developing self-doubts and guilt, is the key to keeping a healthy outlook on the process of aging.*

Above all, ***the greatest feeling of helplessness seems to come the day the decision must be made to admit a spouse or an older person to a nursing home. Spouses and children suffer the same feeling as the person making a residential change.*** But, if you gain nothing else from this chapter, please let me offer a valuable insight to this transition. ***The caring does not stop. The family doesn't give up—caring or hoping. Only the location of the care changes. Believe it or not, there is a bright side to this event. Mom or Dad or Grandpa or Grandma will be cared for by people trained and equipped to offer the best that money will buy***—yours, if you have a ton—the insurance company's—if you've properly prepared—or "the government's," if you are impoverished, or are willing to impoverish yourselves.

In the meantime, nursing homes have made terrific inroads in elder care. Activities, entertainment, medicine, counseling, diet and spiritual help are in place—the rule, so to speak—not an afterthought. Assisted Living facilities abound and are generally fairly new facilities, a mainstream feature of the change in elder options. And Home Care and Home Health Care appear to be the wave of the future, as insurance companies have made home living a valuable part of comprehensive Long Term Care Insurance policies

At the moment, as you ponder what I have written, think about your own situation. ***Count the blessings, and the memories. Yes, keep emotions, keep hoping, keep caring, keep thinking, keep feeling.*** But, above all—learn. Learn to change attitudes. Learn to anticipate the problems, and prepare the solutions, before the problems arise. Learn to accept change. Learn to prepare for the emotions of everyone involved. Lastly, eliminate any sense of guilt. Scratch "guilt" from your vocabulary.

# CHAPTER 5

# THE INHERITANCE AND FAMILY MONEY ISSUES

## *SOME THINGS YOU NEED TO KNOW ABOUT THE NEW AMERICAN "MONIED" CLASS—YOU'RE IT!!*

## MONEY—IT'S NOT JUST FOR THE RICH ANYMORE

***"Inheritance" is not a four-letter word. But "Lose" is.*** Remember that. If you are in a position to bequeath an inheritance, remember that. If you are in a position to inherit a birthright, remember that. Whatever you do, remember that. In my part of the country, countless tales are told of people who lost a major part of an inheritance to the costs of caring for parents or grandparents responsible for paying their own long term care bills for endless years. What would have been a ***decent inheritance evaporated in the space of time that the would-be grantors lingered in a nursing home.*** Worse yet, agricultural communities see prime farm and ranch land sold for far less than market value, in order to liquidate the holdings to pay an older person's long term care bill.

I was born in a small northern Minnesota town, in the heart of an agricultural community but I was raised in Montana farm country. My friends were farm and ranch kids. I live in a rural state. The land is composed of great expanses of acreage, some with large, flat, farm-ranch operations, some with small mom-and-pop operations, most with what we call the "family farm" or "cattle ranch, or maybe just "the place." Two generations, or even three, work to carve out a living. Thirty years ago I published a book about this land, these people, and the growth of both. I've watched it. They've lived it.

I admired both my parents greatly. They were intelligent, hard-working people, and of great inspiration to me. I'm proud of them and my family, my in-laws (thankfully no outlaws), my children and my grandchildren. I'm most proud of the accomplishments of my mother, who was an inspirational poet and had the crafty ability to write articles in a down-to-earth fashion. Most importantly, she knew how to raise a family.

My father, "Mr. Ed," an early Farmer-Labor Party leader and "died-in-the-wool FDR Democrat," inspired me with his natural instinct for fairness. He would have made a great statesman or judge. But greatest of all was his ability to instill a work ethic in me that lives today. Sometimes I didn't always see eye-to-eye with him, but he saw to it that I did, and his influence has shaped my life. As did most children in that day and age, dad started his first full-time farm hand job at age 13, in rural North Dakota. At 17, he worked in the iron mines of the famed Mesabi Range, and later settled with Mom on a family farm in Polk County, Minnesota. I saw a sale bill one time that said they sold the farm for $3,500—the equipment auction proceeds brought in another $700. Probably pretty good for that time.

## Chapter 5

We moved to the beautiful Gallatin Valley of Montana, ninety miles north of Yellowstone Park, arriving there on Columbus Day, 1945, as a better location for my Mother's sinus condition. Dad was "town cop" for several years, getting the job largely because he owned one of the two pickup trucks in town. Obviously, pickups were in short supply after the war. He became the airport manager at Gallatin Field until his retirement, and oversaw the building of jet-age runways. He got around.

Why all of this? Well, here's a chance to say something nice about my folks and I'm going to say it. Don't worry, read on and you'll see why it's important. I suspect that I'm no different than any boy growing up in the fifties, with one exception. My parents were not invested in land holdings, nor did they own commercial real estate, nor did they possess assets of a "considerable nature." They worked hard and raised a family. Mom raised a garden and had me sell carrots, onions and "whatnot" to the local grocers and restaurants. She made me start a savings account. Too bad I didn't listen. I had my first full time job in the summer of the sixth grade. I made frames for beehives down at Myer's Golden West Honey Shop. Got a cent-and-a-half for each frame and on a good day (between B-B gun and rock fights,) I could make six bucks. I was a "rich kid", self-made, or so it seemed, making as much as some adults in that day and age. My folks weren't rich, nor were they poor. We were more than comfortable; money didn't seem to be a big deal. Mom and Dad made sure that there was always plenty, and that was enough for us—investments or holdings were not a factor.

As I said before, most of my childhood friends were farm and ranch kids. They lived, and some still do, on farms that had been passed down from generation to generation several times. **Land, which at one time sold for very little, became quite valuable over the decades. It still is quite valuable.** That, in itself, would seem to be a blessing, and it was, at least until the last twenty years or so. As some of our modern problems have emerged, and farming has become an expensive gamble, **the illiquidity** of agricultural land may become a nightmare upon the death or disability of the family patriarch and matriarch. There is a lesson here.

If you have been raised in a rural setting, you've no doubt heard the phrase, **"land rich, cash poor."** If you are from a city or urban area, you may have heard of people's assets being tied up in **"bricks and steel,"** or **"house rich, cash poor,"** or of store owners and business people who had everything tied up in inventory. Worse yet, you may **see yourself** in one of the above scenarios. **The problem is one of liquidity, or more accurately, illiquidity.** Sure, lending institutions are more than happy to loan money by placing mortgages on valuable property, because they are normally very secure with that type of collateral. But, borrowing doesn't do much for the owner if the business doesn't return enough to pay the principal, interest, operating expenses and living expenses. Add to that **the possibility of a disability, or, for our purposes, a lingering long term nursing home stay, or home care need, and a new monster emerges.** How do we pay all these bills and satisfy the bank, too? All too often, the friendly neighbor down the road sees the financial strife the family is encountering and comes along to solve all the family problems by offering to buy, for say, about half the real value. Heard enough?

It's true, and *families who have been through such an ordeal can attest to the realities of such situations.*

The face of the change in America has created a huge problem. From the day and age when the elderly stayed at home with the family, or simply went to "the old folks home," or a nearby "rest home," we see a culture that expects old people to finish their "golden years" receiving care in a long term care facility, at a high cost. The problem emerges. *What to do with assets of a nature that must be passed down from one family to the next, and how do we protect those assets during the course of a lengthy long term stay.* For those who have assets of an illiquid nature, as many of my farm-ranch friends and business friends do, today's grantors and grantees have a greater generational transfer problem on their hands than did their predecessors. Too many times we hear horror stories of what happened to the family farm, or the family's inheritance, when Grandma or Grandpa had to "go to the nursing home" and the family had an illiquid asset on their hands.

Illustrating how times have changed—when normal middle-class people died, there was usually little left. Not much more than to pay the cost of funerals, final expenses, and a very modest amount of money distributed among the siblings. But, today we see a new "older" generation with some real assets to pass on, and a "younger" boomer generation waiting to inherit. Then we have the "Echo Boomers, the sons and daughters of the boomers. *Each generation, of which, must prepare for a new way of looking at financial responsibilities—primarily that of how to preserve family money.* In fact, it brings to mind bumper stickers that say: *"Money—it's not just for the rich anymore!"*

## FAMILY MONEY—A NEW EXPERIENCE FOR AVERAGE AMERICANS—LEARN HOW TO HANDLE IT.

So, we live in a new world. *Inheritance will be a major part of financial planning for many people.* This isn't just a one-time, one-shot deal. Inheritance and asset preservation will become an important part of the way of life of many families, just as it has been for the "super wealthy" of the past four hundred years of European and American and Asian history. As succeeding generations become older, then much older, and grayer, then much grayer, *they will also have to become more sophisticated in their handling of family money—money in the hands of normal, middle-American families.*

How about this for an eye-opener? In *1992,* estimates were made that around *$15 trillion would be changing hands through inheritance over the next twenty years.* Well, guess what! By *2003,* the Lincoln Financial Group compiled a study entitled, "Wealth Transfer in the 21st Century: The Perfect Financial Storm," which created an even more interesting point. Referring to a wealth simulation model developed by Paul G. Schervish, director of the Social Welfare Research Institute at Boston College, and his colleague, John Havens*, an estimated $40.6 trillion will pass on to heirs by 2052.* Then also, in February 2003, author and estate planning attorney John J. Scroggin, J.D., LLM, raised the bar even further with the statement that, "There has been an explosion of wealth in the United States. *Up to $136 trillion may be inherited in the next 50 years."*

It makes no difference which amount you may wish to choose, the facts are there, and those expecting to inherit now have some real family money to protect. *Up goes the family money for many "middle income" white- and blue-collar families.* Good news. And, *good news for those expecting an inheritance. But bad news, if* even a $300,000 estate melted down in a few short years due to long term care costs suffered by either Mom or Dad, or the family Matriarch, or Patriarch, or both

Agreed, some of the ravages of the stock market that took place in the early 2000's, were preceded by the incredible growth of the market and 401(k) type retirement portfolios of the '90's. But the "ups and downs" of the stock market have never been the only indicator of economic growth and stability in America. Land and real estate values, salaries, and nearly all other types of investment also saw growth during that period. The point is this. It appears that the family wealth figures, and expected inheritance amounts, swelled from $15 trillion spread over a twenty year period beginning in 1992, to $136 trillion over fifty years by 2003 projections. *I believe we are now talking about some serious money!*

*But, notice that I say "expected inheritance."* Those who have the $40 trill, to use the conservative number reported by Lincoln Financial Group, are also those who are getting older. As they get older we will see their numbers not only multiply from 38 million over age 65 Americans, to 78 million by 2030, but also see their health care costs inflate like we have never before seen in America. What does that mean to the $40 trillion? *In one phrase it means that, "Much of the money will be lost to health care costs of all venues." What does that mean to you? It should mean that if you are in a position to bequeath or inherit, you should be taking great measures to protect the asset base.* What sense does it make to build up a family asset, which should become an inheritance, only to have it turn out to be a family disappointment because nobody bothered to get around to *protecting against the realities of what old-age brings?*

Estate planners have long provided life insurance answers to the transfer problems, but until recently, had few solutions to the living problems. But we have them today. In the examples above, I used rural equations, because I am familiar with them, but can the problems be any different for urban people who have parents with a portfolio of stocks, bonds, CD's, real estate, or "bricks and steel?" Certainly not. *In fact, most Americans are not faced with what to do with the farm, but what to do about a portfolio invested in any of dozens of opportunities for capitalistic enterprise in this country.*

Let's talk about the current picture, that of *dealing with the family home.* While many people are faced with challenges of the nature cited above, most are simply faced with a single problem, the family home and the personal property of the elderly. *Most older Americans have their home and personal belongings paid for.* While they may only possess savings accounts or assets of a modest amount, through no effort of their own, their real estate may have appreciated at an astonishing rate. A home purchased in the

1950's for $12,000, may now be well worth $120,000 or more. Add $50,000 in personal property, $30,000 in an automobile or two, $50,000 in savings, and what seemed like a modest amount, starts to look like real money. Throw a fixed income of $1,200-1,700 per month into the mix and something seems to be out of balance. How can people possibly protect a $250,000 "nest egg" from long term care costs on $1,200-1,700 per month?

How can the children be somewhat guaranteed that their birth-right will be passed on, with the specter of any long term care stay possibly eating away at the principal amount? *Believe it or not, we have solutions.* Those solutions can be found in this chapter, as well as the chapters on insurance and retirement issues, but for now, let me continue with *the problems of the generation who will be giving and the generation who hopes to receive.*

*Both generations are caught in a single web.* The older parents want to preserve and keep as long as possible that which is rightfully theirs, and the next generation waits with breath held hoping that the "family jewels" will not have to be sold to pay for an extended long term care problem. However, there are some pervading social and emotional issues, which must be discussed at this point.

What is it about the word "inheritance" that seems to make people regard it as a four letter word? *Why would people spend a lifetime building assets and then ignore the fact that some day they will be passed on to someone, somewhere, perhaps under less than desirable circumstances?* Why is this important aspect of people's lives left undiscussed and misunderstood to the extent that they refuse to face reality? *The reality of death. The reality of preparing for death. The reality of preparing for a continuum of home care, assisted living, and a possible long term care stay in a nursing home. The reality of becoming incapacitated. The reality of aging and "passing down the farm."*

*The answers and solutions are available as to how to sensibly protect, transfer, or dispose of them.* Does the patriarch, or matriarch rule the family and its future with an "iron fist?" Does the potential inheritor have to wait and wonder what is going to take place that he or she is unable to control? Do Grandma and Grandpa really believe that by not discussing the real world, it will go away? Do they think they are going to "take it with them?" Do we all just wait and see? *Does an inheritance have to be lost because no one wanted to discuss how to prevent a nursing home bill from becoming a meltdown?* Does proper planning take a back seat to probate courts deciding who gets what? Does the state become responsible for decisions that should have been made by the family? Does the idea of death or disability create such an image in our society that discussing and preparing for it take a back seat to Neolithic emotion? *Does the bumper sticker that reads, "We're Spending our Children's Inheritance," suddenly seem a lot less funny?*

When an accountant, long term care insurance agent, financial advisor or life insurance agent discusses these matters with clients it seems that the first thing they must overcome is an invisible emotional barrier which seems to say, *"I know you're right, but I don't want to talk about it."* I counter this mysterious aura with a simple statement, "Bill, buying this policy won't make you live one day longer, or die one day earlier, or send you to a nursing home. Preparing now for an event in the future won't keep one from happening, nor cause one to occur. But, in the meantime, you can transfer this risk to my company, and have the peace of mind that you've provided a solution to your problem. Please remember that delay often turns into denial."

From time to time, I am made aware of incidents of real life, which nearly overwhelm me. Not too many summers ago, I gave a group Long Term Care sales presentation for an agent in the Seattle area. *The meeting was held at a pretty fancy nursing home, with some pretty fancy children of the residents of the nursing home.* I enjoyed the group and the setting. Having given nearly fifty seminars throughout the nation in the past few years, I was rambling on about the costs of nursing homes and long term care and using the then current $120 per day figure for Montana. The nursing home administrator reminded me that their charge was more in the neighborhood of *$200 per day.* Gulp. Think fast. Think on your feet, Ron! So, I immediately "finessed" it and switched gears to relatively higher numbers. Nice group, no lynching occurred.

At the end of the presentation, a local banker, Vice President of a banking chain in Washington, and on the Board of Directors of the nursing home, came to me and said, "Ron, see that lady sitting over there with my wife? Well, that's my Mother-in-law. Five years ago my Father-in-law developed Alzheimer's. They went through $250,000 of his Boeing retirement, because he was able to do so, and then went through $300,000 more of their own savings and so on, then Dad recently passed away. $550,000 later, Mom now lives with us, and outside of some Social Security money, we are her sole means of support. *Believe me, you can tell my story, because we now have Long Term Care Insurance on Mom, as well as ourselves. We know what being without LTCI can do, and we know what having it can do. Wish you'd have been here five years ago."* I was dumbfounded, and felt like crying. Last thing I expected to hear at a seminar. But, I guess I found out about the real world! Here's the kicker. Somehow, I had the feeling that this man was not at all concerned about losing an expected inheritance—I have the feeling that he was prepared well enough for the future for himself, and his wife and family. But, I certainly felt that the total loss of an asset picture for his Mother-in-law, had to have created an impact on the lovely lady. *Sharing a personal story of this nature is sharing an inside view of the real world, though not a pleasant one at that.*

Perhaps Jon D. Hull, writing in Time magazine, in an article titled "Waiting for the Windfall" sets the table better. Hull says, *"Although the subject of inheritance is one of the last taboos in the once crowded American closet,* it's getting harder and harder to conceal its prodigious effects on the huge segment of the population born after World War II." *Hull is right, get it out in the open where you can handle it, because if you don't, someone else is going to be doing it for you.*

Noted syndicated financial columnist Jane Bryant Quinn opens a brilliant piece titled "Junior Can't Count on Inheriting" with her first paragraph, *"A word of caution to baby boomers whose basic retirement plan is to inherit. Although the boomer generation, as a whole, will inherit an unprecedented amount of money, no single son or daughter can count on getting everything owned by mom and dad."* One of her most important points is the loss of expected inheritances through lingering nursing home stays. Quinn closes with recommendations, which include purchase of Long Term Care insurance.

## USE LONG TERM CARE INSURANCE TO PROTECT THE FAMILY MONEY AND SAVE THE WHOLE INHERITANCE

The point is simple. Where assets are an issue, both generations must pay attention. Some years ago, I wrote a Long Term Care policy on a beautiful 94-year old lady. She was a delight and much younger physically and mentally than her age would indicate. Because no provisions had been made to transfer *an illiquid estate worth roughly $500,000, her children were at risk of not receiving their birthright should she require an extended long term care need. Obviously, the solution was a Long Term Care policy*, which would provide at least interim financing for the period of time she could be a nursing home resident and until transfer was completed. Keeping in mind that 36 months is the simple transfer rule, and with premium at that age as a consideration, we worked out a plan, which would allow the five children to each benefit from their expected inheritance. *Guess who paid the premium. The children, of course, and they themselves were in their fifties and sixties!*

Now I have illustrated a classic example of what needed to be done, and by whom. The woman's estate could have been largely depleted by a long term stay, a transfer process had not yet begun, and *the children were each willing to pay a their share of premium today to protect that which would one day be rightfully theirs.* Not discussing the problem, facing it, or acting on it had been the aversion to most of the children until one of them invited me to review the situation. Now the peace of mind (for all parties) provided by the insurance policy gave the children and Mom impetus to move forward with proper transfer processes through their attorney.

I like this story a lot better than the ones I constantly hear from friends and acquaintances about someone in their family, or someone they know, who had to go to the nursing home and *the word "spenddown" became an unwelcome part of the family vocabulary.* Remember that "spenddown" is a very real fact of life, since it means that all eligible resources (moneys) belonging to the patient must be spent to pay for nursing home costs before qualifying for help from Medicaid. Unsuspecting children tend to become very upset when the county Medicaid technician, or the *nursing home administrator, must explain the facts regarding nursing home costs,* and who will have the honor of paying them.

Why is it that we wait? The great mystery is all around us, but Mark Twain or Will Rogers or whoever gets credit was certainly right when he said, "Two things in life you can count on, death and taxes." For decades to come, the American who has assets should also count on intelligently defining, understanding and acting on preservation of those (and additional) assets with the solutions recommended in this book. One thing is certain, *forces will always be at work designing "equitable" ways to divest you of your assets, and if you fail to plan, someone you don't want involved will do it for you.*

So, we see the inheritor as a guardian of his/her birthright. What does she, or he, in turn, do to resolve further transfer and estate problems? The answer should be simple enough. ***Use age and good health as allies in providing the solution.*** Seeking a Long Term Care policy at a younger age will amaze the potential buyer as he or she sees the effect age will have on rates. Good health and youth have a way of keeping premiums low. What 50-year old person who stands on the precipice of an inheritance (and someday would be the grantor themselves) would not be able to afford $60 per month ***to perpetuate the family's legacy?*** This is not an off-the-wall figure. At age 40, people can expect an amount closer to $40 per month for an adequate base plan with inflationary features. ***A sound basic plan purchased today, with tomorrow's inflationary factors in mind, is well within the reach of those who have a need to protect current and future assets from evaporation.***

By insuring themselves for their future generations, the person expecting an inheritance has ***covered the future for his or her offspring—but the present still exists. Think about this.*** Suppose, as in the example of the 94-year-old lady, which I referred to above, mom or dad, or grandma or grandpa (the people expected to leave the inheritance) is "house rich, and cash poor." Do something for yourself, which covers all the bases. Pay the premium! ***Yes, pay the premium for an LTC policy on the parents, or grandparents, which will assure you that your birthright will be passed down.*** In all likelihood, you are working and have better resources, and cash-at-hand, to protect what you hope and expect to receive. More than once I have heard "I should have gotten a policy on Mom and Dad, to keep us from losing their home to pay for nursing home long term care costs."

I have also heard this story. "I don't want my parents to be spending money on a long term care policy because it will reduce the size of my inheritance." What foolishness! Talk about rolling the dice! If that's the case, ***have your siblings contribute to the premium payment with you, and keep the family money where it belongs—in the family, not as an ongoing financial drain with long term care providers being beneficiary.*** An LTCI policy will also give you assurance that Mom and/or Dad ***are receiving the best care money can buy—the insurance company's money—not Mom or Dad's, or yours.*** As you can see, this concept (paying for a parents' policy) has several benefits for all involved.

Real life examples of this technique ***are becoming commonplace once the "children" are informed of the pitfalls of waiting to discuss the matter.***

HIPAA '96 gave individuals (and corporations) ***significant tax breaks*** for purchase of LTC insurance, and with the growing number of incorporated family farms and family businesses, the need and the solution fit like a glove, all tied together in an attractive tax deductible package. What more incentive is needed for people to attend to these important inheritance issues now? Additionally, many states now give the LTCI purchaser a tax deduction or credit, regardless of whom, in the family, the policy covers. *Scan the chapter on The Tax Issues to see how you and your family can fit into the tax benefits of purchasing Long Term Care Insurance.*

In closing this chapter, I ask you to please remember some all-important considerations. Financing of long term care costs is done in a variety of ways. Throughout "Guarding Your Gold II" we will discuss them and point out that less than half of current long term care payment is made by private money. Claude Pepper was right when he indicated that most people face impoverishment from those costs. *We can change that.* If you have assets, which are of an amount that you must spenddown to an impoverishment level, you need to at least consider an interim LTC policy which can preserve those assets until proper legal transfer can be accomplished. *If you find spending your own resources to satisfy $42,000 to $60,000 per year of nursing home and long term care bills to be unacceptable to you and your children, seek the logical, sensible solutions we've prescribed for you.*

*If you stand to inherit assets,* and in turn pass them on to future family generations, encourage your parents to purchase, or purchase for them yourself, at least an interim transfer policy and work with them on legal transfer. *Include yourself in this thinking.* Take the guesswork out of their hands and provide adequate coverage for yourself. Insurance companies can no longer be blamed for not providing solutions to this problem. Policies are available, and legal and accounting help, will provide a solid triumvirate in protecting acquired and future assets. As a tender note, older people should not think of themselves as being alone in the evaluation of LTCI needs where inheritance is a factor. *Retirees often find that their children have been thinking about the issue, but perhaps felt just as uncomfortable about broaching the subject as the parents, and often are more than willing to help with the solution.*

Obviously there are additional considerations when contemplating the issues of longevity, hospitalization, and long term care, asset preservation and inheritance. I don't have the authority to provide for the legal issues, and in fact highly recommend the use of an attorney for them, rather than trying to do this with just a simple form. However, when you do consult with an attorney regarding these matters, a very important item should be referenced—in addition to normal inheritance documents—a Durable Power of Attorney, or in what some states or jurisdictions would be called a Medical Durable Power of Attorney. *A simple power of attorney is not sufficient for finalizing the issues of one's death should a loved one become incapacitated.*

Use a long term care insurance agent to explain the benefits of LTCI, and coordinate the accounting and legal matters with your accountant and attorney. Today's family and tomorrow's families will be thankful. *You will have accepted the responsibility of family money in the same fashion as the elite of the world have done for centuries—just with some newer personal variations.* Remember, American family money is a relatively new experience for many average people—and remember also, that it's not just for the rich anymore!

# CHAPTER 6

# THE "TRIAGE" ISSUE

## *NOT EXACTLY A HOUSEHOLD WORD BUT, UNFORTUNATELY, IT WILL BE !*

Ouch!—Why so bold—almost looks angry. No—**serious**—but not angry. There is a story behind it. When I was writing the first edition of "Guarding Your Gold," four years ago, an old pal of mine, **Bob Mead, a Korean War era US Army veteran**, was reviewing some of the chapters, put them down and said, in a word, "Triage." I didn't know what he was talking about. So I asked. "Triage is an old battlefield term," Bob replied, "wherein the most seriously wounded are treated first. On the battlefield, **there are only so many doctors, nurses, and medics available**, and after a major confrontation, **soldiers were treated in accordance with their wounds—the most serious first**—and on down the line until the minor injuries were treated last. **Rationing, so to speak."** Makes sense. Then he added, **"That's what American health care is going to become."** Gulp! My writing reminded him of that word? What's he talking about?

As months wore on, the word kept bothering me, so I went to my six-inch thick Webster's and the word wasn't in it. So what do you do—get a bigger dictionary came to mind. But the library seemed the next best place, and that worked. A number of definitions were available, all pretty much agreeing with Bob's definition. A trip to "Google" on the web was the next stop and 309,000 references were made available. Researched a bunch of them. Found out a lot. In fact, I found out that it's a common term in the medical field today, particularly in reference to ambulances and emergency room treatment. **OK, so where am I going with all of this?**

Let's start with the **word**—it's French in origin, developed early in the 18th century, saw great utilization in the American Civil War, World War I, World War II, and undoubtedly every war since. The word is pronounced, **"trEE-azh,"** according to my sources.

It has come to have **real and common meaning in the medical field**—seriously, and obviously, I didn't know that—in the meantime, here we go.

Why would my writing cause Bob to utter "triage," after he had read the manuscript? Maybe because **most of the chapters dealt with the problems we are going to be facing in this country when an unbelievable 80 million of us need care, in much the same manner as 40 million of us now do.** Surprise? Not to you who keep up with information of this sort, but to most Americans, young and old alike, who have no clue. Young and old alike? Yes. The **demographics tell us that we will have only two workers for every one recipient of Social Security and Medicare.**

Chapter 6

So, what did my work nearly five years ago have to do with "triage"?  Well, Bob saw the problems I was referring to, and could see no way to solve them without—you guessed it—triage and rationing.  Bob wasn't referring to battlefield situations, or even medical care in emergency situations—*he was referring to how 80 million people are going to have their normal medical and long term care needs met, while a workforce of 160 million has some problems of their own to worry about.  Triage and rationing came to mind.*

The research I have done for the past eight months to update this edition of "Guarding Your Gold II," only magnifies the previous data.  What's the difference?  Quite a bit, but mostly it's *what I said would start happening four years ago—ten years down the road—is now only six years down the road.  In addition, very little has been done politically to rectify or alleviate the impending crisis.*  Let me explain.

1)      We already *have the demographics of the situation* in front of us.

2)      *Nothing has been done* to cure the financial problems that *Social Security alone* will present to our country.  There will be changes, and they are more than possibilities, they are *probabilities.*  We are going to see *eligibility ages raise* (some already are)—*age 62 eligibility go "bye-bye—a decrease in benefits* related to a restructuring of COLA—*means testing—greater taxation of benefits—a lowering of benefit formulas*—and last, but not least by far—*increased payroll tax contributions*.  But, *lawmakers have, for over a decade, ignored the warning signs, and seem to be in a "no step" zone.*

3)      *Nothing has been done* to address the real problems of *Medicare*.  Demographics, again, are the problem.  Medicare will crunch costs all they can, and try to address the annual $20 billion graft, corruption, fraud, and overpayment issue*.  But this current $250 billion baby is poised to grow immeasurably each year for the next thirty years, at least, to a trillion dollar a year headache in the boomer's lifetimes.*

4)      *Extended longevity is rampant*.  Longevity and old age issues were well known, but in actuality, they are outmoded, as current figures show us an extended longevity of incredible proportions.  *Some estimates predict that we will have over 1 million Americans over age 100 by the year 2050.*  Seems like a long ways away.  Could be. *But if you are say, 45 or 50 today, you're in the group!*  Happy 100th!  Just count on a comfortable lifestyle taking you to about age 96, and hope that you've hoarded a lot of aspirin.

5)      *The Medicaid issue*—no need to even wrestle with that one anymore.  As budget cuts for nearly every state exist, that situation will worsen.  The warning is very clear— *we are not going to have the money available, at a time when probably three times more people will need it than currently do.  I have a question.*  How can we come down on nursing homes and caregivers, who already have their hands full with—liability problems, staff problems, budget problems, insurance problems, quality care problems,

40

facility problems, investment problems, to name a few—*and expect them to deliver the care we desire at 75% reimbursement of the cost to deliver the care? Then, how do we gear up for proper placement of say, up to fifteen million more residents who will have nowhere to turn, but to Medicaid?* No one in the political arena seems to have an answer. Long Term Care insurance, whether at home, in an assisted living facility, or in a nursing home *has to be the answer.*

6) *The Caregiver issue is probably the most serious of all these items—and leads to the topic—triage.* Who's going to be around to provide for both medical and long term care needs when the projections turn into reality? We are already aware that we are *short some 300,000 nurses currently*, with that number having the probability of reaching 800,000 before it hopefully turns around by the end of the decade.

Not only that, but conditions are already surfacing in the physician arena, which do not bode well for America's current retirees, let alone the retirees of the next three decades. According to studies done In the year 2003, by the AMA, and the AAFP, *doctors are either; declining new Medicare patients, or limiting their practice in proportion to Medicare patients, as much as 48 percent.* How are older Americans going to fit themselves into this dismal picture? And this. With lawsuits and malpractice insurance being deciding factors—*young Medical Doctor candidates are opting out of such fields as surgery and gynecology, and finding easier ways to make a living* by specializing in exotic areas of medicine—and leaving the field of general practice. *Think about that.*

*Not yet convinced* that we are going to have a "triage" and health rationing problem in the near future? One which will continue for decades? *Well, I was wrong. It's already here.* During the month of September, 2003, The Wall Street Journal ran a series of front page articles entitled, "Who Gets Health Care? Rationing in an Age of Rising Costs." The first article headlined *"The Big Secret in Health Care: Rationing is Here--With Little Guidance, Workers On Front Lines Decide Who Gets What Treatment."* The articles all dealt with current examples of rationing, and wrestled with the questions of who gets what in general medicine, as well as Medicare and other government and insurance programs, and prescription drugs.

*As the "Age of Arthritis" is about to begin, doctors, nurses, and caregivers in general, are going to be scarce for the masses*—although I don't think too many of us will be needing gynecologists. When we take into consideration all of the above, don't we seriously have to ask ourselves, as Bob did, *are triage and rationing on their way to becoming a household word? Who's going to be first in line, according to their needs, and who's going to be last? Time, and not enough of it, will tell.*

# CHAPTER 7

# THE RETIREMENT ISSUES

## *PENSIONS, AGING, SAVINGS AND WORK PLANNING ON RETIRING?*

## COMPLETE
## AND
## PROTECT THE PLAN
## WITH LTC INSURANCE

*JUST DON'T GET TOO ANXIOUS!* Most people have forty to forty-five years to think about retirement, so what's the hurry? There is no need to complicate the next—make that—the last, thirty or forty years of your life, with a quick emotional decision. A decision made, in what you hope, are the final five or ten years of your normal working lifespan. *You may well be on your way to a retirement which lasts longer than your working years!* Impossible? No, for millions of American workers, believe it or not, it's already under way.

You've thought about an *early* retirement? Think again. Or maybe you just look forward to retiring at a *"normal"* retirement age. Who wouldn't? Seems reasonable, and that's the way it should be. However, keep in mind that *even a well planned retirement can present some headaches*. I'm not a negative person, but if I were to somehow ignore much of what the *real world tells us, about the final third of most American's lives,* I would be derelict in not informing you of such in this book. As I've said elsewhere, "Please don't shoot the messenger." I rely on hundreds of articles, journals, books, studies, publications, e-mails, and some personal conversations to present sound, factual, "futuristic" information.

In fact, I must admit that I am a "Packrat." In researching and updating this edition of "Guarding Your Gold," I threw away six boxes of research material from the original book, and still kept nine boxes. But, during the interim, I have collected information on *more than twenty new studies* regarding retirement issues. They are not small reports. Many private companies, think tanks, research bureaus, and insurance companies have visited the retirement issues facing Americans, because it is a huge contemporary issue, and not a very comfortable one at that. We will refer to, and quote, some of the studies, but in general the trend is the same in each—*Most Americans have not, will not, or cannot, properly prepare for a comfortable retirement.* That leads to—*"Why" not?*

So, "Why not?" Why do so many people *delay thinking about* and *preparing for* a *sensible* retirement, *especially with a sound "retirement plan?"* It's not just a transition, from working one day, to "turning in the keys" the next day. Planning for retirement means preparing and following a road map, or a blueprint, or a guideline, or whatever you choose to call it. *But, please just do "it"—call "it" anything you want— and follow the plan.* Maybe some parts of the plan are more intent on "how to enjoy the good life" or "how to spend the Golden years." And that's okay, *as long as the plan includes how to finance the enjoyable parts of the plan.*

But, the *plan also has to include how to prepare for the unexpected—or what we should be calling the expected.* The "expected" includes changes in lifestyle and changes in health. Those changes are imminent, and every retiree should know about— and expect—*health and lifestyle changes.* With the exception of a quick death, these two factors are going to have an impact on the retired person, and their plans—count on it. So, part of retirement preparation boils down to preparing financially for the *"expected" changes in lifestyle and health.*

We all know about the "Tooth Fairy." You put the tooth under your pillow and the next day some money appears, all for being such a brave child. But let's remember, it was Mom or Dad who really supplied the money—not the tooth fairy. According to the dozens of studies discussing retirement planning—or rather the lack of it—it would appear that most of America is going to be relying on the tooth fairy to solve their imminent retirement problems. Too bad. *The fairy won't be drifting in through the window and supplying dollars for being brave.*

Here's the point—rather than moving down the road twenty-five years from now, and saying *"I wish I would have..." let's turn the clock back from twenty-five years ahead, to now—the present.* If you are presently considering retirement, or are even currently retired, NOW is the time to prepare for the changes of lifestyle and health. One sensible approach is to *maintain the current health insurance plan you have,* whether it be employer sponsored or individual, until such time that you are eligible for Medicare. *When you are Medicare eligible, purchase Medicare Part B, and a Medicare Supplement plan of no less than Plan C,* or Medicare + Choice, or any variation of plans which are available after implementation of Medicare reform of 2003. That will take care of the *physical medicine of health care—you can't afford to "take a chance" in this area.*

You also can't afford to take a chance with your Long Term Care needs, *which are not covered under health insurance plans, or Medicare.* That means purchasing now, while you have age and good health on your side, *a Long Term Care Insurance policy, which will cover your "care" needs, just as health insurance plan covers your "cure" needs.* A compound inflation rider will be the most important part of proper preparation, since four to seven percent inflation in care needs, will surely accompany 76 million boomers who pass into retirement over the next twenty-five years. Some would say, "Why should I buy Long Term Care insurance, when I may never need it?" Well, you insured your house and cars over a lifetime because they were valuable assets, and because the law and the lender made you do so. But the law and the lender are not going to come along and see that you insure your assets, and your family money, as you prepare for retirement.  This is something that you have to do for yourself, because after all, *you are insuring your retirement planning*, and it takes conscientious preparation to protect those plans.

Years ago, I compiled a list of statements that people had made in regard to their own retirement, and presented a composite of what some have encountered.  Viola! The list looks nearly the same at the beginning of the 21$^{st}$ century.  However, the two dozen studies add a few more complications.  Let's take a look at some actual retirement misconceptions from both the recent past and the present:

1) "We thought we'd have enough for retirement, but that's not so."
2) "I thought I'd be able to retire around age 55, but it's not possible."
3) "Here I am at age 58, out of work, and nobody wants me."
4) "Our savings are being eaten up by inflation and medical costs."
5) "We lost everything we own to pay for Bob's Nursing Home costs."
6) "We were expecting $456 per month in pension money.  Now we find out the pension plan is broke.  We think it's been raided."
7) "We thought the rising value of our home would provide enough."
8) "We were told that moving to a warmer climate would be cheaper."
9) "We thought taxes were supposed to go down when we retired."

Yes, sad as it is, the above are only a few of the examples of problems which seem to have surfaced, *after people had assumed that a comfortable retirement was a guaranteed part of the great American scheme of life.*

*From all indications, the problems will get worse.*  Americans don't, or can't, save enough.  Pension problems combined with turn-of-the-century investment portfolio grief, a continuation of skyrocketing medical and prescription drug costs, inflationary erosion of the current dollar, tax obligations of several kinds, and inflation in normal living expenses, seem to be pretty well entrenched as obstacles to the normal retiree's future.  *In addition, huge demographic problems caused by 76 million (give or take a few villages), of your friends and neighbors joining you in your retirement years,* will exacerbate even more problems of an unusually new and never-before-seen nature.

We have two demographic problems—*extended longevity and population shifts.* We can do nothing about the first scenario—extended longevity— the wheels are locked in, and the final approach is underway.  In the past, we simply referred to the word "longevity." *Not anymore.  We now have "extended longevity."  It's here to stay.*  Every decade of America's existence has seen the life expectancy of it's citizens rise, and we now have a "bubble of boomers" being followed by too few workers—in fact, we are on our way to two workers for every one recipient of Social Security and Medicare.  This bubble has even caused the Census Bureau to predict that by 2050, we will have *more than one million people over the age of 100 in our country.*  Seems impossible, doesn't it?  But look at it this way—the year 2050 is only two and a half generations away— seems like forever.  It's not. Guess what. *From now 'til 2050 includes—you got it— the baby boomer generation.*  Did I say a "long retirement?"  Did I also mention too few workers following along behind to support this "top heavy" baby? Would this indicate a need for protecting yourself during retirement?

The second demographic problem is that America's senior citizens have found a new way of life in the Sun Belt. However, while the living is easier, the **cost of living is no easier.** A lower winter heating bill savings can be eaten up by high air conditioning and utility bills. Add to that, sales taxes, higher state income taxes, and the inflation of normal "cost of living" scenarios. The Sun Belt states have already experienced the imbalances of swollen retiree numbers. The states are in a continuing battle to stay ahead of the situation facing their own budget problems, created in part by Medicaid nursing home costs, and trying to provide general economic planning for the retired hordes. **It's only the beginning.**

In addition to the demographic changes, we have additional problems for **Americans and their retirement dollars.** Let's compile a short list, point out some of the problems, find some solutions in the chapters of this book, and get on with our lives. **Just pay attention to what to expect, face it, prepare for it, solve it, and move forward.** In other words, **educate and solve for yourself now, and do not dwell on "it."**

A) OLD AGE—For a varying period of time retirees feel good enough to **remain active, but doing so usually requires money**—money for travel, money for entertainment, money for dining out, etc.—all of which means that money must be available to **supplement activities of time replacement, which formerly had been time spent at a job.** The retiree normally is active until some incident of bad health sets in.

B) HEALTH AND ITS COSTS—"The Golden Years" really have very little to do with a guarantee of feeling good. Today, we are aware of what many of us have suspected, Medicare will likely see serious revision, even after the "reforms" of 2003. It does not matter the political affiliation of those discussing **how** to reform, **additional reform is imminent. Reform amounts to one simple thing. Dollars.** Where do they come from? One source will undoubtedly be continual increases in Medicare premiums from retirees, and an increase in a beneficiary's supplemental products as deductibles and coinsurances go up.

C) LONG TERM CARE—Nursing Home costs, which range from $120 to $300 nationwide **today** (and are increasing at four to seven percent annually—which exacerbates a compounding inflationary problem), have created a new form of monster for **people who assumed they had enough** money in pensions, social security and savings for a decent retirement. Impoverishment, because of long term care costs, is not an unusual end game for many members of an otherwise proud generation, but, unfortunately, it is a very real specter.

D) EARLY RETIREMENT—A once admirable ambition, now available to only the wealthy, or those who were very well prepared ahead of time. As recently as a decade ago, early retirement was considered a way to get more young people employed or "moved up the ladder," in order to help our tax base. But, as retirement problems begin to surface, *early retirement seems to only mean availability for another job* and a recycling of the "double and triple dipping" of some "retired" folk.

E) INADEQUATE SAVINGS—Starting savings plans, or forced savings plans, at an early age is the only solution to pension and social security (which was not designed to be a total solution) inadequacies. Savings rates for average Americans are deplorable. Many feel that the cost of living and tax burdens prohibit savings. The average middle-aged American had about $2,600 in net financial assets in 1993. 55% of ALL the people in America had less than $5,000 in savings or investments! Ten years later, this situation has improved for many people, but many others—most of the masses—lag far behind. The high market yields of the late nineties—which saw a boom in 401(k) portfolios included as savings—and with the unbelievable growth in real estate values and with other forms of investment gaining considerably, the savings picture improved. At least it improved for those who had money in the market or real estate. But, in December, 2002, a Congressional Research Service analysis of Census Bureau data discovered that *"More than half the paid workers ages 25 to 64 don't own retirement savings accounts of any kind. Of older workers ages 55 to 64, three out of four lived in households with retirement savings of zero to $56,000."* Not exactly good news for the national retirement scene of the next three decades.

Look at some of the problems this way. The oldest boomers turn 60 in 2005, which means that retirement is *beginning to be a more than distant thought.* Expect a totally different approach to retirement as 76 million people retire right along side you— *they (and you) will redefine retirement in America.* In the meantime, we have all been "fore-warned" of the fact that some financial situations are going to change for you. Let's compile a simple list for your consideration as you ponder retirement.

1) *Be prepared for the loss of income from a job,* unless you intend to work part-time or replace job one, with job two, and/or job three. Financial advisors feel that a person needs 70 to 80 percent of his or her pre-retirement income to live comfortably during retirement. Social Security normally replaces no more than 40 percent. What's even more scary is that some people wander into retire-ment *without any thought of decreasing expenses—simply spending at will. You might* even look at it this way—"Let's see now, how do I look into the future and exist for the next thirty years on less money than I am making today?"

2) *Do not overestimate investment returns.* The experience of the last few years should make that a "no-brainer."

3) *Do not overwithdraw from investments.* Five percent or less should be the maximum.

4) *Reduce your living expenses as much as possible, and change your liv-ing habits within the scope of what you have available to spend.* Buy what you need, not what you want.

5) *Eliminate debt. All of it. Be particularly cognizant of eliminating credit card*

*debt.* There is no way you can justify the interest charges of debt, in the face of limited income.

6) ***Do not expect too much from Social Security.*** An already over-burdened system is not going to produce magic COLA results.

7) Question your desire to retire early and revaluate, ***based on your needs.***

8) ***Accept responsibility. Don't look for someone else, or "the government" to take care of you. They won't.*** Wives are particularly vulnerable, since statistics show that women will outlive men by several years, and longevity creates health, health care, long term care and financial issues.

9) ***Don't underestimate longevity.*** Let's make that ***extended longevity.*** The country is getting grayer, much grayer, and extended longevity eventually leads to the need for care. Long Term Care. Prepare for reality.

10) Think about the ***worthy use of leisure time.*** Becoming retired is one thing. Staying retired is another. Finances may dictate a need for seasonal or part-time work, ***but emotional satisfaction with the way you spend your leisure time is another factor.*** Be aware that loneliness is not your personal domain. Many retired ***people "medicate" loneliness with gambling and alcohol, which only creates worse problems***—both mental and physical health are included.

11) ***WHATEVER YOU DO, DO NOT RETIRE UNLESS, AND UNTIL, YOU ARE DEBT FREE—AND CAN REMAIN SO.*** You may not agree with me on this statement, but consider it, please.

All of which says—***prepare for yourself. Prepare for a retirement that may turn out to be less than you expected,*** and ***much longer than you expected.*** As indicated previously, the boomer generation will redefine retirement. Boomers will undoubtedly have attitudes about what they expect from retirement, since they have been accustomed to some pretty good times during their growing years. In short, they may expect everything to be as comfortable and fortunate for them, as it was in their preceding years. So, if it all doesn't work out as well as hoped for, they may look at retirement and say, "I'm used to good fortune, and I still want it, so bring it to me now, in my most important time of need. After all, there are 76 million of us and we intend to be heard." Well, the free and easy "bring it to me now," won't be happening. ***At least from a source other than themselves.*** Aha! Retirement planning—taking care of oneself in life—after a lifetime of good things happening, seemingly on automatic pilot. What the boomers ***had better hope won't happen*** is a little more serious. Read on.

I said sources other than themselves—***government help***—in other words. And I say that ***won't be forthcoming.*** Imagine this scenario. ***Two workers for one recipient. Recipients of Medicare, Social Security, and in some cases, Medicaid.*** That's right. That's what the demographics of the American labor scene around the year 2040 look like. So, is there any reason to believe, that if two workers have to provide for the living conditions of one retired person, those two workers ***are going to agree to, or even be able to,*** provide for anything more than what the retired class already has? Won't be happening. And that's what I have been warning in this chapter, and in fact in this whole book.

*Frankly, I am afraid for our country. I am afraid for our retirees. And most of all, I am afraid for the workers following me.* What happens when we see two workers (and their employer) having today's 15.3% Social Security and Medicare tax raised to 30% or more to pay for the benefits of one recipient? What happens when we see higher state taxes needed to pay for the recipient who is receiving Medicaid nursing home benefits because they failed to provide Long Term Care Insurance for themselves? What happens when the workers say "We've had enough, and we won't do this anymore!"? Open rebellion? Anti-government rallies? Anti-grey strife? Worker strikes? Labor violence? Inter-generational wars which give new meaning to the '60's phrase of "generation gap"? Who knows? I certainly hope none of the above. *But something serious is on the way—it just hasn't been announced, yet.*

I believe the only way that people are going to be able to protect themselves is to expect to *fully prepare for retirement, as closely as possible, to be completely on their own—from day one to day fifteen thousand!* Today's retirees will have to immunize themselves against the coming generational and governmental problems caused by these great demographic and economic imbalances. They can do so with serious retirement planning designed to avoid and evade the problems discussed previously and further on in this chapter.

## PENSIONS, PENSION FAILURES, AND PENSION PROTECTION

In the 1990's, if you, or your parents, were not on a pension, *it is highly likely that you did not feel the sting of pension problems that affected millions of Americans.* Also, as the nomenclature of "pensions" drifted to retirement plans of a *"defined contribution"* and "individual retirement plan" nature, you may have enjoyed the meteoric rise in a variety of investment opportunities in the decade of the '90's. Most dramatic was the explosive growth manifested in 401(k) plans during that time. But, whether we call them "pensions" or "retirement plans," both have a serious impact on the participant and their abilities to foresee what their "retirement years" income will look like. The first few years of the twenty-first century have not treated retirement income hopes very kindly, with many investment portfolios of either a pension, or retirement plan, getting slugged rather severely. *Now, those who didn't feel what "pensioners" felt in the '90's, are getting into the ball game, and feeling the same type of "sting" referred to in the first sentence.*

So, we need to take a look at pensions and what has happened to them over the last dozen years. This topic is huge, well defined, much regulated, and often misunderstood, but we only have time to discuss the basics, and the basic historical pension problems. The history of pensions in America grew out of old European concepts. The US government introduced pensions to civil servants in 1920. Corporate pensions began in the 1930's and are tied closely to events surrounding the Great Depression, the introduction of Social Security, the industrial spurt of WW II, and the influence of labor unions.

Chapter 7

Strong unions fought for and won employer-funded pensions, thus we had the beginning of the Defined Benefit Plan, America's first approach to pensions. Let's take a look at the "linage" of pension and retirement plans:

1) **DEFINED BENEFIT PLAN**—Evolved from the belief that employers have an obligation to provide for retired employees who have worked a life-time for them and made the company successful. Thus, under the traditional pension, the union/management negotiated Defined Benefit Plans, employers funded plans for retired workers, and sometimes, survivors, to provide a lifetime income. The amount of the benefit is normally based on what the worker earned, retirement age, and how long they worked. However, in the past few decades, traditional pension plans have taken a beating, for a variety of reasons:

A) Company goes broke, or is sold. Record corporate bankruptcies created a $3.6 Billion shortfall in 2002.
B) Employee dies before retirement. Spousal problems.
C) Employee is fired, laid off, or quits before retirement.
D) Company mismanages or raids pension funds.
E) Union management mismanages funds.
F) Employee credits are transferred incorrectly, if at all.
G) During the 1990's as many as **sixty companies per day eliminated pension plans—mostly defined benefit plans.** 30,000 plans abolished since 1990.
H) American Academy of Actuaries estimates **1,000,000 workers per year** lost pensions in 1990's.
I) **Pension plan becomes underfunded—By 1992** the tip of the iceberg had surfaced, and had become **a $45 Billion problem**, and growing, with the **fifty largest plans $38 Billion short**. Dozens of famous names involved—Tenneco, Loews, Uniroyal Goodrich, Rockwell, TWA, Bridgestone-Firestone, Bethlehem, General Motors, Budd, Mack Trucks, Westinghouse, Reynolds, Goodyear, Northwest Airlines make the list.
J) **By 2003, the problem had grown to $300 billion, and 32,000+** traditional pension plans, covering 44 million Americans were covered by PBGC, which was declared a "high risk" government agency by Congressional investigators in July of 2003, due to an increase in the number of large failing plans it had been forced to **take over from struggling private employers.**
K) Business Week reported early in 2002 that 78% of businesses had surpluses in their pension funds, and that by the **end of 2002, about the same number would be in the red.**
L) In March of 2003, Reuters News reported that **US Pension** Funds had lost $1 Trillion in the previous last three years due to stock market problems, **and because more retirees live longer.**
M) Gender inequities have been and continue to be a problem.

2) **INTEGRATED PLANS**—A variation of a pension plan, wherein the employer counts a portion of what the retiree gets from Social Security as part of the

defined benefit—and reduces the amount of the benefit accordingly. Yes, *it is legal, but, understandably, not liked by pensioners.*

3) *PENSION BENEFIT GUARANTEE CORP*—The US Government pension insurance agency—which *Absorbs the liability for underfunded pensions.* PBGC regulates and has authority to require funding of federally guaranteed pension plans. Under the Department of Labor, the PBGC is normally about $3 Billion short of funds, which will grow with additional failures.

4) *DEFINED CONTRIBUTION PLANS*—The outgrowth of problems associated with traditional pension plans, the defined contribution plan is a plan wherein the employer agrees to put money into pension funds *without guaranteeing the retirement benefits employees will receive.* The plan offers a variety of investment options. The contribution can run from 15% to 25% of salary, depending on the plan, with a dollar limit for each type. Most employers have chosen to go with the 401(k) plan, which matches contributions from the employee, up to a federal legal maximum. *By 1996, 85% of all pension plans were comprised of Defined Contribution Plans.*

5) *TYPES OF DEFINED CONTRIBUTION PLANS*—Most workers today will recognize or become familiar with these plans.

   A) Money Purchase Plans
   B) Profit-Sharing Plans.
   C) Employee Stock Ownership Plans (ESOPS).
   D) Thrift or savings plans.
   E) 401(k), 403(b), and 457 Plans.

6) *INDIVIDUAL RETIREMENT PLANS*—Have evolved as a way for Americans to personally plan for their own retirement.

   A) Individual Retirement Accounts (IRAS)
   B) Roth IRAs
   C) Simplified Employee Pension (SEPS).
   D) Keogh Plans.

Pension problems led to a totally different approach to pension income during the 1990's. In essence, the most popular form of retirement money, the *DEFINED BENEFIT PLAN, has all but disappeared from the scene*—except for those which are historically left— and which are experiencing a sea of red ink. A multitude of pension problems; companies going broke or sold, pension funds being underfunded, employee death and spousal problems with receiving benefits, one million Americans losing pensions in the first four years of the 90's, decline of unions, pension regulation of companies, and the loss of income due to integration with social security, have seen Defined Benefit Plans drop to only 4% of the nation's pension plans.

Now enter the year 2000. People who had expected their Defined Contribution and Individual Retirement Plans to lead them to believe that a comfortable retirement was well on the way, got a severe shock. Boomers who had seen unbelievable growth in their retirement portfolios, began to wonder if an early retirement, or even a comfortable retirement, was going to become a reality. First the stock market took a severe beating. Then a domino effect started to surface in a series of corporate fraud scandals, which likely could continue into the middle of the decade, as further "bookkeeping" irregularities are exposed and developed.

As gigantic corporations suffered losses, and started declaring various forms of bankruptcy, *so did the pension funds and retirement system portfolios* of thousands of funds involving millions of investors. In 2002, The California Public Employees' Retirement System figured it lost $560 million with the collapse of WorldCom stock alone. Seven other state pension funds reported $700 million losses in the same catastrophe, with similar losses being reported in thousands of various funds. One corporate failure seems to have eliminated billions of dollars from what millions of people hoped were sound retirement futures. The bankruptcies of several more large corporations, which have already been exposed, and the possibility that dozens more will follow, may cause *comfortable retirement plans to disappear for millions of people.* True, restructuring and salvage will eventually probably right most of these corporate ships, but the nervousness of the investor will remain.

In addition, the corporate downfall affected millions of individual employees and investors, who may have had the majority of their own investment *portfolios tied up in a single corporate stock.* New laws limiting the practice of employee stock options and 401(k) portfolios being tied up in the company's stock, as well as dozens of other solutions to corporate accounting and fraud, were passed by Congress and signed by President Bush within a matter of weeks during the summer of 2002. Hopefully, these aberrations will come to an end for America's retired and soon-to-be-retired citizens. But the facts are clear, retirement expectations tied to either, the pension system, employee's retirement systems, or individual investment portfolios, have taken severe punishment in the last few years. People who thought of early retirement in their '50's, and looked forward to pension and retirement portfolios taking them to a comfortable sustaining retirement will have to think again, since *history teaches them not to count too much on "chance," once they divest themselves of a paycheck during their high income years.*

## THRIFT AND SAVINGS

While Defined Contribution Plans, and Individual Retirement Accounts should be considered a form of savings, we find that *traditional savings plans are falling behind, as a source of income for retiring Americans.* In fact, savings rates for average Americans are almost abysmal. Many feel the simple cost of living and high tax rates prohibit savings. 55% of all people in America have less than $5,000 in savings or investments. In fact, *would it be proper to say that many American families spend more than their income in any (every) given year?* That was true in the early '90's, and I would dare say that such an attitude has grown considerably in the last ten years— in light of the ease with which Americans are able to obtain multiple high limit credit cards, the low bank and credit union borrowing interest rates of the last half of the nineties and into late 2003—and the *"buy now, pay later" mindset* of today's consumer.

*Huge credit-card debt and rising personal bankruptcy are commonplace.* According to the Federal Reserve, in May of 1996, total US credit card balances stood at $444 billion. In 1990, the average credit card debt per household was $1,263. By 1995, the amount had nearly doubled to $2,287. I leave it to you to speculate what credit card debt figures will look like as Americans march into the 21st century with the first of the "boomers" expecting to embark on a comfortable retirement ten years later. As an example, according to SRI Consulting Business Intelligence, *in 1992, only about 18% of Americans older than 65 had an outstanding credit card balance. By 2000, that had increased to 46%.* And according to Leonard Raymond, executive director of Homeowner Options for Massachusetts Elders, "When we started the program 18 years ago, credit cards were a non-issue. Today our clients have an average credit card debt of $8,000. But we also see people with $30,000, $40,000, $60,000. One client had $202,000 in credit card debt." Are we starting to see a very uncomfortable trend?

In *1996*, America set a milestone, when, for the first time, *more than one million bankruptcies were filed*. By 1997, bankruptcies increased to 1.4 million (1.35 million individuals and 54,000 businesses) and by 1998, had reached an all time high of 1.44 million, of which 1.39 million were personal bankruptcies! Of course the trend continues upward. *By 2002, the number was 1.54 million,* and during the first quarter of 2003, the amount went over 400,000. Consider the overall significance of these numbers to the entire American savings picture. According to the Consumer Bankruptcy Project, about 24,000 people age 65 and over, filed for bankruptcy in 1991, but over 82,000 people in the same age group filed in 2001, a change of 244%. Could this just be the "tip of the iceberg?" A key to the figures may lie in the fact that *nearly half of elderly people who end up in bankruptcy say they filed because of a medical reason,* according to the Consumer Bankruptcy Project from Harvard University. Also, this from a report compiled by the Commonwealth Fund—"Out-of-pocket health care expenses for seniors increased nearly 50% from 1999 to 2001." A period of three recent years, *reflected in great part by the simultaneous rise in prescription drug prices.*

*"Thrift," as a word, has disappeared from the American way of thinking.* Net national saving rates had already begun a downward trend to 7.2% of the Gross Domestic Product in the 1970s, then fell to 3.9% in the 1980s, and plunged further to 2.3% in the 1990s, *finally hitting rock bottom at 1.1% in 2001*. According to the Bureau of Economic Affairs, a 2001 study shows that U.S. personal savings rates have dropped to nearly nothing, as the percent of disposable income put into savings plans plummeted consistently from the early '80's. And a study conducted by the year 2000 Retirement Confidence Survey, shows that 70% of all American workers have $50,000 or less accumulated for retirement. The Federal Reserve says that *even counting Defined Contribution plans, the typical worker nearing retirement has less than $50,000 in financial assets.*

But, given the embarrassingly low interest rates on Certificates of Deposit, by America's banks, in the early years of the Twenty-first century, who would expect to put money into accounts that would return such small growth? So, effectively, savings at a bank are not sensible. Annuities, even though not federally insured, but which are guaranteed by the insurance company which sells them, have become a market for savings money. Interestingly enough, as laws regulating the sale of insurance products by banks were removed in the late '90's, many banks began selling annuities as a form of meeting the competition for higher interest rates than those offered through their own bank.

Scudder Investments found in 2002, that although **75%** of the nation's 76 million baby boomers believe they'll be financially set for retirement, *two thirds of them don't think they could swing long term care (without insurance) if needed*. This, in the face of a report from the American Council of Life Insurance, which says that 25% of them will need long term care for an average of 2.3 years, at $44,000 of today's dollars. "Because people are living longer, *whatever money they do save is going to be stretched out over a much longer time period than in the past,*" says Leslie Eggerling, vice-president of product development and sales, for Schwab's insurance services. Obviously, *Long Term Care insurance solves this problem, if purchased now,* at a younger age, including an inflationary clause, with premiums stretched over a greater number of years.

In 2002, an "Allstate Financial Reality Check" found that *78 percent of boomers felt they were ready for retirement and 69 percent said they knew how much money they would need to maintain their desired lifestyle. The problem is that an amount of $30,000 was considered the necessary amount,* partly because 46 percent of them felt that *living expenses would increase less than 20% over the next twenty years.* Go figure. Where does this form of insanity come from? What happens if the cost of living doubles (that's five percent simple) in the next two decades? Who knows? Again, stay tuned, and *don't hold your breath on a one percent inflation increase, per year, for twenty years!*

Perhaps the crux of the savings dilemma in America is found in a January 4, 2002 editorial in USA Today, which portrays the reason people are not taking advantage of the many options available to people today—is that of confusion. "Congress loaded up last year's tax cuts with another dozen or so new offerings for workers, the self-employed and families with college-bound children. All of the changes are supposed to boost the nation's anemic savings rate. Few likely will." The editorial continues, "Not because the country is inherently profligate or shortsighted. But because *a once-simple savings concept has grown to an incomprehensible thicket that can be sorted out only by high-priced accountants.*" Confusion, and the lack of discretionary dollars to save, seem to be the biggest drawbacks to financial prudence.

An Allstate Financial poll conducted in the spring of 2003, and reported in PR Newswire, March 5, put a somewhat different slant on the idea of borrowing, and the idea of saving for retirement. The headline read, "Allstate Poll Shows That Many Who Say Saving for Retirement is a Priority, Have 'Other Priorities'." Figure that one out. The article says, "93 percent of Americans surveyed said they believe it is up to individuals to ensure their own financial security during retirement. Yet, ironically, the same poll showed that as many as 70 percent of this same group said that *present financial obligations preclude them from saving as much as they would like for the years ahead."* Not only that, but the same poll reported a statistic from the 2002 Fannie Mae National Housing Study: "Well over one half the cash being raised from record home *refinancings*—nearly $170 billion in 2002 alone—*is being used to directly finance more spending,* on everything from home improvements to vehicle purchases, vacations and even general living expenses." "…many Americans may be *forgetting an important savings strategy—pay yourself first."* There we have it, refinance a home which may be nearly paid off, and put yourself further into debt just to buy more stuff.

Is it time for America to start thinking in terms of *zero tax on simple passbook savings and CD's,* in order to encourage its citizens to save more and depend on entitlement less during their retirement years? Do not think this is an idle possibility; some countries do not tax simple savings in order to *encourage savings and less dependency on their government in the retired person's later years.*
As a matter of common sense, Americans need to overcome this insatiable desire to overspend, and realize that retirement is not going to be a simple matter of "the end of punching the time clock," and the beginning of enjoying the good life. According to the Employee Benefit Research Institute, *twenty to twenty five percent of retirees are financially troubled. I would think the figure would be much higher, but perhaps the key word here is "troubled."*

No matter how we look at retirement, financial planners say that *fewer and fewer people are actually able to enjoy the lifestyle they had counted on, because of—you guessed it—inadequate finances.* Saving seems to be an afterthought with millions of people who count on their employer and "the government" to provide answers, rather than planning and saving, for themselves, as a career-long resolve. My point in all of this, is that *current retired lifestyles all require whatever combinations of incomes the retiree can put together.* But what happens to a couple when one or the other, or both, *outlive their good health, and increased norms of longevity for this nation's citizens extend another three, four, five, or more years onto the retired person's life?* One solution is to visit your banker, annuity sales person, or insurance/investment counselor and ask them to show you how a compounded 5% interest table on a one hundred dollar monthly deposit will look over a lifetime. We are talking about EXTENDED lifetimes here, and you will be pleased to see that the miracle of *compounding interest* will follow hand-in-hand until your final days, and at least keep you even with that old nemesis—inflation—which is the major threat, other than health, to a lengthy, happy retirement.

## WORK

*"Work?!"* As Maynard G. Krebs, the consummate hippie on Gilligan's Island, exclaimed forty years ago, *"Work?!" Yes, work.* No matter what measures are taken to "correct" all the economic and entitlement problems facing America's retirees, one thing is certain. The four-letter word, *"WORK" will become a huge part of a new "four-legged stool" of retirement.* Yes, downscaling, thrift, and cost-cutting will become a part of the retiree's rethinking, but *"work" will be commonplace for many.* As the lack of a large work force, which is needed to fund the elderly and their entitlements, the "entitlement ethic"

will hopefully subside in future contemporary thinking. But, then again, who knows what our crazy future is going to bring us.

***Work will be of major necessity, and "subsistence wages" will take on a new, real, and unwelcome meaning for a great number of the retired masses.*** If, it could be said, that there is a "bright" side to this enigma, it would be that jobs will be plentiful. Working for wages has already surfaced as a survival tool for many of America's retired people. Don't expect that scenario to change. At all. More and more "retireds" are finding that their mere existence, excluding the frills of a fancy retirement, is dependent on having a job, ***assuming they can work. And then assuming that they are happy with the type of work and wages available to them.***

In fact, the work trend for "retired" people has already started. The Census Bureau reported in 2002 that ***13.2 percent (18% of men and nearly 10% of women) of people age 65 and older were either working or looking for work.*** The major reasons for working are those cited throughout this book—inadequate Social Security income, dwindling retirement savings (if they existed in the first place), concerns about health coverages, and pension losses. Deborah Russell, manager of economic security and work, at AARP, defined the work issue as such: ***"Retirement is now seen as part of an employment cycle, rather than as the end of employment.*** Some retirees decide to work part time; others choose volunteer work." Also, a 1998 AARP survey ***indicated that 80 percent of boomers said they expected to work after retirement.***

So, maybe work, as a necessity, is not all that bad. Various articles presented by the National Academy on An Aging Society see ***work as somewhat easier*** for the 70 and over crowd, with about 21 percent involved with service work and 32 percent holding professional and managerial level jobs. The biggest surprise is found in the Academy study, which shows that 34 percent of workers over age 70, are ***self-employed***, compared to just 14 percent of workers age 40 to 59. That's good news. In addition, one Academy report says that many older workers ***do not feel stressed at work.*** That's another piece of good news. No need to be stressed if you want to work, are able to work, and maybe really don't even have to work. We should all be so lucky.

***The work ethic for retirees will be revived, and such phrases as "work expectancy" and "productive aging" will become synonymous with "life expectancy." After all, will there be any choice anyway,*** in the face of rising Social Security age requirements, Social Security and Medicare question marks, pension problems, demographic imbalances, gender iniquities in longevity and wages, savings problems, and health and long term care issues? ***We may be better off—with work.***

# CHAPTER 8

# THE SOCIAL SECURITY ISSUE

*THE SYSTEM NEEDS ATTENTION IMMEDIATELY—
IF NOT SOONER—
BUT, LAWMAKERS ARE IN A "NO STEP" ZONE!*

Assumptions. Assuming. Assume. We "assume" something is going to happen. We "assume" that the future will be there in a fashion that will make us happy, and one that we will find comfortable—*based on our assumptions. Don't assume.*

There was supposed to be this "three-legged" stool of retirement. It went like this. When people get ready for retirement they should be able to count on *pensions, savings and Social Security, as the three legs, to comfortably see them through their final years.* It has worked—to a fairly respectable degree. It has worked with some variations—depending on how much a person could save and how well their pension plans delivered. It has worked for millions of people who had nothing to count on except Social Security. Thank goodness—and thank the taxpayers. *The solution of the three-legged stool was not a fancy answer, but has worked nonetheless, for nearly seven decades. It will continue to work—assuming we are all ready to take a beating—now that's a fair assumption.*

The "savings" leg of the stool has taken some pretty hard hits recently, assuming the retiree had a "savings" leg. The "pension" leg has been nearly turned upside-down for many retirees—assuming they had a pension. *That leaves the third leg—Social Security—it has been there, and will continue to be there, but it too, will take a beating—no assumptions.*

We've all seen a piece of equipment, or an airplane, that has a stencil-lettered warning that says *"No Step" zone. That's where Social Security is right now.* We have the warnings all over the program, have had for over a decade, and Senators and Representatives, and the President, the people in Washington, D.C., *both parties included*, who need to address the warnings, *are deftly avoiding them as gingerly as if they were "No Step" zones.* In fact most serious students of the issue have very grave concerns about the future of the plan, *unless great changes are made, and soon—very soon. Demographically, the numbers verify the problem.*

*The "No Step" zone—hear me out.*

It's refreshing to know that some politicians, *or at least some former politicians, are joining forces in providing the nation with information that it's citizens don't really want to hear, but need to know about,* and which my readers, in particular, need to know about. The Concord Coalition, by its own description *"is a nonpartisan, grassroots organization* advocating fiscal responsibility, while ensuring Social Security, Medicare, and Medicaid are secure for all generations." It is co-chaired by **Bob Kerry, a former Democratic senator from Nebraska, and Warren Rudman, a former Republican senator from New Hampshire**. These two statesmen delivered a compelling editorial to the Washington Post of August 12, 2002. No matter what anybody's political affiliation is, this piece is significantly important to everybody in America. The entire article warrants your attention, but, unfortunately, I can only offer you some compelling portions, which indicate how serious the problems are, and how quickly Social Security problems must be addressed.

"...In just six years the baby boomers begin receiving Social Security checks. Then, the number of workers whose wages are taxed, relative to the number of beneficiaries who receive the proceeds of the tax, begin to decline sharply. Before Tiger Woods turns 50, **the number of beneficiaries will grow by at least two-thirds, while the number of workers will barely budge.**"

"Doing nothing **means deep benefit cuts or steep payroll tax increases in the future**, which is why Social Security trustees warn that prompt action is essential."

"...It is certainly fair to criticize reform plans on policy grounds. But it is fundamentally unfair to judge **them against a standard that assumes the current system can deliver everything it promises. It Can't.**"

"**Today's Social Security system promises far more in future benefits than it can possibly deliver.** The relevant comparison for any reform plan is **with what current law can deliver, not what it promises.**"

"**...We should stop playing political shell games with this issue. If we do not have the political will to solve the Social Security problem now, we can't hope to do so when the baby boomers start collecting benefits—not just for Social Security but for Medicare and Medicaid as well.**"

"The problems facing our health care programs are much more daunting than Social Security. **These three programs together are expected to double as a share of the economy within 30 years, putting unthinkable pressure on tax rates, the economy and the budget.**"

"**Not acting is itself a choice—one that has grim consequences for today's midlife adults and even bigger ones for their children**. Politicians of both parties should get behind specific reform plans or be held accountable for supporting the consequences of the **Do Nothing Plan.**"

Well spoken, gentlemen. Well spoken. Thank you for sharing honest information with my readers. Information which they need to have in their possession as they prepare for retirement. The quotes probably won't rank up there with the Gettysburg address, but certainly should be **as important as the work that Paul Revere did. The "Do Nothing Plan," huh? Shameful in the heartland of America. The "No Step" zone at work.** Perhaps we all begin to suspect that personal savings, investment, and debt freedom will be considered paramount to that "third leg" of government help over the next two, three, or four decades.

Nor do the warnings of the last decade stop coming. In July of 2003, no less an authority than the General Accounting Office challenged the system with some unsettling information. In a small column hidden on page 10A, of USA TODAY, on July 30, the headline read "GAO: Social Security cuts of 33% likely without changes." The story reported, *"If no changes are made to shore up Social Security finances, benefits to retirees would have to be cut 33% by 2039 or payroll taxes would have to be raised 46%,* the General Accounting Office said. The report by Congress' investigative arm said that *the sooner Congress addresses the decline in Social Security revenue that will occur when baby boomers begin retiring in five years, the easier it will be for future generations to keep the system afloat."*

"President Bush's Commission to Strengthen Social Security outlined in 2001 three proposals to establish individual investment accounts with the retirement system, *but the plan has gone nowhere. Other options include raising the retirement age and cutting benefits."*

*But, is anybody with the responsibility to act on this "No Step zone" going to move on the matter? Not yet.* And obviously not as soon as should have been done. Clearly we're going to need some heavy-duty "heavy lifters" to tackle this problem. So, now that we're in "it," and need to find a way around "it," how did we get where we are?

Let's take a moment and look at the history, background, definitions and development of the Social Security program—find out where we were, where we are, and where we're going as a nation. *First of all, Social Security was never intended to be a total retirement package. The problem is that until recently, most Americans viewed it that way. They now know differently.* Another problem is that while the Social Security Trust Fund is huge, Congress, has consistently raided the fund to pay for spending bills which it writes. The US government gives the Trust Fund Treasury notes in return for the money it "borrows." *That's where most of the national debt lies.*

For the last decade, deep concerns about the soundness of Social Security have been issued (though ignored,) and the retirement benefits of Social Secutiry seem to be under siege. *A demographically unsound "top-heavy problem of longevity," will not be supported by an inadequately sized American labor force for the next thirty years.* A two to one ratio of workers to recipients in about thirty years, will not work without serious changes, as Senators Kerry and Rudman point out.

*Social Security is an "Insurance Contract."* In fact, the provisions of the Social Security Act make the United States government and the Social Security Administration the largest insurance company in the world. *The system of "social insurance" is as real as if any corporation had invented the product and sold mandatory policies to the American public.* The definition of an insurance policy is "a contract binding the company to indemnify an insured party against specified loss in return for a premium paid." The Social Security program meets this definition.

In fact, the program is similar to the "Defined Benefits" model of early pension concepts. Benefits are based on amounts contributed. This determines the amounts payable to recipients, with *some variations designed to achieve parity for lower income retirees.* According to the Social Security Administration, "Social Security is the nation's primary means of *assuring a continuing income to a family when the breadwinner retires, dies, or becomes disabled."*

The transition from an agrarian society to an industrialized economy created the underpinnings of the need for this social insurance program. Families, who had made self-sufficiency a way of life, were no longer "down on the farm," but were isolated in urban areas, with no way to keep up with some of the lifestyle changes and standards of living brought about by new economic factors. The Great Depression of the 1930's indicated that millions of people were unable to cope with national economic, and personal financial, problems beyond their control. Thus, Congress passed, and President Franklin Delano Roosevelt signed, *"The Social Security Act of 1935."*

Again, we must remember that the intent of the Social Security program was not to finance anyone's retirement, but to guarantee a *"floor of protection."* Social Security was designed to provide basic economic security; a system of "social insurance," with *three types of benefits: retirement, survivor's, and disability. A fourth program—Medicare, was added in 1966.* For purposes of this discussion, we will only speak to Social Security retirement and Medicare.

Let's list the basic provisions that guide Social Security retirement to achieve the "floor of protection."

A) Statutory right: *Benefits are not based on need.*

B) Compulsory participation: *Nearly everyone who works* participates and receives benefits.

C) Contributory financing: Payroll tax from employers and employees, and taxes from self-employed. *Employers and employees pay a tax rate of 7.65% each, which adds up to 15.3%. The self-employment tax rate is 15.3%.* The tax rate is applied to earned wages, and that ceiling historically has gone up. Expect this rate to go up again, as soon as congress applies a much needed overhaul to the entire system. (Both Social Security and Medicare funding are included in the 15.3% figure.)

D) Work-related benefits: *Tax amounts are based on earnings, and* benefit amounts are based on earnings.

E) However, we have weighted retirement benefits: According to "Social Security &

You", the **program attempts to achieve social adequacy as well as individual equity.** (Authors note: Read that definition as "parity.") Let's explain:

1)   Lower-paid workers receive proportionately higher benefits.
2)   **Increased benefits are paid to married couples**, and under some circumstances, divorced spouses and children.

Social Security helps meet the goal of financial security in retirement, and minimizes the risk of financial disaster. **For some, it is the only planning that keeps them above the poverty level, or formerly did, if that is even possible.** Because Social Security is compulsory, the "safety net" of social insurance is supposedly in place.

The nearly seventy-year-old plan, however, is thought by some economists, politicians, "think tank" experts and futurists, to rear its head as a monster soon. Very soon. Others see the problem, but feel it is under control and manageable through 2030. We shall sift through current thought regarding the problems and changes, which seem necessary and eminent. Keep in mind that Social Security has undergone several changes through the decades, **but none was precipitated by the urgency of demographic facts now facing us.**

Some definitions will be helpful to this discussion.

A)  **SSA**— Social Security Act of 1935, also known as the Federal Old Age Insurance and Survivor's Act.
B)  **SSA**— Also the acronym for Social Security Administration.
C)  **FICA**— Federal Insurance Contributions Act— set up to fund the Social Security Act by the first party—the employee, and the second party—the employer.
D)  **SECA**—Self Employed Contributions Act—for the self-employed to provide both parts of FICA.
E)  **OASI**— Old Age and Survivors Insurance (Trust) Fund.
F)  **DITF**— Disability Insurance Trust Fund— Merged with OASI in 1994 in an attempt to prevent DITF from going bankrupt.
G)  **NRA**— Normal Retirement Age— "Normal" in current question.
H)  **EEA**— Early Eligibility Age— Now in question as to propriety.
I)  **COLA**— Cost of Living Adjustment.
J)  **CPI**— Consumer Price Index— to which COLA adjustments apply.
K)  **PIP**— Personal Investment Plan— A new, yet not approved, plan which would allow people to fund part of SS with their personally owned participating plans.
L)  **SSI**— Supplemental Security Income— Extra income for those on Social Security below the poverty line.

Let's discuss one of the most important of these acronyms, the **OASI (Old Age and Survivors Trust Fund),** and relate it to the warnings that have been issued by observers during the last decade. The following statements taken from the booklet, "The Raid On

Social Security" (pages 57, 58, and 59) published by The Senior Exchange, Inc., April, 1996, concludes what has happened to the OASI Fund for several decades.

*"The long term threat to Social Security does not lie in the offices where benefit checks are written, user services are performed or eligibility is determined.*

*The real threat lies at the Department of the Treasury and the Office of Management and Budget at the White House, where the United States government has been spending $50, $60, even $70 billion of our Social Security nest egg each year. The system is still run and controlled by politicians and political appointees and not by actuaries, independent of political manipulation.*

*Today, one out of every six Americans receives payments from Social Security. Currently, cash benefits are provided to forty-two million retired and disabled workers and to their dependents and survivors. Likewise, in 1993, one hundred and thirty-five million workers paid taxes to support the program. This enormous number of workers represented almost one out of every two people in the American population."*

***Now, here's the "kicker" to the last sentence above.*** When Social Security was adopted in ***1935***, (and set up for the first recipient to draw benefits in 1940), ***the worker-beneficiary ratio was 40 workers to 1 recipient.*** By 1960, that ratio had become 5 workers to 1 recipient. ***In 1996, the ratio was 3.3 to 1***, and estimates for ***2040 indicate a ratio of 2 to 1.6 workers, for each recipient. That demographic factor is what is making observers of the Social Security retirement system nervous.*** Social Security is by far our largest government program. In 2001 it paid $378 billion in retirement benefits—more than 20 percent of the federal budget. In the past 50 years, the payroll tax deduction has risen from 2% to 12.4% (Medicare not included.) And yet, ***with a top heavy enrollment in entitlement programs, without great change, how can we expect a 2 worker to 1 recipient ratio to work? Looks like we'll be needing some "New Math."***

Since a major overhaul of Social Security tax contributions (increase) in 1985, the surplus of payroll taxes has created an ***excess*** over benefit payments by about 10%, thereby leaving the OASI Trust Fund with excess contributions. This number has fluctuated from $50 million per hour at one point around 1991 to $9 million per hour by 1996. Seems like that would leave plenty of money, and in fact, supposedly left the trust fund with about $578 billion in reserves at fiscal year end 1996. By year end 2002 the reserve was calculated at $1.049 trillion largely due a healthy economy during the last half of the '90's. ***That type of growth would seem sufficient, except for the population figures soon to affect this reserve***. Some boomers will start to retire at age 62 around 2008, and the clock winds down on the expected imbalances of some 76 million boomers swelling the retirement ranks.

However, the 1999 Report of the Social Security and Medicare Trustees, projected that payroll taxes would stop generating a surplus in 2014. Then, in the 2001 Annual Report, the commission revised that year to 2016. In reality, a few months difference in predictions is unimportant. **At some point the "pay ahead" program becomes a "pay as you go" program, and the surplus in reserve in the OASI fund for "rainy days," will see some pretty ugly clouds on the horizon.** According to the 1999 report, after a time line of rising benefit costs and dwindling reserves has been crossed around the year 2014, the reserves are exhausted by 2034. Again, the updated 2001 report revised that figure to the year 2038, but you get the idea. **That's right—money sent ahead to be put in the bank will be gone.**

**Also, benefits outstrip tax incomes in 2016 and the system is left with two choices, raise taxes or increase deficit spending.** Assuming no change in retirement ages (other than those already in place), no increase in payroll tax revenues, and an increase in beneficiaries, we find that the Social Security program is at ground zero by the year 2016. Not coincidentally, we will have been in the sixth year of boomer retirements and, 2016 is the year that **"most" of the Boomers will start their age 65 retirements.**

Serious reform of a sweeping nature is gaining attention among the nation's citizens. Considering that **100% of the assets of the Social Security system are found in about 170 various treasury notes locked in a file at the Office of Public Debt Accounting in Parkersburg, W. Va., prospective retirees have a right to get a little nervous about the stability of all this.** Ask yourself, where does the government go to borrow to make payments on that which is already borrowed? To Parkersburg? **Yes, to Parkersburg.**

In the May, 1996 issue of Atlantic Monthly, Peter G. Peterson summed up the scenario after 2010. Though the reference is somewhat dated, the message is still apropos.

> **"By 2030, when all the Boomers will have reached sixty-five, Social Security alone will be running an annual cash deficit of $766 billion.** If Medicare Hospital Insurance is included, and if both programs continue according to current law, **the combined cash deficit that year will be $1.7 trillion. The horse, in other words, will be quite dead.** By 2040 the deficit will probably hit $3.2 trillion, and by 2050, $5.7 trillion. **Even discounting inflation, the deficit that year for these two senior programs will come to approximately $700 billion—four times the size of the entire 1996 federal budget."**...

> "By 2040 the cost of Social Security as a share of worker payroll is expected to rise from today's 11.5 percent **to 17 or 22 percent**—depending on whether you accept the official or the high-cost projection. Add both parts of Medicare, which currently cost the equivalent of 5.3 percent of payroll but are growing so rapidly that **they will eventually overtake and pass Social Security in size, and we're talking about 35 to 55 percent of every worker's paycheck before we even start to pay for the rest of what government does."**

So, what does all of this mean? Depending on whose numbers you choose to use—calamity or complacency. Mortimer B. Zuckerman, Editor-in-Chief of U.S. News and World Report stated in a May 13, 1996 editorial, **"Social Security is in a slow-motion** slide that will sap the system and pit 20-something's against their grandparents." An Associated Press article urged Americans to "**Prepare for Age**." An AARP publication pleads, "**Don't take the Security out of Social Security**." USA Today, in a cover story, asked, "**An Old Age of Rags or Riches?**" Pete Peterson's Atlantic Monthly article is entitled "**Will America Grow Up Before It Grows Old?**" and in that article refers to **America's impending "economic meltdown**."

In November of 1997, **Alan Greenspan, Federal Reserve Chairman opined that the Social Security system was "badly underfunded" and that congress should fix it sooner, rather than later. "If we procrastinate too long, the adjustments could be truly wrenching,"** Greenspan said. In May of 2002, White House Budget Director Mitch Daniels stated that returning to a balanced budget without using Social Security remains **"a very important aspiration. But it isn't a realistic goal in the short run."**

Then, in the spring of 2003, after six precious years had passed, with no action taken by Washington, and his warnings (above) going unheeded, Greenspan returned to the Senate Special Committee on Aging with some further admonitions. Referring to the "abrupt and painful" adjustments needed to prepare for baby boomer retirement, Greenspan stated in a story reported by Sue Kirchhoff of USA Today:

> **"The aging of the population in the United States...makes our Social Security and Medicare programs unsustainable in the long run, short of a major increase in immigration rates, a dramatic acceleration in productivity growth well beyond historical experience, a significant increase in the age of eligibility for benefits, or the use of general revenues to fund benefits."**

Kirchhoff reported further that, "Greenspan repeated his call to change the inflation index used in calculating benefits and **suggested another increase in the retirement age might be needed. He said increasing taxes is the least attractive way to solve the problem.** Greenspan further stated, "The first challenge was to do everything possible to improve economic growth, **or else, 'I don't think there's a solution here, period.'** 'If we can get, first, maximum economic growth, and then make certain types of adjustments as we phase in the marked increase in the commitments that occur after 2010**, then I think this is a solvable situation."** Further timely reinforcement of the problem—**but still talking to people in the "No Step" zone.**

Fortunately, we have politicians and former politicians warning us of what lies ahead. But, no action in Washington. And, yes, we have had Social Security reformations in most of the past decades—but, those alterations and corrections were **not even closely presented with the type of problem which faces us today—that of the demographic imbalances we have discussed.** We would hope that America's leaders would soon start to change their "Do Nothing Plan" to at least a "Tread Lightly and Carry a Big Stick" plan, **before the "abrupt and painful" solutions discussed by Alan Greenspan become reality.**

We shall see what we shall see, but the following are some predictions you can be sure will take place within the next decade:

A) **A raise in retirement age to 68, 70 or even 72.** The man who designed the Social Security Act, Robert J. Myers, says higher retirement ages are coming, and that age 65 was never meant to be a magic number.

B) **A decrease in benefits** related to a restructuring of COLA and CPI assumptions.

C) **Means testing** of retired people's incomes.

D) **"Work" as a fourth leg** of the original three-legged retirement stool of savings, pensions, and Social Security.

E) **Personal Investment Plans** will be allowed for individuals and credited as part of their Social Security contributions.

F) **Reduction or total disallowance of age-sixty-two benefits.**

G) **Greater taxation of benefits.**

H) **Increased payroll tax contributions**.

I) A change **(lowering) of benefit formulas**.

When will all this happen? In the previous edition of this book, I stated "Sooner than you think," but I was dead wrong. **Four years have passed and nothing but talk has been accomplished, and obviously, nothing was done as soon as was needed.** 1998 thinking was that 1999 would have been the appropriate time; the same in 2001, as a "window of opportunity" appeared for all politicians who did not have to worry about reelection. But for political reasons the needed legislation had still not been attended to through the fall of 2003. The truth is that **no real action has been taken on the reality of the warnings listed above, many of which are well over a decade of being ignored.** In fact, with the war on terrorism, we find the vulnerability of a financing vehicle, by conveniently raiding the Social Security fund again; yet few people speak out about such a travesty.

The problem **has the attention of the American people, but nearly everyone avoids acting in some manner, nay, any manner, on this important "time bomb" issue.** Each month passes by with news articles pointing out the problems, and asking when something will be done, but the message generates little more than rhetoric from our statesmen. USA Today quotes Robert Reischauer, a former Congressional Budget Office director who now heads the Urban Institute: **"Nobody wants to talk about it, because to do so, you have to lay out a plan to fix it. By not talking about it, we don't have to admit reality."** So true, Robert, so true.

Young voters have started to form nationwide organizations to educate each other about their **"inheritance" from an older generation** of voters. Boomers are afraid of any immediate action, having watched billions of their dollars evaporate with losses in retirement plans mounting as a result of the downturn of the stock market extending from 2000 and into the winter of 2002-03.

The **problem of a smaller work force exacerbates the projections** of people hopefully getting all the benefits of Social Security, on which they are counting. America has already seen a downturn in the growth of the workforce, but the situation worsens and the plot thickens, as we see less than a one percent growth in available workers from 2000 to 2010, less than one-half percent growth from 2010 to 2020, and a near halt to .02 percent growth from 2020 to 2040, according the Social Security Trustee's report of 2001. Personally, I *dispute these figures, because I believe that we will see about thirty to forty percent of the over age 65 crowd in the work force, as full and total retirement becomes available to only the very well prepared, the very old, or the very ill.* The income derived from "productive aging" jobs however, will not be of major consequence—"subsistence" will be a closer definition.

So, we have a continuum of problems which surface within a few years of each other. *Around 2008 to 2010 we see boomers starting to qualify for benefits, the annual cash surplus beginning to shrink, and the growth of the work force stagnating.* Sometime around 2014 to 2016 the trustees project that Social Security's cash flow will turn negative, and about 2038, the trust fund will be depleted, containing only enough annual income to pay only 73 percent of the benefits. I suppose these predictions will vary in detail over the next few years, depending on whoever is making them and whatever legislation is finally enacted to address them, but the message is clear—this will be a *very anxious time for about eighty million Americans who assumed that Social Security would "be there for them."* How much, and in what fashion, will be the answers to skeptical questions.

We truly have our "head in the sand" on this important issue of our country's future, and eventually, politicians will be forced to listen and will be forced to react, regardless of party affiliation, or the need to be reelected. But in the meantime, we ignore the facts, and sit and wait while the situation deteriorates. *In short, the "talkin' part's done."* Remember when we said that the first of the Boomers turned 50 only eight years ago? Well that means eight years have passed and the clock ticks down to seven years remaining, until 2010. *Then all we have to do is sit back and wait for the boomers to start taking their Social Security retirement and Medicare benefits—and live with the calamity we've created.*

Indeed, "The times, they are a'changin'" and it will not be a pretty sight unless ALL Americans accept themselves as part of the problem and strive earnestly and honestly to be a part of the solution. *Prospective retirees have the recipe in front of them— prepare now for your retirement in all ways; finances, debt reduction, investment, savings, health, health insurance and long term care insurance—since current government entitlement programs are going to alter the way you were intending on looking at your financial retirement well-being.* Take care for yourself, because as you think about retirement, keep in mind that 76 million of your friends and neighbors are thinking about the same thing.

## NOW, LET'S LOOK AT GOVERNMENT SPENDING

Analyzing the government's spending and seeing where the benefits are directed, is a huge factor, is more difficult to track, and occupies thousands of volumes of writing. But, for our purposes, let's list the major factors by their common popular terms.

***The Federal debt, interest on the Federal debt, Federal deficit, and Federal deficit spending, are four different items***, and need to be discussed and understood in their own separate realms.

A)  In ***1980*** the **FEDERAL DEBT**—what the government owes because it has borrowed to finance its spending— (Government bonds and various Treasury Notes), stood at ***$910 billion.*** By 1990, this debt had risen to $3.21 trillion. By mid 1995, the legal limit of $4.8 trillion had been reached and Congress had to raise the limit to $5.1 trillion, which, in turn, was reached in June of 1996. Sadly, another raise in the limits to $5.9 trillion was exceeded rather rapidly, and by August of 2002 the Federal Debt had increased to what appeared to be about $6.1 trillion. Not enough. ***2003 saw this "permissive*** indebtedness grow to $7.3 trillion in 2003. Is your head hurting yet? Look at the growth in the federal debt from ***1980 to 2002—twenty-two years—about a 600% growth!*** And we're told not to worry. Tell it to retirees—and boomers—and young people in the work force. Tell us not to worry.

B)  ***The INTEREST on this debt*** was roughly $362 billion (per year) in 2000, a 70% increase from 1988, and is now our government's second-largest expenditure (excluding social programs; medicare, social security, medicaid,) about what we were spending on national defense before the events of September 11, 2001, which created a need for new billions being pumped into the war on terrorism.

C)  **FEDERAL SPENDING** currently amounts to about 21% of our Gross Domestic Product (all spending in the nation internally), while State and local spending is at about 11% of GDP. However, with HUGE expenditures for coming Social Security, Medicare, and Medicaid entitlements already built in, some economists fear federal government spending coud soar like a mountain slope to 37% of GDP by 2030. Add state and local spending bill to this 37% and America could see government taking 48% of a wage earner's salary.

D)  In the meantime, the **FEDERAL DEFICIT**—the amount of money that the government underfunds itself each year—has the possibility of soaring to 18% if current entitlement formulas remain in place. During the last four years of the 90's, **FEDERAL DEFICIT SPENDING** went down, and would hopefully have done so for the next decade. But a war on terrorism, a recession, and several tax cuts resulted in deficit spending occurring again in 2002, to an amount announced by the White House in ***July of 2003 at $450 billion***. It has an expected possibility of running as high as a half a trillion dollars in 2004. In fact, as scary as it sounds, some economists predict that this debt will amount to $2 trillion over the next five years. Unless someone gets government under control, some analysts feel that the number ***could reach $1 trillion in the year 2007alone***. Then, the first big boomer retirement year of ***2010 will undoubtedly cause a dramatic*** increase in further deficit spending, as the boomers start to utilize their Social Security retirement and Medicare benefits. Remember, this is not a long ways away—for all of us—recipients or workers.

*At no time in our history has the combination of federal spending and indebtedness—and known and expected (but ignored) future economic pressures—encountered such a recklessness with our nation's lawmakers, as that illustrated in 2002-2003.* It's almost as if some mystical doctor had written a prescription for disaster—delay and denial on the part of lawmakers, and delay and denial, and waiting, waiting, waiting for the hammer to fall—on each generation of Americans.

Even though common people, retirees, pre-retirees, housewives, executives, observers, insiders in both the executive and congressional branches, and think tank experts can clearly see the warnings and have continuously alerted lawmakers of the "runaway freight."—*the people in charge do not act as if they can distinguish red from green.* The differences between public trust and political cover are going to haunt some politicians forever. *But the worst of it is—they are going to haunt the rest of us for at least the next three or four decades—unless self-reliance becomes the operative phrase—as well it should, in the face of current and coming events.* Stay tuned.

# CHAPTER 9

# THE MEDICARE ISSUE

## *PUTTING THE MEDICARE ISSUE INTO A PROPER PERSPECTIVE*

Medicare…Medicare…Medicare… Where are you going? *I didn't think this would actually happen*, but, in November of 2003, the House and Senate passed the new *Medicare bill*. What started out as a *"Medicare Prescription Drug" bill, became everything but that*, by the time the bill had grown into the "2003 Medicare Modernization Act." I have a great deal of reservation about the new law, as do many Americans, but it looks like we are going to have to live with what happened, at least until some further legislation over the next two years, modifies this "piece of work." We are told that this measure will cost about $400 billion over the next ten years. It will be more. *Let me hit some highlights for you*, *and discuss the apparent "winners" and "losers."*

The *"winners" include Medicare HMO's*—no doubt about that—what started out as a Prescription Drug Bill suddenly became a full blown Medicare *revision* bill, with HMO's, (the "private sector"), gaining in several ways, including $12 billion in subsidies to compete with traditional Medicare.

*Drug Companies*—There is just *no explanation for what was achieved by the drug lobby.* The new law now *prohibits the government from forcing price controls or price reductions in prescription drugs.* Talk about protectionism! It looks like there is now no way that Medicare or Medicaid can *collectively approach drug companies for price reductions in their products, no matter how inflated they may be.* Let's apply the same principle to automobiles. Would a state highway department, or the U S Forest Service, or any other governmental entity, now have *no* clout in going to automobile manufacturers and saying, "We need 2,000 four-wheel-drive vehicles, and because of the volume involved, we would like your best bid on the deal." "Just charge what you want," seems to be the message. I suppose this would be acceptable if prescription drug costs were not increasing at about 13% per year.

In addition, the bill kept the *"importation" prohibitions of Canadian drugs*, although some in the Administration immediately began to reassess that stance.

*Rural hospitals and doctors*—After being underpaid by Medicare forever, the new law provides that *rural health care providers will be seeing an allowable increase in their services.* It's about time.

*Medicare beneficiaries whose drug costs are over $5,000 per year*—Well, that's helpful, but the numbers for those who need less, are not very appealing—the bill simply *does not help the average Medicare recipient a great deal*. This part of the bill does not take effect until 2006, but in the meantime, Medicare beneficiaries will be allowed to purchase a drug discount card for $30. Low income seniors will have a card "loaded" with a $600 benefit built into it.

The reason this provision does little to help *most* people, is found in the expense of the "benefit." First of all, there will be an "approximate" $35 per month charge for the feature. That adds up to *$420 annually*. Then there is a *$250 annual deductible*. This adds up *to $670.* Then, the benefit will pay 75% of the next (after the deductible) $2,000 of allowable covered prescription drugs, in other words, $1,500. So, now the drug benefit purchaser has expended *$1,170,* and received *$1,500* in benefits. Next, there is a vacuum, or coverage gap, on the next $2,850 of drugs, so the recipient has now used *$3,950* of his or her own money for this "feature." The final provision calls for a 95% payment by Medicare on the amount over $5,100. Obviously, this a fine feature for people requiring more than $5,100 in prescription drugs during a year's time, but, as I said before, this bill *does little to help most recipients, which will, in turn, discourage a great number of people from purchasing the drug benefit.*

So, what started out as *a "prescription drug" bill did not hit it's mark in the fashion originally intended, but certainly did a lot toward changing traditional Medicare.* We have a couple of years to chew on this legislation, and see where it really fits into the scheme of things in the total, overall Medicare program, but I don't see it as the answer to changes which need to made over the next thirty years.

The *"losers",* at this time seem to include *Medicaid recipients,* for a variety of reasons— *retirees,* who may see their former employers dump them from their existing group health plans—and the *older, sicker, and more frail Medicare beneficiaries,* who will be left in traditional Medicare as the HMO's try to pick off the younger and more healthy retirees. This would cause traditional Medicare costs to rise, as the old principal of "adverse selection" kicks in. How did all of this happen? For starters, let's go back to the beginning, and see why the economics of Medicare are scary.

Medicare carries an immensely large bill in America. In 1995, Medicare Benefit Payments for Elderly and Disabled went over $190 billion. The turn of the century sees costs in the $250 billion neighborhood, and not-too-distant "baby-boomer" retirements will continue to fuel an incredibly astonishing spiral in Medicare costs. Now, here's the distressing part. Medicare projections from the Congressional Budget Office in 2000, concluded that "Medicare spending will resume growing at an average rate of 7 percent in the decade after 2000, and when the baby boomers begin enrolling in Medicare after 2010, Medicare spending will increase at an even faster rate." Hang on to your hat!

*The current $240 billion* (Medicare spending for 2001 was nearly $241 billion according to the Centers for Medicare and Medicaid Services, who administer Medicare) *will look like play money when we compare the figures in say 2020, or 2030. It looks like an annual half-trillion dollar baby will be born over the next thirty years. An "old" baby, with less than the necessary number of parents (taxpayers) to support it.*

Unlike Social Security's suspected problems, Medicare's problems have been analyzed and officially announced from time to time.  On June 5, 1996, the Medicare Board of Trustees, in it's annual report announced that Medicare's Part A (Hospital) Trust Fund would be broke in 2001.  It didn't happen.

In actuality, by 1999, the report of the Social Security and Medicare Trustees, changed that projection, and decided that because of higher than expected payroll tax revenues from the strong economy, and a shifting of home health care from Part A to Part B, that the fund would remain solvent until 2015.  This, in spite of the fact that the 1998 Part A deficit was $8 billion and similar deficits were expected through 2006.  However, many observers question how this difference was changed so quickly, whether or not accurate accounting techniques were employed, and even if so, *how the trust fund can possibly sustain itself in light of 7-9% annual growth in utilization inflation.*  After the decline in the country's economy in the first three years of the twenty-first century, one has to wonder how this projection and deficit differences will actually play out.

To put this information in a text that will make sense, we need to provide some background as to the financing of Medicare, and a look at how Medicare health care utilization has increased and will increase, in proportionally far greater amounts than ever seen before, during at least the next thirty years.  *First, remember that Medicare is the nation's second largest social insurance program, exceeded only by Social Security.*

In the 1930's, at the time of the New Deal and the birth of Social Security, *all levels of government spent only $1 annually per person on health care for the elderly.*  By 1965, the figure was closer to $100—by 1975, roughly $1,000 and—by 1995 Medicare spending reached nearly $5,000 per person per year.  By 1999 the spending per beneficiary had increased to $5,500 (not including any Medicare Supplemental Insurance privately paid), *and is expected to reach $10,700 by 2009!*  The total bill for all health spending in the US is about 15% of GDP, and is expected to rise to 18% by 2005.  In fact, over the past 25 years, Medicare spending has gone up at a rate of 5% per year, twice that of inflation.  Remember, that was for a *25 year period.  But during the last ten years* have seen Medicare inflation in the 9-11% range, and as the demographics tell us, these percentages will be compounded by even greater utilization during the next thirty years.

*Medicare is paid for by two separate Trust Funds.  Part A, the Hospital fund, gets its money from payroll taxes of 2.9% on wages.*  The fund has been little better than a pay-as-you-go program, and had amassed around $300 billion by 2000.  But since spending is outstripping payroll tax income by 2-to-1, and the interest in the fund is consumed along with the principal, one has to wonder how much longer this program changes from a "pay ahead" to a "pay as you go" program and *where the "pay as you go" comes from.*  A raise in tax "contributions" is surely going to be the only solution.  Part A covered the Hospital bills of more than 38.8 million Americans in 2002, *with additional annual increases of around 2 million people per year starting in about 2010.*  This fund, the Part A Hospital Trust  fund, is the fund in serious jeopardy of remaining solvent as boomers begin to expect to receive benefits.

***Part B's fund covers doctor's services and some limited home health care***. This fund, from the US Treasury's general fund, is already a pay-as-you-go operation, with recipients paying $66.60 per month in 2004, (compare that with the original $3 per month payment when the program started) and ***supposedly pays for 25% of the actual cost of Part B type expense. Taxpayers pay the remaining 75%.*** Since income taxes fund the greatest part of Part B expenses, income taxes must go up, spending must go down, or other Medicare benefits must be cut. As the cost in 2004 is $66.60, (and will increase in large proportions annually for the next three decades,) the question begs, "Is $66.60 per month getting the job done, or are there some surprises in store for the American taxpayer and Medicare recipients." In reality, annual Part B Medicare costs have been increasing about 10% per year during the last decade, and a 1997 solution (Balanced Budget Act of 1997) to implement Provider Payment reforms (cutbacks) to the health care providers of Part B, worked to some extent. Unfortunately, the cutbacks were laid mainly on the backs of good health care providers.

Why has this happened? Obviously, the answer refers us back to our original premise of the demographic problems, and promises to get much worse. Another factor is the simple cost of new medicine, inflation, and the increase in beneficiary's lifetimes. Health care for the "old old" (85+) is more than 2 and one-half times as costly as for the "young-old", (65-84). ***Imagine what the picture will look like in 2010, when the Boomers start retiring, the worker-beneficiary ratio starts its drop to 2-to-1, and the "old old" are really old.*** One projection is for America to have over 1 million people over the age of 100 by mid-century. That seems like a long ways away, but in reality, includes—you guessed it—some of today's "baby boomers."

***Since the inception of Medicare, the deductibles for both Part A and Part B have grown.*** In 2004 the part A (hospital) deductible was $876. Seems simple enough. Except that the benefit period for that deductible is limited to ***sixty days***, with a $219 PER DAY deductible beginning on the sixty-first day and another $438 PER DAY deductible beginning on the ninety-first day with no payment beginning after the one hundred-fifty-first day. True, very few hospital stays go into sixty days, but unless you go back to the hospital for the same or related illness within the 60 day period, the ***DEDUCTIBLE STARTS OVER***. So quite possibly a person may face one, two, three or more deductibles in one year. For example, bronchitis treatment in January, influenza in May, and a heart problem in October. The deductibles now total over $2,600. Again, ***check that against the original $50 deductible in 1966 when Medicare was established!***

The point of all this is that these deductibles are going to go up. The ever increasing Part A deductible will soar and the Part B annual deductible ($100 in 2004) will either increase or take on a different scope. Count on it.

In addition to dollar problems, ***we have seen a growing number of physicians who do not wish to accept Medicare patients because of the continued cut in payments to the physicians by Medicare. This problem will worsen.*** Physicians who accept Medicare patients know in advance that they cannot charge those patients what they would charge under age 65 patients. Most doctors have even ***"cooperated" with their*** *elderly patients and Medicare, by accepting "assignment,"* a process in which they agree to accept whatever Medicare will send for a certain service. Usually, that payment, which is 20% less than the Medicare "allowable" charge for such service, will be accompanied by a payment from a patient-owned Medicare Supplement policy, which would seem to restore the physician's charge to a full payment. But, it really doesn't, in light of the Medicare imposed limits on physician charges.

Remember here, that we are talking about the growing number of physicians who feel they cannot afford to take on *new Medicare patients* period*, not those who already treat Medicare patients and accept assignment.* In January of 2003, American Medical Association President Yank Coble, Jr., MD, stated that in a survey conducted by the AMA, "Nearly half the physicians surveyed—*48 percent—will begin limiting or further limit the number of Medicare patients they treat because of the impending Medicare payment cut*. A full 61 percent of primary care physicians and 44 percent of specialists intend to impose new or additional limits on the Medicare patients they treat."

And this from a news release July 24, 2002, from the American Academy of Family Physicians—"A new study released today indicates that the number of family *physicians who are no longer taking new Medicare patients is 28 percent higher than one year ago.* The annual survey of its members by the American Academy of Family Physicians finds that 21.7 percent of physicians surveyed in June, 2002, report that they can no longer take new Medicare patients, a significant increase from last year's figure of 17 percent."

So, with the number of Medicare patients doubling in the next three decades, and the number of physicians willing to accept Medicare patients already on the downturn, *how will older Americans fit themselves into the grand scheme of health care in the future?*

Doctors are also aware that the Physician's Reform Act totally limited the charge they can apply for a certain service; and that charge is limited by law to 115% of the amount Medicare says is "allowable." That means the doctors know from the outset that they will be *limited to a maximum charge for any service which they may perform on a Medicare patient.* Period. They can perhaps charge more, but they cannot legally collect more. Therefore, the physicians know that by accepting Medicare patients, their income will be limited to an amount set by Medicare (assignment), rather than receiving payment for what they actually feel the service costs them to perform.

*The above scenario develops two problems. The physician must either: 1) stop accepting Medicare patients, or 2) transfer the costs of his business operation to other patients, thereby increasing the cost of health services to the under age-65 clientele. The situation has been for some time, the same for hospitals.* The terminology used to describe this dilemma is called "cost shifting" and it has been with us for some time. No matter what health care reform is brought about by any administration and subsequently the Congress, this problem will not go away.

*In the long haul,* Medicare's shortfall is expected to be three times as big as Social Security's. *In fact, according to the Health Care Financing Administration, (currently CMS—Center for Medicare and Medicaid) Medicare spending grew 11% from 1993-1994, and roughly 11% each year through 1997.* Makes no difference if the actual amount was 9%, 10%, or 11%, the number is scary—*and with the demographics illustrating the seriousness of things to come, we had better be working on some answers soon, very soon. No matter what legislation develops regarding Medicare and additional prescription drug encumbrances, Medicare is in trouble. However, one of the answers already sits within current Medicare dilemmas. Read on, brave souls.*

## WHY DOES NO ONE SEEM TO CARE ABOUT GRAFT, CORRPUTION, FRAUD, AND OVERPAYMENT IN THE MEDICARE SYSTEM?

Why is it that thousands of articles about fraud, overcharging, corruption, double bookkeeping by hospitals, graft, organized crime, mega-corporate profits, etc., in Medicare grew until the problem became a *$23 BILLION dollar mistake in the single year of 1996 alone?* The age old question, "Who's minding the store?" seems to have some great implications here. *A $23 dollar theft from a church would likely land somebody in jail. But $23,000,000,000.00?* Now hold on to your hat. In 1997 this amount was still at $21 billion, and by 1998 was "reduced" to $12.6 billion. So for three years this overpayment gaffe totals over $56 billion. Let's assume that this problem didn't just surface in 1996. *Is it possible that graft, corruption, theft and overpayment reached $100 billion in the 90's?* Very likely. More than likely—very probably.

*This hemorraging red ink blood bath doesn't seem to stop.* The General Accounting Office reported that *in 2001, the Medicare waste bill was back up to $19 billion, "down" from the amount of $20 billion reported in 1999.* Wouldn't even half of this amount have either bought a lot of prescription drugs for the Medicare program, or perhaps even have gone a long way toward preserving the credibility of both Part A and Part B trust funds?

Common citizens in this country watch television, read magazines and newspapers, listen to the radio, or television, and hear these things, and just assume that at least somebody in Washington or Baltimore (CMS headquarters) is also hearing them, but that doesn't seem to be the case. Let me quote the April, 1998 issue of the Reader's Digest. Out of hundreds of articles on this sordid issue, they seem to encapsulate it best.

> *"Last July, Inspector General June Gibbs Brown of the U.S. Department of Health and Human Services (HHS) released an audit of the Health Care Financing Administration (HCFA), the federal agency that administers Medicare. It calculated improper payments of $23.2 billion in 1996—14 percent of all Medicare fee-for-service payments. "And falsified documents and medical records would not necessarily have been picked up in our audit," Brown told Reader's Digest. "So the actual fraud figure could be even higher."*

Really!  Maybe the problem was really a simple mistake made by doctors, hospitals, nursing homes and home health care agencies who just didn't understand Medicare's 45,000 page rulebook (which by 2002 had grown to 100,000 pages.)  False alarm, no big deal.  *Would thirty years worth of little mistakes add up to say, a half trillion?* Nooooo problem.  *Just charge the taxpayers.  The lion's share of the estimated 23 billion went to the nation's hospitals at 32%, while doctors "found" 22%, and nursing homes, home health care agencies and laboratories "shared" in the remainder.*

Stephen J. Hedges, who authored a Special Report in the Feb. 2, 1998 issue of "U.S. News and World Report", must have lived on a steady diet of antacid and antidepressants as he coped with the information he developed during a lengthy investigation of...get ready for this...drug dealers and organized crime (including the RUSSIAN underworld) involved in Medicare fraud.  Listen to this little tidbit from Hedges:

> "...Hernandez, authorities say, is only one of a horde of hardened criminals who saw Medicare for what it really was—an unguarded, $250 billion-a-year pile of cash just waiting to be had."

And this:
> "Over the past decade, many of the criminally inclined have moved out of the drug trade to start careers in Medicare fraud, a crime where penalties are low and rewards stratospheric."

And this:
> "To realize this windfall, they have set up thousands of phony clinics, Medical-equipment outlets, and laboratories—a vast underworld of health care that investigators find particularly difficult to understand, let alone penetrate."

I don't know Hedges, but I'll bet he didn't get a Pulitzer for this expose, probably not even a bonus, and *that's indicative of how little anybody has cared about this problem.  What a shame.*

## MEDICARE NEEDS A NEW ENFORCEABLE ACTION PROGRAM NOW!  A "BULLDOG WATCHDOG" AGENCY

So, with billions in resources, how does this happen?  I think it happens very easily.  If you put some numbers to this outrage, it's fairly easy to figure.  Take the $20 billion fraud and overpayment bill for 2001 alone.  CMS genuinely seems to be concerned about the amount of fraud and overpayment.  If that's true, and we have to suppose it is since the numbers are their own, *why not spend say 10% to recover the other 90%?  Too easy?  Or too hard?*  Spend $2 billion just to catch crooks?  Well, the Balanced Budget Act of 1996, legislated a whole bunch of new ways to get the bad guys.  I would never say that no one has been trying, and in fact in 1997, more than 3,000 individuals and businesses were barred from doing business with Medicare.

HIPAA allowed a new $104 million to pay for 370 new agents, lawyers, and other personnel to prosecute fraud. I realize that money is in addition to what enforcers already spend. ***BUT IT'S NOT ENOUGH! You don't send a Poodle to do the work of a Pit Bull.*** You don't look at a full pool of a quarter of a trillion dollars and expect that a few hundred million is going to repair a $23 billion crack in the dam. So the hospitals double-booked and made off with 32% of $23 billion, something under $8 billion. So what? So this. ***Ten thousand young accountants, working in pairs, each auditing 5,000 hospitals, at a $50,000 per year individual salary would cost "only" $500 million. But look at the trade-off. A net $7.5 billion!***

The only problem is that it would take another 10,000 accountants to keep up with new tricks, so now we've cut the net gain from overpayments to "only" $7 billion. I know I'm oversimplifying, but think about it. If a program is worth $250 billion today, why wouldn't we spend at least 1%, or $2.5 billion to guard that worth. ***We need a completely new "bulldog watchdog" agency NOW, before we see the years (and not too far off) when we are spending $500 billion on Medicare annually, and would hope that enough progress has been made by the new agency to keep fraud, graft, corruption, etc. to a mere $10 billion.***

Honest, hard working doctors; and hospital, nursing home, and home health administrators, who do their books right, should be particularly upset that thousands of crooks took money out of a system which is in endangerment. This group alone has the most to lose, because new measures, which were instituted after HIPAA, have come down hard on them. The $115 billion "savings" in the Medicare program (over a period of five years) is about what we seem to have found in fraud and corruption. In reality, the good practitioners are being penalized in an almost identical proportion to the bad actors. Does this make sense? ***Why not just spend the total amount on defeating fraud and forget any decreases.***

Home Health agencies (which seem to have created about $3 billion of the $23 billion fraud and overpayment in 1996) have really been slugged. In the attempt to correct overspending in the Home Health Care system of Medicare, Congress in the Balanced Budget Bill of 1997, unsuspectingly did some serious surgical cutting to America's most desired type of non-acute care—that of Home Health Care. A message from Val Halamandaris, in "Caring" magazine cuts to the heart of this issue. Halamandaris, President of the National Association for Home Care and Hospice, brings the severity of what, in reality happened, to our attention with the following comments.

> *"In 1997 the Congress of the United States inflicted a deep wound on the nation's senior citizens by deeply cutting the Medicare Home Care benefit. Congress set out to trim the rate of growth by $16 billion over five years through 2002,* **but actually wound up cutting more than $70 billion from the**

*program.* *It is clear to everyone that they not only moderated the rate of growth* **but actually cut into the bone and muscle of home care services."**

*"It is important to take stock and fully understand what has already occurred. For example,* **approximately 1 million fewer Medicare beneficiaries now have access to home care services** *than in 1997. The* **number of home care agencies** *in the United* **States has been reduced by one-third, leaving hundreds of counties with so much as one home care agency within their borders."**

*"The* **home care agencies that have survived have seen their budgets reduced by approximately 50%.** *...All of this has meant that* **good people** *(executives, nurses, and home care aides)* **have left the field of home care in droves.** *There is now an* **acute shortage** *of personnel because* **thousands of nurses would rather retire than put up with the mountains of paperwork that they must do to qualify each and every patient."**

As I have pointed out, Home Health Care and Home Care are the number one choices of care delivery systems in American thinking. And now we have injured a most vital part of this health delivery system, with the "sanctions" and limitations, placed on good HHC agencies. I believe in getting the abuses under control, but to do so, at a time when that particular area of health care utilization is the prescription of choice *(and in turn saves even greater billions of otherwise utilized nursing home dollars), for millions of America's elderly, is a recipe for disaster.* As the old saying goes, "This needs to be corrected immediately, if not sooner." CMS needs to act quickly to get corrupt Home Health agencies out of the hair of those who operate properly, and reward good agencies with immediate reparations.

I can't help but offer a few examples of personal experience gleaned from a number of years in this business. While I have been "favored" with several (as has any agent,) *let me share two classics which illustrate what we as a nation have been dealing with in Medicare fraud and related problems.*

I have a very close and personal friend whose mother was dying of Leukemia. The friend went to spend the last few months with his mother, and was privileged to spend a few hours with her at one of the nation's larger hospitals while she received a transfusion of two pints of blood. Some weeks after, as he was handling her mail, he came across an Explanation of Medicare Benefits, which indicated that the *Medicare provider had been paid for transfusing 20 pints of blood.* He called the hospital, told them of the error and mentioned, that not only was this an error, but, incidentally, that this was *physically impossible.* He was assured that "there was some kind of error," and not to worry because his mother wouldn't have to pay anything since Medicare had already paid the entire bill. Not content with the non-interest in the obviously incorrect billing and EOMB, he called the Medicare contractor in that state and repeated his concern. The response from the administrator's employee was simple. *"Well, you're not the patient, and besides, what do you care anyway, the bill's been paid."* Over $2,000 of Medicare money had been wasted, and all my friend could do about it was utter in disbelief, *"Lady, I'm a taxpayer, and I do care."* Before a zealous employee of CMS calls me to pin me down on the details, let me say now, that it all happened long ago, in a far off land, and besides, they don't keep records that far back anyway. Do they?

Incidentally, a very good idea has made it's way to the front in this regard. *As of January 1, 1999, Medicare will offer rewards of up to $1,000 to Seniors who alert Medicare about fraudulent billing.* A good move, and one that should be very easy for Medicare patients to help with, in this big picture. All they have to do is check their own bills (some providers will send a copy to the patient), then check the EOMB and the benefit statement from their Medicare Supplement insurance company. Hey! Maybe some of this new stuff will work!

The second sad story happened shortly after the implementation of the Physician's Reform Act, which limited doctor's payments to a 30% additional charge (at that time) over what Medicare deemed allowable. The mother of an agent in my agency had gone to the hospital for some sort of a minor head operation. After successful surgery, a copy of the bill was received by the agent's mother. She called her son and informed him that she could not stand to have bills laying around and was going to pay it that day. *The agent asked her how much the bill was and she replied about $9,000.* Being in the Medicare Supplement business, the agent knew she should pay nothing, at least until Medicare and her supplemental policy, which he had sold her, had paid. The lady was upset with the thought of delay, but agreed to wait. Within a few weeks, the woman forwarded the EOMB, which she had received from the Medicare administrator (this was before "automatic claims") to the claims department of the insurance company. The EOMB indicated that *Medicare had allowed somewhere around $2,000 for the procedure, and accordingly, had paid the proper $1,600, or 80% share.*

After a few days, the agent "followed" the claim for his mother and was enlightened during a rather interesting phone call with the Medicare supplement company claims auditor. It seems that the doctor had charged *about $7,000 more for the procedure than Medicare had allowed for.* The auditor had called the doctor and asked him if he was aware that he was in violation of the Physician's Reform Act. The doctor answered, *"Sure, just send me what I've got coming."* Now this story seems to end innocently enough, but only a trained agent will recognize what was wrong here. Can you guess? Millions of retirees don't like bills, and pay them as fast as they can, when they can, if they can. So now you see the picture. *If "Mama" had paid the bill without the knowledge or advice of her son, do you suppose the doctor would have so cordially refunded nearly $6,500 involved in a simple billing procedure he knew to be fraudulent?* Only when an auditor identifies himself and informs him of his legal problem, does the doctor cheerfully capitulate.

How often do similar events occur across the nation, especially after HIPAA '96, in which we see that *Medicare contractors (who pay Medicare claims) are paid ahead of time to aggressively be "proactive" in discovering fraudulent claims, and simply aren't doing the job.* According to a DHHS audit developed late in 1998, the administrators of Medicare, (dozens of companies nationwide) have nearly *ignored the requirements of Medicare contracting in generating fraud cases* other than those based on an outside complaint, such as in my first friend's personal story related above. *What a sad state of affairs when people who are supposed to be in charge don't care, and the faucet just runs.*

In 1998 a fresh new face was given the job of fixing Medicare. The new face belonged to Mr. Bobby Jindal, a 26-year-old Louisiana resident, who received rave reviews for his work in restructuring that state's welfare program. Jindal headed up a Washington, D.C. commission which was *in charge of cleaning up, clearing up, and thereby saving Medicare from itself.* Many recommendations addressed all of the abuses and misuses of Medicare and Medicare money, and offered solutions to more problems than Medicare. *The hope is there, and I'm not saying that our Medicare people are not trying,* but whatever was hopefully going to happen after 1998, does not seem, in reality, to have taken place. *Again, this is evidenced by the fact that the problem, by 2001, still lingered at around $20 billion per year,* even though proportionally less, due to larger Medicare expenditures, but far less than acceptable.

So, what's the cure? As Joe Spiers so succinctly said in the May 27, 1996 issue of Fortune magazine, "As the baby boom moves from the Age of Aquarius into the Age of Arthritis—beginning in 15 years or so—expect an era of triage in which Medicare simply won't pay for every high-cost, low-benefit service that modern medicine has to offer."

"An era of triage," huh? Not exactly a common household phrase in the American vocabulary in this day and age. But one, which will be working it's way into our thinking during the next decade. "Triage" is a French word, which refers to wartime battlefield scenes, was developed early in the 18th Century. The word became very familiar to those in the military during World War I and World War II, and I am surprised to find out that it is still used in the field of medicine in regard to ambulance service and emergency care. In short, it describes the rationing of care, or preference of treating those with the most serious wounds first, the less injured second, and so on down. Well, we won't be talking battlefield conditions in American healthcare, hopefully, but I have so much respect for the term that I have dedicated a short chapter in this book to the issue—"The 'Triage' Issue"—and agree with Joe Spiers. *Like it or not, rationing is on its way.*

*Expect also, the following in the Medicare program, and believe it or not, soon,* as politicians finally begin to understand the *seriousness of the total aging problem.*

1) A raise in the eligibility age from 65 to 68, or 70.
2) Payroll taxes will take another small hit soon, larger—later.
3) Beneficiary "premiums" for part B will rise rapidly.
4) Lower payments from Part A to hospitals, perhaps with a complete overhaul of the DRG system, which will then cause a renewed cry, and further cost-shifting by hospitals.
5) A push for more HMO, managed care systems, even though the current structure of many Medicare HMOs has failed.

6) Reduction in Home Health Care Benefits and Skilled Care.
7) Raise in deductibles for both Parts A and B, followed by another raise in Medicare Supplement premiums.

On October 1, 1996, the government announced a 2% increase for Part A hospital payment for the nation's 5,200 hospitals which participate in Medicare. The reason given by HCFA: "More Medicare beneficiaries and hospital admissions, and an increase in the severity of illness of patients treated in hospitals." The landslide continued, and in 1998, HMO's received the bad news that they would be receiving only a modest 2% increase in their monthly per member rates after becoming accustomed to 5% to 10% raises in previous years. *The result has been the closing of a large number of HMO's and the resulting loss in HMO coverage for over 2.1 million elderly Americans by Dec. 31, 2001*

## MEDICARE, MEDICARE SUPPLEMENTS, MEDICARE + CHOICE, AND THEIR RELATIONSHIP TO LONG TERM CARE

## MEDICARE—THE BASICS

Legislation was developed and enacted from 1966 to 1968 to provide an answer to America's elderly and the problems of their rising health care costs. *The program became known as MEDICARE.* To date, by virtue of turning 65, Americans are now eligible for the hospital and medical benefits of Medicare if they have been registered under the Social Security Act or Railroad Retirement Plan.

Medicare is divided into two parts—*Part A and Part B. Part A* of Medicare provides for *hospitalization and some limited nursing home* benefits. *Part A is provided "free" to all Social Security and Railroad Retirement beneficiaries upon registering for Social Security.*

*Part B* of Medicare provides for *medical and some limited home health care* coverage for Social Security and railroad retirees. Part B, however, is purchased (or optionally rejected) and is withheld from the retirement check. The cost in 2003 is $66.60 per month, and the retiree has to purchase Part B to be eligible for a *Medicare Supplement Plan. The Part B premium will undoubtedly raise annually, as it has in the past, since it traditionally has represented about 25% of the actual cost of medical (doctor's) care, which in itself is ever increasing, and as beneficiaries increase their utilization of the home health care benefits.*

The Balanced Budget Act of 1997, called for a name change in Medicare to the *"Original Medicare Plan"* as it introduced several new and confusing alternative programs to the original Medicare plan. These new programs were invented in response to ways of controlling Medicare spending. They were not really requested by older people and retirees, and will do little to solve the coming demographic and financial problems facing Medicare. For the moment, we will concentrate on what is now being called the "Original Medicare Plan" because it, at least, is understood by generations of people on Medicare. In retrospect, as this change was introduced, the majority of recipients of Medicare had little interest in sorting through this manufactured confusion in hopes of finding anything of value to them.

As hospital and physician charges grew during the '70's and '80's, HCFA (the Health Care Financing Administration, now known as CMS, Centers for Medicare and Medicaid Services,) which administers Medicare, saw a **need to change the way in which hospital and physician's charges were treated.**

Because of the geographic and demographic variation in hospital charges, **"DIAGNOSTIC RELATED GROUPS," or DRG's as they came to be known, (486 of them) were selected as reasons a person would go to a hospital.** Medicare decided to allow a hospital a certain payment for each group—example: Broken hip— 8 days. The certain payment is determined by zip code in the USA and is made to the hospital regardless of whether or not the patient is hospitalized for the duration of the fixed number of days allowed by the particular DRG. DRG's (correct terminology is the Prospective Payment System) spurred an incredibly rapid growth in the nursing home industry **and terminology such as "extended care", "swing units", and "skilled care in a nursing home" became commonplace.** What was originally intended as a cost saving measure to get people **out of expensive hospital beds, became its own monster, as people now go to expensive nursing home beds.**

Medicare itself has deductibles and coinsurance amounts. The first Medicare deductible was **$50 for hospitalization (Part A) and $0 for medical services (Part B).** By 2004, the Part B deductible has only increased to $100 per calendar year. However, Part B has a coinsurance portion, which says that Medicare will pay 80% of what it considers an allowable or reasonable (approved) charge.

The Part A deductible has increased every year (and will continue to) since its inception. By 2004, this Part A deductible had become $876 PER BENEFIT PERIOD. Remember, this is not a calendar year deductible, it is a Benefit Period deductible, which only has a 60 day duration unless the hospitalization is repeated within 60 days of admission. Unrealistic as it is, that means the person could face as many as six $876 deductibles in a year's time. Example—Mrs. Jones goes to the hospital with pneumonia in January. First Benefit Period, first deductible. Then she returns in March with a broken hip. New Benefit Period, second deductible. Then in July, she has a bronchial problem. Third Benefit Period, and third deductible, and so on. This may or may not be a likely scenario.

Medicare Part A also allows for **some LIMITED NURSING HOME coverage in that it will pay for the FIRST 20 DAYS OF SKILLED CARE in a nursing home.** Beyond the first 20 days, (in 2004) there is a $109.50 PER DAY DEDUCTIBLE for SKILLED CARE ONLY for 80 days, and **THERE IS NO PAYMENT OF ANY KIND FOR INTERMEDIATE OR CUSTODIAL CARE.**

## MEDICARE SUPPLEMENT

Since Medicare itself has deductibles and coinsurance amounts, the need for a **MEDICARE SUPPLEMENT Insurance Policy arises.** Government, CMS and Medicare itself refer to Medicare Supplement as "Medigap." Do not be confused, **Medicare Supplements and Medigap coverage are the same product.**

The history of Medicare Supplements and their sale until recently was less than admirable. Given the over 65 market, and an often ill-informed public, unscrupulous traveling agents abused many elderly people in replacement (or duplication) of existing policies in order to receive new (higher) first year commissions each year. Much legislation resulted. Without delving into the details, let us suffice it to say the **STANDARDIZED MEDICARE SUPPLEMENT** was the major outgrowth, with a lowering and limitations placed on new and renewal commissions**. It would be an understatement to say that the technique worked well.** Seldom are former Medicare Supplement problems with agents now revisited.

Medicare Supplement Policy provisions have been standardized for several years. You can locate and review a copy of the **"Outline of Medicare Coverage" and the Plan A (Basic Benefits) as guidelines.** Your Medicare Supplement agent will provide one for you, and perhaps you have a "dated" one from an original sale. Please note the first line, "Medicare supplement insurance can be sold in only ten standard plans." As you will see, the plans are labeled A through J. You will also note that **the higher the letter, the greater the benefits. Premiums follow accordingly.** Also note that the major difference in plans H, I, and J, as opposed to plans A through G is the addition of prescription drug coverage. As you can see, the most comprehensive coverage, excluding drugs, is plan F, which leaves the typical Medicare Supplement policyholder with no deductibles and coverage for excess charges under Part B physician's charges.

Again, these are the traditional, or "original" Medicare Supplement coverages after standardization. These plans are still available after the introduction of Medicare Plus Choice in November, 1998. In addition, two new options were made available in the ten standardized Med Supp plans after Medicare Plus Choice became available. The two new options are a high deductible Plan F and Plan J, which allow the policyholder to choose either plan with a $1,500 deductible with the trade-off obviously being lower premiums. **That in essence, makes a choice of twelve Medicare Supplement plans, from which to choose.**

**Medicare Select** was introduced in addition to the ten standard policies, as a cost saving measure to Medicare beneficiaries. The plan works, but the policyholder must understand that they have selected a plan which insures them only at a specific hospital, or network of hospitals, and may be limited to the services of specific physicians at those hospitals. **The trade-off is that the chosen hospital will waive the Part A deductible for services received at that hospital**. As a result, premiums may be from 10% to 30% lower. **Medicare Select is normally used as a tool for competitive hospitals within a community.**

*Medicare + Choice utilizes Medicare Health Maintenance Organizations (HMO's),* which contract directly with Medicare and receive a *fixed monthly fee from Medicare per enrollee.* Although, at its highest point, only about 18% of Medicare beneficiaries chose HMO coverage, cost savings to the patient (as compared to Medicare Supplement policies) seemed to be the chief motivating factor for enrollment. Unfortunately, the late 1990's saw a significant disappearance of a large number of Medicare HMO plans due to rising costs and limited Medicare payments, which led to bankruptcies of the plans. *By the end of the year 2,001, over 2.1 million people in Medicare HMO's were told to find insurance elsewhere, according to Weiss Ratings, Inc.* By mid-summer 2003, another 400,000 people had seen their HMOs close down.

*Again, enrollees must be made aware that HMO's require that Medical services be utilized at their hospitals with their doctors.* Some HMO's offer additional benefits not covered by Medicare, but recent developments have seen some HMO's dropping those features, and others totally closing down their contracts, as Medicare allowances for the HMO services are squeezed.

After *voluntarily disenrolling* from the traditional Medicare HMO, depending on state and federal laws, *you may not be able to qualify for traditional Medicare Supplement policies due to pre-existing conditions,even though you will be allowed to stay in Medicare.* This is as opposed to the new Medicare Plus Choice wherein people will be allowed to return to traditional Medicare Supplement one time, within the first twelve months of enrolling in a Plus Choice program. Please remember that, as with all new variations in Medicare choices, disenrollment will require careful consideration by yourself, agents, and companies to see that you can comply with the new rules. For that reason, be careful in your choices and don't expect immediate action on any switching of policies. Also, *due to the closing down of many Medicare HMO's, many people began to seek coverage back at their traditional Medicare Supplement companies. The law allows a 63 day "window" in which to requalify for Medicare Supplements (plans, A,B,C and F), with no pre-existing condition limitations if the client can provide proof of the termination of the Medicare HMO plan.*

In 1999, all states were informed of the new choices available under Medicare Plus Choice. Original Medicare, Original Medicare Supplemental plans, Medicare Select, and Original Medicare HMO's remained available and most Medicare beneficiaries remained with their existing plan. *Individuals must be enrolled in both Part A and Part B to be eligible for a Medicare Plus Choice program, and the plan is not considered a Medicare Supplement insurance policy.* The "alphabet" choices are listed below, even though very few of them, with the exception of the HMO's, have actually been utilized by Medicare enrollees, with most enrollees regarding the "new plans" as experimental and remaining with the traditional Medicare Supplement Plan choices.

A) HMO with Point of Service—A Health Maintenance Organization with a Point of Service option. Patient uses the HMO hospital and doctors for most services, but for an extra fee, may go outside of the HMO to seek services.

B) PPO—Preferred Provider Organizations. Physician networks that charge less if beneficiary utilizes them for discounted fee.

C) PSO—Provider Sponsored Organizations. Plans owned and operated by hospitals and doctors that provide most of the services to the beneficiary like an HMO, but supposedly are more user friendly.

D) PFFSP—Private Fee For Service Plan. Operates similar to traditional Medicare with some exceptions. There is no limit to the premiums or charges for service, so beneficiaries may be paying substantial costs. Government subsidized private insurance. The Plan gets a fixed amount per beneficiary.

E) MMSA—Medicare Medical Savings Accounts. MMSA's are a private insurance policy with a deductible as high as $6,000 with thepremiums paid by Medicare (deposited in the MMSA account which is tax free) which can then be used for any health care expenses, including the deductible. Beneficiaries are forced to pay for medical bills out-of-pocket for the amounts under the deductible.

F) Private contracts between doctors and beneficiaries are now allowed under certain conditions, however, claims cannot be filed with Medicare or Medicare Supplement policies, and limiting charges (Physicians Reform Act) on physicians doesn't apply.

G) Religious and Fraternal Benefit Society plans are authorized.

What is the outlook for Medicare Plus Choice Plans and traditional "Original" Medicare and traditional "Original" standardized Medicare Supplement plans. Who's to say? We shall see what we shall see. But one thing is certain. Most people, even federal and state advisors, are saying, *"Go slow in making the decision to enter into a new program, particularly if you are satisfied with your current plan.* Again, these plans were not requested by retirees, *but were sought out as solutions to enable Medicare to cut costs.* Rural vs. urban interests played a part.

As a point of interest, and to help you protect yourself against someone who may take advantage of you, the following educational items will help you *determine the difference between proper (ethical) and improper (unethical or illegal) replacement of Medicare Supplement policies.*

A) Some Medicare Supplement products sold prior to July 1,1993 were better than the current "standardized" policy series. Some policies contained provisions, which paid the client an automatic 80 (or more) days of nursing home care at any level of care—skilled, intermediate, or custodial. In today's environment, that amounts to about a $10,000 benefit which was included automatically as a built-in feature. *Replacement of that, or similar products, would result in a loss of benefits to the insured, a practice which is unethical,* since the policyholder may not be aware that the feature is not available in any standardized plan sold subsequent to July 1, 1993.

B) *Replacement of an existing policy in order to obtain a new first-year commission is unethical.* Most states by now have enacted legislation which allows only level commission on policy renewals. This is to discourage, and

# OUTLINE OF MEDICARE SUPPLEMENT COVERAGE — COVER PAGE
## BENEFIT PLANS A, C, D AND F

Medicare supplement insurance can be sold in only 10 standard plans plus two high deductible plans. This chart shows the benefits included in each plan. Every company must make available Plan "A." Some plans may not be available in your state.

BASIC BENEFITS: Included in all plans.

Hospitalization: Part A coinsurance plus coverage for 365 additional days after Medicare benefits end.

Medical Expenses: Part B coinsurance (generally 20% of Medicare approved expenses) or, in the case of hospital outpatient department services under a prospective payment system, applicable copayments.

Blood: First 3 pints of blood each year.

| A | B | C | D | E | F | F* | G | H | I | J | J* |
|---|---|---|---|---|---|---|---|---|---|---|---|
| Basic Benefits | Basic Benefits | Basic Benefits | Basic Benefits | Basic Benefits | Basic Benefits | | Basic Benefits | Basic Benefits | Basic Benefits | Basic Benefits | |
| | | Skilled Nursing Coinsurance | Skilled Nursing Coinsurance | Skilled Nursing Coinsurance | Skilled Nursing Coinsurance | | Skilled Nursing Coinsurance | Skilled Nursing Coinsurance | Skilled Nursing Coinsurance | Skilled Nursing Coinsurance | |
| | Part A Deductible | Part A Deductible | Part A Deductible | Part A Deductible | Part A Deductible | | Part A Deductible | Part A Deductible | Part A Deductible | Part A Deductible | |
| | | Part B Deductible | | | Part B Deductible | | | | | Part B Deductible | |
| | | | | | Part B Excess (100%) | | Part B Excess (80%) | | Part B Excess (100%) | Part B Excess (100%) | |
| | | Foreign Travel Emergency | Foreign Travel Emergency | Foreign Travel Emergency | Foreign Travel Emergency | | Foreign Travel Emergency | Foreign Travel Emergency | Foreign Travel Emergency | Foreign Travel Emergency | |
| | | | At-home Recovery | | | | At-home Recovery | | At-home Recovery | At-home Recovery | |
| | | | | | | | | Basic Drugs ($1,250 Limit) | Basic Drugs ($1,250 Limit) | Extended Drugs ($3,000 Limit) | |
| | | | | Preventive Care | | | | | | Preventive Care | |

*Plans F and J also have an option called a high deductible Plan F and a high deductible Plan J. These high deductible plans pay the same or offer the same benefits as Plans F and J after one has paid a calendar year [$1580] deductible. Benefits from high deductible Plans F and J will not begin until out-of-pocket expenses are [$1580]. Out-of-pocket expenses for this deductible are expenses that would ordinarily be paid by the policy. These expenses include the Medicare deductibles for Part A and Part B, but does not include, in Plan J, the plan's separate prescription drug deductible or, in Plans F and J, the plan's separate foreign travel emergency deductible.

even **outlaw, the practice of "rolling, which meant that agents switched people each year to obtain higher first-year commissions.** The legislation has been highly successful.

C) The practice of **"stacking" (selling more than one policy to a client) is illegal under Federal Medicare Law,** but some unethical agents still ignore or overlook the law and continue to take advantage of the client in their desperation to seek new sales. **Duplication is illegal.**

D) **Replacement of Medicare Supplement policies is legal, and in some cases, very beneficial to the client.** Since all Medicare Supplement policies currently sold are identical by Plan (Plan A, Plan B, etc.) there can be no variation as to the benefits of any single plan. **However, the agent must compare "apples with apples."** Comparing a Plan C (which is less expensive) with a Plan F (which offers more benefits), means that **the client MUST BE MADE AWARE OF A LOSS OF BENEFITS, EVEN IN CONSIDERATION OF PREMIUM.** You, the client, must evaluate what is in your best interests, or at least, what is in your pocketbook, when considering loss of benefits. **In all instances, a replacement form which discloses the reason for the replacement (lower premiums, change of plan, etc.) must be taken at the time of the replacement** and forwarded to the replacing company, for it to determine if the replacement procedure is in fact, suitable to the client.

E) Variations in premium (between two companies) may be as high as $300 for a Plan C Product, and as high as $700 for a Plan J product, depending on the age of the client. **Reduction of premium for the same plan would be an example of an ethical replacement of an existing policy— "apples to apples."**

F) The client needs to be aware that should they choose to replace a policy, after comparing benefits and premiums, that a REPLACEMENT form, must be signed and submitted to the company. **Not indicating that the new application is a replacement is illegal.**

As you can judge from the above maze, we have seen a great deal of legislation passed within the past dozen years, which deals with the way Medicare has tried to cut costs. Most of the grand experiment has gone ignored, with the possible exception of Medicare HMO's, which flourished for several years, and in many locations, still do. What will the future bring? As we pass into a new era of a greatly increased utilization of both Medicare and Medicare supplements, and with the obvious need to solve this country's prescription drug problems, as well as inflation in health care costs, **no one can predict with certainty, or even optimism, what Medicare will look like a decade from now.** We will live through it, some people will be satisfied and others dissatisfied, but one thing is certain, **you will have to protect yourself as well as you can, and prepare today, against all future health care costs. As you know, in the long term care arena, and even in the Home Health and Home care delivery system, you will not be receiving a great deal of additional consideration from Medicare. Stay tuned.**

# CHAPTER 10

# THE MEDICAID ISSUE

*THIS IS AN ISSUE?*
*NAY, THIS IS A KIND AND GENTLE WARNING*

## SO NOBODY HAS TOLD YOU ABOUT THE "MEDICAID POLICE."

Nowhere else in "Guarding Your Gold II" have I started a chapter with personal experiences. ***But the importance of this information must be placed first, lest a reader not understand the seriousness of setting themselves up for Medicaid long term care assistance.*** There are three major phrases that the reader must become familiar with—***Lien laws, Estate Recovery Laws, and Medicaid Recovery Units.*** They are real, necessary, and effective. They were designed to protect a program set up years ago for those truly in need, but which has been invaded by people who chose to simply "skirt" the intended use of Medicaid, and "get my long term care needs covered by the government."

Unfortunately, many well-meaning and well-intentioned people are not aware that ***the program is not an entitlement***, and are unwittingly cast into the Medicaid situation simply because of poor or misdirected advice. ***They are honest, law-abiding citizens who "went along with the system,"*** usually during a time of crises, when urgent and immediate action had to be taken, because proper planning had not been achieved. You can avoid such scenarios—this chapter will show you how—but first, a couple of real life examples of honest folk who, after the fact, were notified that their best intentions, had indeed, gone astray.

My first experience with such a case came about four years ago, when a friend of mine called with the following story. He said, "Ron, I've got a rather large problem on my hands and I wondered if you could help me. Two years ago, when it became apparent that my mother was going to need to go to a nursing home***, we called a lawyer here in town and asked how we could get her on some kind of state assistance.*** The lawyer told us how to do it, and we transferred the title of my mother's home to my sister's and my name, as joint tenants. Well, my mother died a few weeks ago and ***now we have a letter from the state wanting the $78,000 they spent on her nursing home costs.*** The letter says they want us to reimburse them."

I said, "Obviously, they want it from the sale of the house, or ***whatever other means they can get from her estate***—and you and your sister are now in charge of the estate—so you are the proper party for them to look to for reimbursement. That's what they are doing, and they are well within their right to do so, because the transfer was legal, but the simple transfer "lookback" period has not run it's three years."

Chapter 10

My friend asked, "What can we do?" as if he assumed I had the answer. I did. I said, "I guess you had better call your attorney and ask him who he has his E&O insurance with, because it looks as though you will be asking them for some answers." I wasn't being flip, but *I was making sure that he and his sister knew that they had not escaped paying for their mother's care by simply following the advice of an attorney, who did not know (or did not explain) all the facts about the transfer of "eligible resources" to qualify for Medicaid.* Keep in mind, these were common people who were not trying to "skewer" the government, but simply thought they were doing the right thing by following their attorney's advice. The state felt differently, and recovered their $78,000. The attorney did not help in the aftermath of the "sweet deal." *The Recovery Unit won. Bad loan. More on this later.*

Then, recently, an agent acquaintance gave me an *actual copy of another case letter.* It's not quite like the one young men used to get from the Selective Service Draft Board which began, "Greetings, you have been selected by your friends and neighbors..." (to report for a physical because you were being drafted), but it's about the same.

The letter is from "The Recovery Unit—Estate Division", is dated, addressed, and reads:

> **"In the matter of the estate of: Recipient; _____, Our File #: _____**
>
> **'NOTICE OF INTENT TO FILE A CLAIM AGAINST THE RECIPIENT'S ESTATE'**
>
> **The Department of Public Health and Human Services** *would like to extend It's condolences for your recent loss.* **This letter is to inform you of the laws concerning Estate Recovery. Pursuant to ___(state)___ , statute __(number)__ , the Recovery Unit, on behalf of DPHHS intends to file a claim against the estate of the above named individual. According to the Department's records**, *the above named was a recipient of Medicaid* **benefits. The Department is seeking reimbursement from the estate for Medicaid payments made on the recipient's behalf..."**

Of course, there is much more detail in the one page letter, but the surprising thing was that it had been sent within a few days of the recipient's death, and *received much to the amazement of the son of the recipient.* The point is this—*do not take recovery units lightly. They are fast, efficient, and serious.* Of course there's a way to avoid all of this. It's called Long Term Care Insurance—and for those of you in the four "Partnership" states, it's even a better deal.

The above examples show that there are ways to imperil the objectives of your long term care needs, but *there are also ways to avoid the aftermath of poor planning.* Before we discuss the ways which can be legal, and which, when combined with a sufficient LTCI policy as a base, could make financial sense; we need to describe the background of the problems which face Americans in protecting that which they have earned, inherited, or accumulated.

For our purposes, let us suppose that the average American wage-earner has been fortunate enough to accumulate assets of a nature that would make government view him or her as "non-poor." What that really means then, is that the person or couple would be considered at least "middle-class." It then follows that since most middle-class Americans have assets of some amount, *they are not "poor," "impoverished," or "destitute," and they are therefore ineligible for welfare, or Medicaid benefits.*

For openers, we need to look at how both Medicare and Medicaid fit into the national health picture in general, and long term care in particular. In short, we need to *understand the differences in qualifying for each program.*

The explanation works like this. You can be a millionaire and *qualify for MediCARE simply by being a citizen of the United States,* eligible for Social Security, receive Medicare Part A, purchase Medicare Part B for $58.70 per month (in 2003) and you're set for governmental payment of medical bills for acute or intensive care, or what we would refer to as "cure" services. You can also be *eligible for, and receive MediCARE, if you are a pauper.* So, essentially America takes care of all of its sixty-five-year-old-plus citizens (for their medical "cure" services) through Medicare. *Thus, Medicare is regarded as an "entitlement program."*

*Not so with MediCAID.* There is a world of difference. *MediCAID is not an entitlement program,* although a large segment of our population from generation to generation have been taught to *believe that it is* an entitlement. The difference between the two programs—and the entitlement feature—can be found in one word—*qualification.* There is no qualification for Medicare, it is pretty well guaranteed to everybody reaching age 65. *There is a qualification for Medicaid*—in a word--impoverishment. In another word, Medicaid is—*Welfare.* Medicaid was designed for the *truly poor, regardless of age,* and is available to people who can demonstrate to the state that they qualify for Medicaid assistance through a low asset or income base. Remember that we said, "can demonstrate to the state" because, later in this chapter, we are going to visit the issue of "artificial" impoverishment, by "demonstrating" how this is achieved in order to receive Medicaid assistance.

*Medicaid is funded by both state and federal governments*, and the payment of benefits of the program is dictated by the feds to some extent. But interpretations of, qualifications for, and administration of Medicaid are defined by *BOTH* the state and federal government through various laws, mandates, rules and regulations. The *state's governments have permission to change those rules through a waiver*, which can be accepted by the Department of Health and Human Services of the U.S. government. In other words, *each state has the right to regulate and interpret the MediCAID program in its own manner.* That's why your state's Medicaid rules will be different than the next person's state. No problem. Or at least it hadn't been until the rise and swell of health care unrest in the early 1990's.

What started as a noble gesture on the part of our state and national governments has become somewhat of a nightmare. *Welfare programs seem to have a way of getting out of hand at best, and out of control at worst.* We have been seeing some of the worst. Current state budget problems are only recent reminders of the problems both the state and federal governments have in regard to keeping up with welfare, or Medicaid financial requests, including nursing home benefits.

While a person with a million bucks may be lucky enough to not need either medical care through Medicare, or nursing facility benefits through Medicaid, America and its states have NOT come up with a solution for the average middle American and his or her desire to expect governmental payment of long-term nursing facility costs. *Nor will they be doing so in the near or very distant future.* Simply, since the payment would ultimately wind up on the back of taxpayers, *America's workers cannot afford to contribute to a national nursing home payment system, which has already begun to deteriorate.* In other words—*a third entitlement program*—which would be in addition to Social Security and Medicare. Also, in light of the coming demographic problems of extended longevity and a top-heavy ratio of elderly to working age people, Medicaid will have it's hands full in simply correcting and modifying existing qualification and eligibility standards.

The American Medicaid program started simply and honestly enough, but unfortunately, as it has been allowed to develop, it has become a major part of American healthcare budgeting—even without being an entitlement program. Though the nation's nursing home bill comes nowhere close to Medicare's expenditures—and accompanying supplemental (actual) expenses—it is, in itself, huge—and becoming greater. According to the Health Care Financing Administration, *long term care expenditures for nursing home and home health care rose from $64 Billion in 1990, to $106 Billion by 1995, and to $124 Billion by 2000, an 8% annual increase.* Depending on which year you choose to use, total public funds for payment of nursing home and home health care, varied from 48% to 57%, with *Medicaid picking up the greatest part of the total public funding* (of nursing home and home health care expenses).

How did nursing home expenditures grow to be so large? *They grew as the result of a restructuring of the way Medicare paid hospitals in 1983.* Within a few years nursing home utilization soared, and costs of that utilization followed. This increase was the result of the "invention" of the Prospective Payment System or Diagnostic Related Groups (DRG's); in which a hospital is paid for a certain number of patient days, according to any particular diagnosis. The PPS, or DRG factor, which supposedly lowered Medicare hospital payments, also *influenced* the rise in costs to Medicaid, since about 40% of the welfare bill in most states goes to pay Medicaid funded nursing home bills.

## MEDICAID— WHY IT ISN'T WORKING AS INTENDED— AND WHY WE CAN'T BLAME THE NURSING HOMES

First of all, you may be aware that Medicaid pays most of the nation's nursing home bill, but *you may not be aware of the problems this reliance on Medicaid has caused the nursing homes.* In this chapter we discuss how people qualify for Medicaid, and how others, who have no right to Medicaid paid for nursing home assistance, imperil the system. To simplify, let's resort to some basic facts. Medicaid is welfare. Welfare is paid for by state and federal governments. So, it follows then, *that welfare programs are not going to be plush; that they are going to be as bare-boned as tax dollars will allow. It further follows, then, that nursing homes are at the mercy of what Medicaid can afford to pass on to them in the form of monetary payments, derived from limited tax sources, thereby perpetuating a never-ending dilemma.*

So, let's take Nursing Home A, and make the supposition that 90% of its residents are on Medicaid. Not just this year, but for the ten years previous, and for probably ten or twenty years into the future. What kind of past does that represent, and what kind of future does that project? Simply, that *the nursing home must survive on the very lowest monetary support that tax dollars will allow. Low wages are inevitable. Poor care and sometimes, poor meals are the result.* Low pay for hard work leads nursing homes to employ people of less qualification than they would like to recruit. *Less than desirable working conditions* lead a great percentage of the labor force to shun caregiving jobs for better opportunities—leaving the institutions with a very small percentage of capable workers to choose from. *Turnover of existing employees (as high as 135% in some locations in one year)* becomes a never ending merry-go-round. *Worker's Compensation rates skyrocket.* Mounds of regulations must be complied with, *causing care dollars to become administration dollars.* All the conditions combine, and create an incredible specter of uncertainty. Nursing Home A suffers a *continuing cycle of inadequate dollars* on which to operate, and less than hopeful prospects of improving their conditions. This, because Nursing Home A is reliant on Medicaid dollars and regulations, which in turn are reliant on government dollars and regulations, which in turn are reliant on taxpayer dollars and limitations.

As a measure of the importance in being fair to Nursing Home A, we must give you an explanation of at least part of the problem. That "part," is the system in which the nursing home is forced to operate. In actuality, if the going "street rate" for one day's care is $120, you will be surprised to know that Medicaid pays only 75-80 percent of that rate, in most cases. So, if the cost of care is really $120 per day multiplied by 100 residents, that amounts to a total of $12,000 per day. If Medicaid is only able to pay 80% of the bill, the amount is $9,600, which means the cost of care went short by $2,400 that day, for a *net loss of around $876,000 for the year*. Now, where does any business go to make up this kind of shortfall? Normally, bankruptcy is the answer, and about 10 per cent of the nation's nursing homes have chosen this route in the last few years. Or, the deficiency might be made up by the county, in which the nursing home exists, or some other benevolent sources. But mostly, it is made up by the private pay patients in that old phrase, which our country has come to know and accept in government driven health business, as "cost shifting." That's right, *because of the deficiencies in the Medicaid system, the actual expense is shifted to the private pay patient*, to make up the difference.

Now let's add to Nursing Home A's problems a fairly new predicament—that of liability. Several sources are reporting a significant rise in general liability and professional liability premiums for nursing homes. In other words, *monies made available by Medicaid for patient care, have had to go to liability insurance premiums to defend the new found "cash cow," of suing nursing homes for not providing excellent care.* Try to understand this—I can't. In other words, get grandma eligible for nursing home welfare benefits, and when the care isn't perfect, file suit. Is it any wonder then, that Nursing Home A has less and less dollars available to pay for the quality caregiver they would prefer to hire, and to achieve what is expected of the nursing home—quality caregiving?

Nursing Home B, on the other hand, learned to circumvent Medicaid dependency and has perhaps ten percent Medicaid occupancy. Nursing Home B accepts only, or nearly only, private (personal, family, or insurance) pay patients and avoids the limitations of Medicaid payment and regulation, by doing so. *Yes, the cost of the care is normally higher, because people, or insurance companies on their behalf, are paying for their care. Nursing home B thrives as a business and can offer amenities and quality care that Nursing Home A struggles to provide.* What? This works? Really.

In the meantime, *nobody seems to care about whether a "well-to-do" person gets themselves artificially qualified for Medicaid* by hiding or transferring assets, thereby adding to the already heavy existing burden of Nursing Home A. Ah, yes, the old "Medicaid Planning" trick, in which an attorney enables clients of substantial means, to artificially qualify for Medicaid, and charge the public to pay for care which the recipient is not really entitled to. In other words, we are faced with a sort of reverse "Robin Hood" scenario, which says "steal from the poor to enable the rich," to receive benefits that are supposedly rightfully available only to the poor. *As an added insult, the state of Massachusetts enacted legislation in July of 2003, which will tax "nursing home beds"* to relieve the burden of Medicaid nursing homes in that state. Tax all beds to pay for Medicaid—where the money goes, anyway? *Not really. Tax the "private pay" nursing home beds to direct the money to the Medicaid nursing home beds— that's what's really going on. Cost shifting at its ultimate craziest.*

I will never forget giving a presentation about the value of Long Term Care insurance to a group of nursing home, assisted living, and home health agency administrators. During my presentation, the administrator of an assisted living facility stood and said, "I'm sorry to interrupt you, Ron, but I just have to tell our group how pleasant it is to deal with insurance companies, that have their clients as our patients. We send the bill and they send the check. It's nice not to have all the paper to deal with, and it's a very easy way to do business." *Easy, indeed. The current and coming thing, for those who look to LTCI to solve the problem now.*

With the "all-too-real" costs of Medicare and Medicaid, statesmen during the last decade have finally understood that the *demographics just won't support three huge entitlement program.* Since Medicare is firmly entrenched as an entitlement program, and *the American public is unable to fully absorb the costs of long term care, as another entitlement,* limitations on Medicaid nursing home eligibility needed to be implemented. Obviously, the problem preceded the solution, and during the last decade, restrictions on eligibility and availability became more than talking points.

## SO—WHAT'S THE KIND AND GENTLE WARNING?

Now we must back up a minute. Let's take our millionaire and let him or her develop a serious medical problem. Let's just use cancer as the malady. Mr. or Mrs. "M" will immediately qualify for benefits for THIS health problem through traditional MediCARE. No matter the ability of this person to pay, they will only be subject to the Part A Deductible, the Part B deductible, and the Part B co-payment up to a certain amount. The grief of financial indebtedness under the Medicare program is limited.

Not so under **MediCAID.** Since Medicaid was established to **provide limited public funds for the care of the truly needy**, our millionaire friend is obviously ineligible for the "public" paid services of Medicaid. Should the need arise for a "care" service (meaning an extended nursing home stay) the "M's" of America simply will not qualify. Seems fair enough. The "M's" should have the wherewithal to pay a nursing home bill, or the premiums to insure against such, and not suffer a financial calamity. We can all understand and live with that.

The eligibility problems which surface however, are not relative to millionaires, and are twofold. First, **what do we do for people who are not millionaires**, and through their own prudence and perseverance **have been able to build a "nest egg" of say $100,000** to see them through an ever lengthening retirement span? Perhaps the "hundred thou" is not even liquid. Perhaps it is tied up in home ownership, a farm, ranch, business or other similar venue. Perhaps they do not have accessibility to the "nest egg" and are only receiving the interest, or rent, or payments from the asset. **Will they qualify for MediCAID under these circumstances?**

I can most assuredly answer. "No!" As long as they have a considerable amount of assets, "middle Americans" will not qualify for Medicaid, unless they choose to become involved in what has become known as "Medicaid planning," which may not be the best answer.

Second, what do we do for people who have the "misfortune" of not contracting a "cure" service eligible disease which would not be covered by Medicare? Can't happen? Guess again. Without entertaining a morbid discussion of which unfortunate disease to acquire, suffice it to say that our cancer patient was "lucky" to develop a malady, which was covered under Medicare.

But, **what do we have for the American citizen who is less fortunate** and contracts Alzheimer's, Parkinson's, or one of a dozen or so subtle insidious diseases, which wrack the mind, as well as the body, **and require "care" services?** What do we have for the unfortunate soul who suffers a stroke and must live for years under the watchful eye of caretakers to accomplish even the simplest of otherwise normal tasks? What do we have for the lady who spent thirty-five years working for wages and along with her husband raised a family of three children, sending them off to school and high income jobs, but who is worn out at age seventy-four? What do we have for the farmer or grocer who took the biggest gambles of all in keeping America fed, and scraped enough money together to settle in for their "Golden Years," only to be brought down with a debilitating disease that doesn't qualify for more than a few days of hospitalization and twenty days of skilled care in a nursing home? *Not much. Unless they can prove they are poor, and can do so to qualify for welfare.*

Thus, what is an unpopular and bitter pill for Mr. and Mrs. Middle America to swallow (no pun intended), is that the average person, or the above average financially sound citizen, has no governmental program in which to seek relief from ever increasing nursing home, home care, or assisted living expenditures. Guess what. *That dilemma is not going to change. It "ain't" gonna happen. It simply will not get any better for people who have assets.* In fact, the trend is toward an opposite extreme. People with assets will face a much tougher task in qualifying for any type of governmental assistance in the area of Medicaid. In addition, their personal payment of Medicare services will increase.

Americans with assets must understand this situation. *Don't count on government of any kind to pay for your long term care of any sort if you have assets.* Why? *Because, as we said, government cannot lay another expensive entitlement program on the backs of a proportionally smaller taxpayer base.* As recognition of this funding problem, governmental programs in 1993 began to change existing rules. The Omnibus Budget Reconciliation Act, commonly referred to as OBRA '93, directly affected both Medicare and Medicaid recipients, and qualifications for Medicaid.

## PROBLEMS WITH MEDICAID START TO SURFACE

The portion of OBRA '93, which is of GREAT IMPORTANCE to our subject—that of protecting assets legally—deals with the various state regulations in qualifying individuals for Medicaid Nursing Home benefits.

Let's explain the existing qualifications for Medicaid. A simple definition will have to substitute for thousands of pages of welfare and Medicaid rules, which, in themselves, are different in each state. *Simply, to qualify for Medicaid (i.e. Nursing Home payment assistance under welfare law) a person must prove "impoverishment,"* a term which the government would probably like to redefine, but nevertheless is attributed to that late great champion of the Senior cause, Senator Claude Pepper of Florida. At any rate, a person applying for Medicaid must prove that he or she has no countable (eligible) assets (excluding some exempt personal assets) over $2,000 if single, and roughly $80-90,000, if married. This amount will vary (sometimes greatly) by state.

*Originally*, to avoid a "spenddown" of the assets over a period of several years, the federal government set a guideline of allowing assets to be transferred over a two-and-a-half year period (30 months) into irrevocable trusts, or as an outright transfer to heirs, etc., outside of the thirty month period. That meant that people with assets could transfer those assets to their children and, thirty months after the transaction date, ask to qualify for Medicaid. Well, OBRA '93 included a provision that eliminated the "30 month lookback period" and, retroactive to May 11, 1993, *allowed the states to establish their own limitations for "lookback" up to 60 months.* So, as the states have now attempted to patch up their various Medicaid budget problems, *we have seen most of them increase the "legal transfer period" to 36 months for a simple transfer, or 60 months for transfer to a trust.* Look for the simple transfer to increase further to 42 or even 48 months within the next decade. In 2002, some states started the movement to ask for a 42 month waiver.

This is in marked contrast to the *states who have entered into "partnership" agreements,* whereby the individual has a right to purchase an LTCI policy for "X" number of dollars, and the state will then allow a like number of dollars to be paid for by it's Medicaid program, with no time limitation on transferring assets during that period. *The advantage of partnership programs allows the individual to avoid transfer (for the same period as the dollar limits of a LTCI policy allowed), and still be eligible for Medicaid if the client purchases a "partnership policy."* The partnership program works well in the four states where it is allowed—*California, Indiana, New York, and Connecticut* (with slight variations of the program in each state). In view of the success of the partnership program, and in view of state budget problems exacerbated by an ever growing dependency on Medicaid, *Congress should seriously consider allowing implementation of this program in all other states.*

## MEDICAID GETS WHACKED BY ARTIFICIAL QUALIFICATION

Not only was the transfer period extended under OBRA '93, but a number of "loopholes" in Medicaid law were eliminated. The jargon used in skirting the intent of laws designed to assure American taxpayers that only the poor qualify for welfare programs, became known as *"Medicaid Planning."* In the "old days," I clearly remember telling seminar attendees about the mechanics of some of these techniques. At the same time, a part of the legal community was applying them to actual clients' cases. In fact, books and videos were made available to the public at large on how to accomplish "impoverishment" in order to qualify for Medicaid. *The legal maneuvering of converting "eligible" assets such as cash, certificates of deposit, or stocks and bonds, into "exempt" assets of personal property such as large diamond rings, expensive artworks, etc., became somewhat commonplace.*

Other versions of illustrating impoverishment for the purpose of artificially qualifying for Medicaid were used (divorce, for example, was a severe solution), and soon the general public had found a new cash cow to milk. However, *OBRA '93 supposedly closed most of the doors which allowed people of means to "impoverish" themselves,* and within a few years, the states had adopted laws which implemented the federal legislation. In 1996, the Health Insurance Portability and Accountability Act took even more serious steps to eliminate what had become known as "Medicaid Planning". HIPAA imposed criminal penalties of up to one year in prison, a $10,000 fine, or both, on people (or anyone who advised people,) to knowingly and willingly dispose of assets (including by any transfer in trust) in order for an individual to become eligible for Medicaid assistance.

Even though this "putting granny in jail" legislation, as it came to be known, was passed, it has not been enforced. These two pieces of legislation were designed to effectively close the door on Medicaid Planning, but a small number of members of the legal profession continue to practice the technique of artificially qualifying their clients for Medicaid. This has resulted in serious debate within many states over how each state allows its residents to qualify for Medicaid assistance.

There seems to be two camps in the legal field. *One group of attorneys has had the foresight to educate themselves, and understands the value of utilizing the tax enhancements of HIPAA '96 (as well as state income tax deductions in states that allow for such), and advise their clients regarding the benefits of purchasing LTC insurance.* We are aware that asset preservation is the common goal of the attorney, the client, the client's families, and the LTC insurance industry. My guess is that, fortunately, far more attorneys educate themselves and direct their clients to solving asset preservation needs with LTC insurance, than the second camp, who advises risky transfers of assets in order to qualify clients for Medicaid.

*The second camp will not consider their techniques as artificial, but legal, and therein lies the problem.* Medicaid (welfare) is designed for people who honestly do not have resources to pay for the costs of long term care. But, a small number of attorneys in this country feel they have found ways to take middle-Americans, or even wealthy ones, with assets, and legally qualify them for Medicaid.

The drill usually goes like this. Hold a seminar. Get people who know little about long term care, its costs, Medicaid, Medicare, and saving and sheltering assets, to come to the seminar and inform them that they needn't waste their money on LTC insurance. "Waste your money on me," should be the title of the seminar. At that point, inquisitive people are invited to free consultations (after all, "inquiring minds want to know," don't they?) where they are advised as to how their assets can be sheltered, or transferred, and qualification for Medicaid will be illustrated as the "value" received for the fee charged for "boilerplating" each particular client's needs and supposed desires.

But some problems develop. *First* of all, it is no secret that nursing home payment by *Medicaid is not well handled in many states, and in fact is deteriorating, as public money dries up, partly due to the overburden of paying for more than the truly needy.* In July of 2002, Carrie Teegardin authored an excellent in-depth project for the Atlanta Journal-Constitution, in which she reports a scathing observation of the Nursing Home industry in Georgia. The project describes many of the short-comings of nursing homes in general, and the *problems of nursing homes being reliant on Medicaid money to provide quality care for nursing home patients.* This should be required reading for any attorney who is advising, or a *prospective nursing home patient, who is contemplating, getting themselves eligible for Medicaid.* Sure, the project was written about the Georgia situation, but, can other states be any different than Georgia, when *Medicaid money and rules are the foundation of what has the possibility of becoming a national nightmare?* Stay tuned for further information, as the nation's "over 65" population nearly doubles in the next few decades, and more people expect Medicaid to be the solution to their nursing home care payments.

*Secondly*, in their anxiety to divest their assets and get on the "gravy train" to "keep those nursing homes from getting my hard-earned money" does the attorney's client *overlook what people most want from long term care?* It's no secret that Americans want, in this order; 1) Home Care, and Home Health and Community Care, then 2) Assisted Living care, then 3) if need be, Nursing Home Care. Well, guess what, *there is no "tooth fairy" or "godmother" who is going to come along and pick up the first two most desired types of care—Home and Assisted Living.* The client is left with a very nasty surprise. "Huh? *You mean I gave all my stuff away and all I did was get myself set up for going to a nursing home?"* Undoubtedly the Medicaid Planning attorney has answers to that small problem. "Stay with the kids until you absolutely have to go to the nursing home," comes to mind.

As a *third* item, the *"prospect" for artificial Medicaid qualification should ask their advisor if he or she has done for themselves what they are recommending that the prospect do.* Oh, oh! Maybe, maybe not, but unlikely—highly unlikely. What attorney is going to start divesting themselves of their assets, put a smile on their own face, and sit around and wait for Medicaid to kick in. I seriously doubt if one has.

A *fourth* problem is poised for reaction, when today's attorney artificially "qualifies" someone for Medicaid, and *several years later the reality of estate recovery and lien laws kick in*. Is that same attorney around to clean up the mess created for the families of those involved? Will a solid defense come up missing when a new attorney and the heirs have to provide solutions to the problems created by what seemed to be such a slick deal?

A final *fifth* issue. *In what other legal arena do attorneys advertise and hold "seminars" for the general public?* As I said before, thankfully only a few attorneys use this approach to asset preservation, or whatever nomenclature they wish to use, to describe "artificial qualification." I'm sorry to get so base here, but I just can't help it. *Having come from rural country, another phrase comes to mind, that of "artificial insemination," which seems to better describe the scenario.*

Yes, Medicaid Planning was, and in some cases *still is, legal*. But two important viewpoints surface. Dealing with the hassle and risk involved, *Medicaid Planning may be more than average people want to encounter. Second, getting a generation of independent, hard working people to agree that the techniques may be legal, is somewhat easier than getting them to agree that the "planning" is moral or ethical.* I have found few retirees, who felt that a *"legal" approach* to qualifying for Medicaid by hiding their assets, was a *moral or ethical way to pass inheritances on to their children.* I've had more than one seminar attendee who was highly offended, and in some cases downright upset, that I would even mention the issue, let alone discuss it with them. Keep in mind that, at that time, my seminars informed people about asset preservation, including a variety of options. Obviously, changes in law have led to Long Term Care insurance as nearly the only sensible, efficient, and logical solution, and I have learned to avoid bringing up qualification for Medicaid as a part of my seminars. Live and learn.

## ENTER ESTATE RECOVERY AND LIEN LAWS

OBRA '93 was the first indication of government's recognition that it could not continue to take on larger and larger responsibilities for American healthcare. Not only did the Federal government **recognize that it could not continue to give money away under Medicaid, but forcefully began to inform the states that they needed to tighten up the rules for qualification for welfare,** and resultant nursing home assistance under Medicaid. Additionally, OBRA 93 required the states to **aggressively recover money it had paid to some recipients,** who may have had no right to it in the first place. As a result, during the next two years, **most** state legislatures were busy enacting legislation which effectively gave the state the right to recover Medicaid nursing home payments, **to which the patient appeared to be LEGALLY qualified, from two sources—Estate Recovery laws and Lien filing laws.** We italicize the term **"legally qualified" here, because the recipient would be assumed to be legally qualified until Medicaid personnel, or a Medicaid recovery unit, discovered differently, as in the two examples I cited at the beginning of the chapter.**

Basically, although there is one combination of recovery efforts, it is based in two separate laws regarding estate recovery and lien laws. Let's discuss **lien laws** first. You will find that the department of the state government which deals with Medicaid, under whatever name it functions, will have **the authority to place a lien on the Medicaid recipient's real property, within certain parameters.** Real property is defined as land, buildings, or improvements to that land. The lien will be imposed on the real property of any permanently institutionalized recipient, who is not expected to be discharged and return home. After that determination, a notice will be given and an opportunity for a hearing will be provided before the lien will be imposed. **Filing of the lien in no way requires that the property be sold, only that if, or when, the property is sold (perhaps several years later), then the lien must be satisfied.** An important factor is, that no lien will be filed if the property is the recipient's home, and the home is lawfully resided in by the recipient's spouse; the recipient's child, under 21 years of age, blind, or permanently and totally disabled; or the recipient's sibling was residing in the recipient's home for a certain period (depending on the state of residence) immediately prior to the recipient's institutionalization. Again, this is the general rule, but each state will have different laws regarding the lien law, and in addition, differing interpretations of the general rule.

The **estate recovery** plan works in much the same way, in that the state (again depending on that state's laws) **may have the right to recover Medicaid nursing home assistance money from a deceased recipient's estate.** Each state's laws are different, but basically the estate recovery program says that assistance paid on behalf of people age 55 or older, may be subject to recovery from the individual's estate. **The amount of the claim may be for all Medicaid moneys expended on the patient's behalf. The estate may include all property of the recipient, including jointly owned property.** Also, again, no recovery may be made if the recipient is survived by a spouse, a child under 21, or a blind or disabled child. In addition, individuals affected by the proposed recovery have a right to apply for a hardship waiver.

I doubt that any reader would dispute the existence of active, aggressive recovery units, but let me **point out how extremely effective these units have been, because it should act as a big red flag** for those who are considering following the advice of Medicaid planners, to hide, transfer, or dispose of assets to qualify for Medicaid. According to HCFA's figures, as the states "geared up" to comply with the new laws, **the first five years (1994-1998) saw recovery of nearly $800 million nationwide**, with California leading the way with over $150 million recovered. As momentum grew, from $99 million recovered in 1994, to $207 million in 1998, (for the last year of available records) would it be hard to believe that Medicaid recovery units totaled over $1 Billion by the year 2000, after only six years of determined effort? **Certainly a large percentage of that amount had to be attributed to recovery of what appeared to be "legally qualified" long term care beneficiaries, who were found later to be in non-compliance with Medicaid's statutes.**

Now, I ask two things. First, **do the above figures substantiate my viewpoint that Medicaid, in the case of those who have assets, might only wind up being a loan, giving people a false comfort until the death of the recipient?** And, secondly, what person would want to risk the advice of an attorney to use Medicaid planning, in lieu of LTC insurance, to **answer the needs of "asset preservation"? In reality, then, if Medicaid wants its money back, you didn't preserve anything!**

Only a few years ago we told people to exclude their real property and personal assets from the list of eligible assets which they should protect, because the home and personal property were (and still are) considered exempt assets from Medicaid eligibility. But, if the people would qualify for Medicaid because a $100,000 home and $50,000 of personal property is considered exempt, and **they apply for and receive Medicaid, only to have liens filed and estate recovery techniques implemented, what was the point in the first place?** The end result is that Medicaid in effect became a loan, and a rather expensive one at that. **What does a person gain by using Medicaid and reducing the estate when, as an alternative, an LTC policy with comparatively smaller cash outlay could save the entire asset base (estate) for the enjoyment of the family?** Even the use of a **reverse mortgage on a line-of-credit basis to pay LTC premiums is far superior to the realities of lien and estate recovery.**

Remember that the Union has 50 states, and nearly every state, has by now, literally enacted its own laws regarding how to recover Medicaid Nursing Home assistance money, even though it appeared to be legally granted. So, the basis for that legislation will somehow tie in with recovering the money spent on nursing home assistance from the estates of deceased recipients, or recovering the money spent by placing a lien on the real property of the deceased recipient. The reader should call their state office on aging, or department of human services, to see how the state in which they reside treats this recovery effort. **This will enable you to prevent doing something that looks good today, from becoming a family problem tomorrow.**

Keep in mind that the four *"Partnership" states* of California, New York, Connecticut, and Indiana, *will have an entirely different set of rules*. The rules are very advantageous to citizens of those states. Remember what we said previously, if a resident of one of these states purchases a partnership approved LTCI policy with benefits paid for a certain number of dollars, the state will provide Medicaid nursing home assistance in a like amount (after the benefits of the policy have been exhausted), without the requirement of transferring assets to achieve a poverty level. That is the main theme, but remember, again, even each of these states will treat this feature a little differently, so a call is in order to the department of human services in your state to determine that particular states' rules. In reality, this program is very well accepted and very worthwhile.

An important item, which should be discussed in *reviewing the Post-OBRA '93 recovery techniques of lien laws and estate recovery laws, is that they are ongoing. Not only do prospective Medicaid nursing home assistance recipients have to qualify initially for this care, but they must also re-qualify through an "annual redetermination" of their eligibility to continue to receive assistance.*

Examples of the forty sources from which information may be obtained include relatives, friends and neighbors, landlords, employers, financial institutions, medical providers, health care facilities, Veteran's Administration, Social Security Administration, County Assessors, Treasurer's and Clerks of Court, buyers of contracts for deed/negotiable instruments, Social Service Agencies, Federal-State-Local Governmental Agencies and insurance companies. In short, *most people would prefer to avoid this sort of intrusion if at all possible, yet Medicaid qualification decision makers must cover these items,* to ensure that tax money is only being spent on the truly needy, and that the goals of Medicaid recovery are possibly avoided.

So, since OBRA '93, the lesson is obvious. *Government,* after years of allowing lax interpretations and qualifications for Medicaid through the use of Medicaid trusts and easy transfer techniques, *closed the window on most legal maneuvering.* Still, there are those who are figuring ways around the law. If you are in a position to attempt artificially qualifying for Medicaid, *you may wish to consider what you give up by way of freedom in selecting where you would prefer to receive your care, as well as the possibility that your intentions would go miserably astray, should Medicaid decide that they want their money back.*

## WANT TO TRANSFER YOUR ASSETS?  HANG ON A MINUTE!

One more issue needs to be addressed. Remember that *Medicaid Planning has, as its foundation, the transfer of assets. Nowhere is it written that elderly people are anxious to transfer their assets. In fact, in my experience, just the opposite seems to be the norm.* The section of this book entitled "Personal Inventory Booklet" has a page dedicated to "Legal" aspects of your personal inventory. Four questions are crucial. The first one (about two thirds of the way down the question list) is simply, "Have I transferred assets to my children?" The second one is, "Have I considered transferring assets?" The third question is, "Do I have an aversion to transferring assets?"

And the fourth question, the one most apropos to this discussion, reads: "Is qualification for Medicaid eligibility the only reason I would consider transferring assets?"

Each question has its own merit, but questions three and four seem to be the ones most people find discomforting. **Transfer not only means giving the assets away, but giving up control. Total control.** That little item is a hard-core dilemma for most people who spent a lifetime building what they have, still have, and still control. In this day and age, many older people may not have a high level of confidence in their children, and **transferring assets simply to qualify for Medicaid assistance may be much more than people want to encounter.**

First of all, the "child" may have no financial common sense, may be headed for a divorce, (which in many states says that half of what you gave to a child, may be given by a court, to a **soon-to-be former** son or daughter-in-law), the child himself or herself may not be healthy, or a dozen or so other problems may rear their head. The absolute worst scenario, and one which seems to be gaining momentum as "baby boomers" begin wrangling with their siblings over new-found possible "wealth", is, **"Who is going to do what for the parent after the transfer has taken place?"** Let's say that the transferring parent needs long term care, or actually becomes a patient in a nursing home under eligible welfare and Medicaid rules. **"Don't worry, Mom, we won't let that happen to you,"** is sometimes forgotten after the legal battle regarding who gets to control Mom's assets is over and the transfers have been made.

**Strange things happen in families when money becomes an issue, and the Patriarch or Matriarch finds himself or herself abandoned in the welfare wing of a nursing home.** I'm not suggesting this is the usual case, but I can tell you it's not unusual. Several articles have appeared in magazines and newspapers recently written by people who have researched this "late stage" sibling rivalry and the resultant legal battles over who was going to take care of Mama or Papa, and take control and ownership of their assets. In short, the family infighting, both legal and emotional, is not a pretty picture.

Having said all of the above then, the reader should be reminded that when used in combination with an LTCI policy, Medicaid money could be considered useful, after the exhaustion of the benefits paid under the LTCI policy, much as the case in the "Partnership States." **A policy of at least three years duration, or more preferably four, allows the policyholder time to make any transfers, starting near the beginning of the benefit period, and passing through the "lookback" period, as the benefits of the policy are being paid by the insurance company.** This approach would somewhat replicate the intent of the "Partnership" program, except for the nearly automatic qualification for Medicaid benefits without transfer of assets used in the "Partnership" program. In short, the LTC policy provides coverage during the first years of a long term care need, even at home, and **allows time for the patient and family to work on transfer, should they so desire.**

Chapter 10

A few years ago, a policyholder asked me what newly passed Welfare Reform Legislation had to do with Medicaid. There was a simple answer. Medicaid is welfare. In many states, nearly 40% of the cost of welfare is used up by Medicaid recipients in the form of Long Term Care. *As Medicaid money becomes more scarce, the requirements for qualifying must become more strict.* Solutions will be very hard to come by, and the *"entitlement mentality"* which assumed that entitlements are here to stay sees some major cracks developing. *The idea that one generation goes into debt to support another may very likely be demolished by those unwilling and unable to support such a system.*

From here, the discussion is very short—*THERE WON'T BE ANY HELP FROM EITHER FEDERAL OR STATE GOVERNMENTS TO ABSORB A GREATER SHARE OF NURSING HOME COSTS OTHER THAN THROUGH INFLATIONARY RAISES. Simple.* As you can see by now, with the problems of federal spending, demographics, Social Security, Medicare, pensions and savings, *government is TOTALLY UNABLE TO ABSORB ANY MORE EXPENSIVE PROGRAMS, regardless of the pleas of senior lobbyists.* Consider a prediction I offered in 1995:

> *"What we will see, is major reform of Welfare laws, with the emphasis being placed on state interpretations of how to regulate nursing home admissions and qualifications for benefits, and tax incentives for Americans to purchase Long Term Care policies."*

HIPAA '96 made this prediction reality in 1996, in relatively quick time. I include it here because, as simple as it was, the prediction is not unlike the heavily capitalized and italicized paragraph preceding it—which hasn't changed in four years—and will not for at least another forty years. *So the choice is crystal clear*—prepare now, to protect yourself against the needs of Long Term Care with an LTC insurance policy—*since there will be a very limited amount of help available from "the government" for people with assets. Amen.*

# Chapter 11

# The Women's Issue

## "THE SILENT CRISES"

## LONG TERM CARE IS A VERY SERIOUS WOMEN'S ISSUE!!!

Don't shoot the messenger. You are about to be exposed to a compilation of facts, which illustrate the importance of Long Term Care Insurance to women. You won't be very happy with most of what you read. But, let's start by saying that **all of the issues** discussed here **have a greater impact on the female population,** than they do on their male counterparts. I have tried to present these "hard facts" in a clear and concise manner, without the sophistication of an academic rendering. But **let me be very clear at the outset—the seriousness of the women's issue is a national problem, and every American—women and men—need to be aware of the problems that the disparity creates.**

Until we accept the viewpoint that **several things must be done to address and rectify the inequities associated with aging, healthcare, and wages, for the women of this country, this crisis will remain "silent. And the solutions will go overlooked and ignored. None of us can afford that.** Hopefully, this publication will help enable us, as a nation, **to "outshout" the silence**, and to accept that we need to prepare now for sensible solutions. **One more thing—I dislike statistics, and perhaps you do too,** but to accomplish the objectives of this writing, **proof is needed, and we have the statistical proof.** So please humor me, as we work our way through the information relative to the content of the women's issues we are going to discuss.

Let's start by itemizing the **various components of the overall picture**. For some, **the information will not be news, but the updating will reinforce** what we have known for some time. For other readers, **much of what develops will be new surprising, shocking, and startling information,** or will at least include a new and complete understanding of the problems of women, and the inequities associated with the process of aging, as well as the current disadvantages associated with employment.

1) *The demographics of the women's issue*—the basis of the problem.
2) *Medicare utilization as a measure*—of the imbalance of longevity.
3) *Nursing home and assisted living utilization*—another measure.
4) **Informal caregiving—wherein women provide the largest share.**
5) **Holding down a job—and holding the family together.**
6) **Salaries, Finances, and Social Security—wherein—disproportion, disadvantage, and disparity, are brutal realities, which must be changed.**

## FIRST, *THE DEMOGRAPHICS* OF THE WOMAN'S ISSUE

The first factors deal with demographic issues. We've known for years that women outlive men. Traditionally, the numbers have been regarded as a seven-year spread, with women outliving men, during the last quarter of the twentieth century, by about seven years. By the end of the '90's, that spread was reduced to about five and a half years, but the difference is still dramatic.

What are the hard numbers, then? Let's use the actual population statistics of men and women **age 65 and over** in the United States, and provide a backdrop for the **disproportionate problem that women face with longevity**. For the vitals, we go to the US Census Bureau, and the Census of 2000. Take a quick look at the tables below, as we diagnose these elderly gender disproportions.

### U.S. POPULATION BY AGE AND GENDER, 2000 (ROUNDED)

| AGE BRACKET | MALE | FEMALE | DIFFERENCE |
| --- | --- | --- | --- |
| U.S.TOTAL | 138 MIL. | 143 MIL | +5.0 MIL. FEMALE |
| 65+ TOTAL | 14.4 MIL. | 20.5 MIL | +6.1 MIL. FEMALE |
| 65-69 | 4.4 MIL | 5.10 MIL. | +0.7 MIL. FEMALE |
| 70-74 | 3.9 MIL. | 4.95 MIL. | +1.0 MIL. FEMALE |
| 75-79 | 3.0 MIL. | 4.37 MIL. | +1.3 MIL. FEMALE |
| 80-84 | 1.8 MIL. | 3.10 MIL. | +1.3 MIL. FEMALE |
| 85+ | 1.2 MIL | 3.01 MIL. | +1.8 MIL. FEMALE |

Source: U.S. Census Bureau, 2000

Let's use the figures for the year 2000 above as a foundation. According to the 2000 census, we had a **total population of over 281 million**, about 138 million males and 143 million females, for **a 5 million female majority**, or nearly a 96% male to female ratio.

When we look at the 2000 **age 65+ total** above, we find close to 35 million people. (Incidentally, this age bracket was comprised of 31 million people in 1990, a **12% growth in this age group over the past ten years**.) When we review the **85 and over** bracket, we find about 4.2 million people in 2000, (compared to 3 million in 1990), **or an incredible 37.6 percent growth in the 85+ age band!** Starting to get the picture? Extended longevity has started to go rampant in only ten years!

Now let's analyze the 35 million people in the age **65+ bracket by gender,** and see what happens.

1) In essence, right from the get go, the numbers are already dramatic, with **females outnumbering males 20.5 million to 14.4 million. That is roughly 141 women for every 100 men,** in the total age 65 and over population.

2) **The imbalance occurs beginning in the first age bracket** (65-69) where we see 5.1 million females to 4.4 million males.  Fairly significant so far, with **less than a million difference.**

3) At 70-74**, the gap widens,** with 4.95 million females and 3.9 million males, or **something over a million difference**.

4) At age 75 to 79, the numbers **start their steep climb** with a ratio of 4.37 million females to 3.04 million males, or a **1.3 million female majority.**

5) The age 80 to 84 bracket **the ratio remains about the same**, with 3.1 million females compared to 1.8 million males, or *still holding* at about a 1.3 million majority.  But what is this age group (80-84) beginning to reflect**?** **It** reflects the male population beginning to die, and the female population **continuing to live.** Which leads us to 6), wherein we find a **huge** difference.

6) The final analysis presented by the Census Bureau reflects the **85+ age** group, and herein you will be startled.  Look at this.  At age 85 and over, we have **a female population of slightly more than 3 million, while the male population has declined to about 1.2 million!**  Now we see **a tremendous disparity** in female to male ratios.  As a matter of fact, look at it this way.  At age 85 and over, for every four people living, **three are females and one is** a male!

These numbers alone indicate that the problem is not going to go away, and in fact, when compared with 1990, we see the problem with *extended* longevity worsening. *So, fact number one is established. Women have been living longer than men. Women are continuing to live longer than men. And, it appears that this trend, for whatever biological reason, will continue.*

These demographic statistics illustrate the basis and foundation of the long term gender situation, and set the stage for the following scenarios.

## *MEDICARE UTILIZATION* AS A MEASURE

One of the ways to relate to the **imbalance in longevity and female to male ratios**, is to cite statistics on the *utilization of Medicare*.  Again, as in the census figures, let's take a look at the total number of the elderly **Medicare** population and then establish the male and female recipients by age.  **Look particularly at the male to female ratios in the last line in the following table.**

## AGE AND GENDER OF ELDERLY
## MEDICARE POPULATION, 1996

| AGE BRACKET | TOTAL | MALE | FEMALE |
|---|---|---|---|
| 65-74 | 18.4 MIL | 45% | 55% |
| 75-84 | 12.0 MIL | 40% | 60% |
| 85+ | 4.2 MIL | 29% | 71% |

Source: Kaiser Family Foundation 1999

We use the above table to **set up the discussion regarding utilization of Medicare**. But for the moment, notice that in all age bands above, the **female gender far outnumbers the male gender in Medicare Population**, again due to the imbalances of female to male longevity. First, look at the Age Bracket 75-84 above and below (you will see a slight variation), and see proportions of roughly **60% for women, to 40% for men**. Then compare that category with the 85+ Age Bracket, which shows roughly a **72% to 28% ratio**, a very significant spread of female over male Medicare populations. *We will discuss this in greater depth on the next page, but the table is set.*

Martha H. Phillips recently prepared a significant report entitled "A Primer on Medicare," for the Concord Coalition, a highly respected "think tank" that watches and influences national policy making in Washington, DC. We want to refer to the resource of the tables below, which were developed in the Phillips "Primer," and which identify the importance of understanding the differences in "Utilization of Medicare." Keep in mind that the statistics sometimes vary slightly depending on the source of the study, the years involved, and the purpose of the study. What I am saying, is that if you look at the following Concord Coalition study it will vary slightly with the preceding Kaiser Family Foundation study referred to above. **Makes no difference. While the variations are slight, keep in mind that the message is the same—that women significantly outnumber men in these older age brackets—and that is where our concerns lie.**

## UTILIZATION OF MEDICARE

### TOTAL AGE 65 AND OVER ENROLLEES—
### YEAR 1997—
### 33.7 MILLION TOTAL ENROLLEES

| AGE BRACKET | TOTAL | FEMALE | MALE |
|---|---|---|---|
| 65-74 | 18 MIL. | 55% | 45% |
| 75-84 | 12 MIL. | 61% | 39% |
| 85+ | 4 MIL. | 73% | 27% |

Source: A Primer on Medicare, 2000 Update, The Concord Coalition

First of all, the list of tables for utilization of Medicare manifests the demographic problem for women rather significantly. Of the "age 65 and over enrollees" receiving Medicare, the age bracket 65-74 indicates that there are about **55% female recipients, in comparison to 45% male recipients.** So, as before, with the Census numbers, through age 74, we see some disparity, indicating an overwhelming female to male ratio.

But, it gets more disparate! In the age bracket 75-84, we find that about **61% of the recipients are female,** and **39% of the recipients are male**. Are we starting to see a trend here? Yes. Now look at the age 85+ table, where we see an even more astonishing female to male ratio imbalance of **73% female to 27% male!**

Does this information indicate that men are more healthy than women, because their utilization of Medicare is so much less? **Absolutely not!** It indicates, just as the preceding census figures did, that there are *more women alive in these older age brackets.* Obviously, then, utilization of Medicare becomes a necessity for far more women than men, because there are more of them. It's just that simple. Statistically, *women outlive men by a greater amount, and yet, not always in the best of health,* as indicated by the numbers referred to above.

That's what nursing homes have been telling us. That's what home health agencies have been telling us. That's what Medicare, Social Security and Medicaid have been telling us. That's what hospitals, senior organizations, women's groups and associations, *and, yes, even* Long Term Care insurance people have been telling us. And that's what the nation's women must prepare for. Simply, the numbers prove they are going to live longer than men. The facts are there. The demographics are there. They cannot be changed to protect the innocent, which in this case, happens to be the women of this country. They are facts of life (no pun intended) and *need to be paid attention to, in order to prepare for even more serious utilization problems, which, in turn, will be exacerbated by the "ready for delivery" oncoming baby boomer generation.*

Now, this longevity and *extended longevity* for women may not seem to be a severe problem, until you *tie the costs of long term care and related medical care* into the picture. It is no secret that the costs of care and medicine can be far greater in the last few years of one's life than in the total years of their preceding lifetime. That scenario is not unusual. But aging experts are informing us that *this life expectancy, itself, is lengthening,* and has been since the early 1800's. So to be brief, not only are we faced with longevity and extended longevity, but, in addition, *life expectancy <u>continues</u> to increase!*

If that is true, then, how do the last few years of today's fifty year old lady play out? Does it mean that an *additional year or so* of questionable health and care needs will descend upon today's middle age woman? An article in "BMJ" Volume 324, May 18, 2002, seems to summarize this dilemma by saying, *"increases of just a few years in life expectancy can have an enormous impact on health and social services."* Indeed, when the label has been read, the dosage becomes clear. Prepare for your future, as well as you can today, because, *the needs have already been calculated by your predecessors*. Use the message created by statistical proof to your advantage, and provide yourself with all the protection you can afford, with an eye towards the expected utilization of Long Term Care Insurance, and normal, natural medical needs, with sufficient Medicare Supplement Insurance.

## *NURSING HOME AND ASSISTED LIVING UTILIZATION* IS PREDOMINATELY FEMALE

Not only do the numbers relating to Medicare utilization magnify, due to the extended longevity of women, but also *the utilizations of nursing homes, assisted living facilities, and home health and home care (professional and personal), are correspondingly more severe for women.* For instance, The American Health Care Association, whose members are composed of owners and managers of long term care facilities and like providers, has done numerous studies over the years with the results indicating that *approximately 75 percent of all nursing home residents are women.* One such letter printed in 2001 profiles the typical nursing facility resident as such:

> *"The typical nursing home resident is a* **women in her 80's** *displaying a mild form of memory loss and dementia.* **Although physically healthy for a woman her age,** *she needs help with approximately 4 of 5 activities of daily living..."*

> *"A typical resident has managed to set aside a total of* **only $20,000 for her retirement.** *With the average annual cost of nursing home care running approximately $41,000, she is unable to afford the care she needs beyond the first six months. The typical resident, however,* **will spend more than** *three years in a nursing facility due to her cognitive and physical* **disabilities.** *Her health insurance is limited to Medicare only, with a modest Social Security check for income."*

> *"Financially incapable of meeting the costs of her care, the female resident must rely on Medicaid to pay for her 24-hour care and supervision. In order to qualify,* **she must impoverish herself** *to no more than $2,000 in total assets."*

Those are the hard facts as seen by the AHCA, and who would be a better authority than the nation's nursing home providers—professionals in the care business? *Would this be a call for the solution of Long Term Care insurance?* In addition to the "profile" of female nursing home residents, the indication is that the typical female patient will encounter a *cost of two to two-and-a-half times what their male counterparts will require during their lifetimes*, with again, the numbers being higher because of more utilization brought on by longer lives. Another AHCA study done in 1995, says that, "The average American man can expect to spend **$56,895** on LTC. The average woman will spend **$124,370.**" Remember, those are 1995 figures, therefore, they **cannot reflect the 5% average annual increase** needed to bring the numbers up to any current cost-of-care amount.

In a particularly savvy publication, "The State of Older Women in America," the OWL organization (formerly known as the Older Women's League), presents a graph of significant interest showing the disparity between men's and women's occupancy of Nursing homes. (I have changed the presentation slightly to highlight our discussion, but the statistics remain the same.)

## NUMBER OF NURSING HOME RESIDENTS AGE 65 OR OLDER BY SEX AND AGE GROUP, 1985, AND 1997, IN THOUSANDS

|  | MEN | | WOMEN | |
|---|---|---|---|---|
|  | 1985 | 1997 | 1985 | 1997 |
| 65 OR OLDER | 334 | 372 | 984 | 1,093 |
| 65 TO 74 | 81 | 81 | 132 | 118 |
| 75 TO 84 | 141 | 159 | 368 | 369 |
| 85 OR OLDER | 113 | 132 | 485 | 606 |

*Reference Population: These date refer to the population residing in Nursing Homes. Persons residing in Personal care or Domiciliary Care Homes are excluded.*
*Source: National Nursing Home Survey*

Now a very careful look at this table will show some serious recent developments.

1) First, notice the increase in women's occupancy between 1985 and 1997— From 984,000 to 1,093,000—a **growth of over 10% in twelve years**.

2) In the age bracket 65 to 74, the men's numbers stayed the same while the **women's numbers actually decreased**. My suspicion is that **the difference really reflects the growth in Home Care** due to the fact that Home Care became another entire growth industry during the decade of the '90's, and younger recipients, both men and women, began to **use Home Care as the** care delivery system of first choice.

3) We don't see a great deal of change in the age 75 to 84 bracket, except that now we see male utilization growing, with the **curve continuing upward** for men into the 85 or older bracket.

4) **The most significant number is the final one.** Look at the 85 or older occupancy for women and recognize that it confirms what we have discussed thus far. From 485,000 female occupancies in 1985, to 606,000 occupancies twelve years later. **An astonishing 25% growth rate, which** verifies the conclusion of the female demographics and statistics we have been illustrating!

Unfortunately, we have also concluded that extended longevity is increasing, and that less-than-perfect health conditions, brought on by older ages, seem to manifest themselves in medical concerns (Medicare utilization data) and Long Term Care needs (Nursing Home utilization data) discussed thus far. **Do the data verify the need for today's woman to be particularly concerned about purchasing Long Term Care Insurance? I should think so.**

## *ASSISTED LIVING* PICKS UP PART OF THE BURDEN

So, are the **numbers** any different **for assisted living needs**? Not really, nor should we expect that they would be. Again, an AHCA article profiling the typical assisted living resident, points out the demographic similarities.

> *"The typical assisted living resident is an* **82-year old woman** *who is mobile, but needs assistance with one or two personal activities.* **Although most** *elderly assisted living residents are female, due to women's longer life* **expectancies,** *29 percent are male.* *The average age of elderly residents,* *men and women combined, is 82 years, according to NCAL/AHCA survey findings..."*

> *"Residents of assisted living facilities* **stay an average of 3.3 years**, *and leave the facility when a higher level of medical care is needed. (NCAL/AHCA, "Survey of Assisted Living Facilities," 1996.)"*

The above information would conclude that **all needs for care, whether they be Medicare, Nursing Home, or Assisted Living, would also reflect the needs for Home and Home Health Care (which we will discuss next), in about the same proportion.** So, what's the lesson here*?* **A Medicare Supplement (upon enrolling in Medicare) and a Long Term Care insurance policy purchased as soon as possible, should be regarded as commonplace rather than the exception, particularly for women, in light of the above information.** If the demographic problems facing women were the only ones, the answers would be simpler, but **additional issues carve out a need for women to protect themselves as well as they can for the later stages of life.** Let's address those issues, for they full well illustrate the compounding of problems for women as they approach middle-age and the later stages of their lives.

## *INFORMAL CAREGIVING* AND HOLDING DOWN A JOB

Ask a woman and she'll tell you. Ask the women who provide care in their homes (or men who do the same) for a loved one, other than their children, and they'll *really* tell you! Caregiving will change your life! The assumption is that caregiving is a normal fact of life, and to a certain extent, that is true. In the continuum of life, logic tells us that parents take care of their children, then those children will have children of their own, whom they, in turn, take care of, and so on. That's to be expected, and yes, that's a matter of nature and common sense. Generational caring for children has been the norm since day one.

As a matter of fact, caring for older generations, within the family home, was a common practice for centuries, and is still "the way" in some cultures and societies. We can all live with that. Even to the extent that we look at it as a virtue, which it is, and obviously should be. Who wouldn't want to be cared for by those closest to us; those we have raised as children, and those we love and respect? But something changed a part of that and went astray somewhere along the way. It was called the 20th century. A multitude of conditions changed.

No longer were we an agrarian society, wherein people pretty much stayed within the same house, same farm, or even the same community, in which they were born. People followed jobs, and some people followed their spouse to wherever those jobs were. Others moved to large cities, as the industrial revolution created a less rural society and a far larger urban society. Soon a movement to "sun belt" states became the goal of a large number of people; young, middle-aged, and retired. Then, towards the last quarter of the century, immigration numbers began to swell, and even more people contributed to changing the "old customs" and "way of life" of the previous century. That's what happened, in a nutshell.

But, one other thing happened along the way. People who considered age 65 as a "ripe old age," began to see *"real elderly"* people living into their 70', 80's, even their 90's. Actually, many of us have had time to see the change occur, and have been able to watch this "aging" take place from afar. But, for those who have seen these aging processes take place in their own families, the story is quite personal. Suddenly, the question became, "Who's going to take care of my father, or mother, or grandfather, or grandmother, or in-laws?" Or, probably the more accurate question became *"Who's going to take care of me?"*

Well, that's been decided. Absent a Long Term Care insurance policy, the "children" do the caregiving, and in **about 75-80% of the cases, women, both young and old, are the care providers**. Sorry, but that's the case. **Women do most of the caregiving. End of story.** We've suspected such, and now that we know about it, will soon present the statistics which bear this out. We simply cannot ignore the issue of informal caregiving in the home, and of the caregiver perhaps trying to hold down a job at the same time. Keep in mind that middle-age "children," or even those in their sixties and seventies, seem to accept the conditions of caring for their older loved ones, and very likely, some of them would have it no other way. But, for many women, **especially working mothers with children of their own, the care-giving situation is indeed a heavy burden.**

For starters, let's hear what a few of the nation's respected political leaders have to say on the issue of caregiving. Not surprisingly, I would like to quote two women United States Senators who delivered their message to the U.S. Senate Special Committee on Aging in February of 2002. First, from Senator Barbara Mikulski (D-MD) who offered:

> "Women are more often the ones who provide care to loved ones and who eventually need care themselves. **Three quarters of caregivers are women.** Women live longer than men and are more than twice as likely to live in a nursing home. Caregivers and their families face mental, emotional,

physical, and financial stresses and strains. Some caregivers **work three shifts**—caring for children, working a full-time job, **and caring for an elderly parent at home."**

Pretty well said, as the overall picture, but let's hear what Senator Debbie Stabenow (D-MI) had to say about the effect of caregiving on the **economic conditions of the working female caregiver:**

> "You have all heard the statistics and what they tell you is that wives are caring for husbands, mothers are caring for children, and grandmothers are caring for entire extended families. **Our economy is reliant upon this uncompensated care** provided by loving family members, **most of who are women.** Many of these women face difficult choices between family and work and **because of time away from the workforce may jeopardize their retirement savings, as well."**

So Senator Stabenow introduces the economic factors involved for working caregivers. We shall discuss that in a moment, as several corporate studies have been conducted which verify both the **economic and physical** ramifications for job-holding caregivers. But for the moment, consider these numbers, as laid out by the U.S. General Accounting Office, and found in the Family Caregiver Alliance Clearinghouse.

> "An estimated 12.8 million Americans of all ages need assistance from others to carry out everyday activities. **Most, but not all, persons in need of long term care are elderly.** Approximately 57% are persons aged 65 and older (7.3 million); 40% are working-age adults 18 to 64 (5.1 million); and 3 percent are children under age 18 (400,000).

> "Most people who need long term care live at home or in community settings, not in institutions. **Of the 12.8 million Americans estimated to need long term care assistance, only about 2.4 million live in institutions,** such as nursing homes." "...It is estimated that **the number of older persons needing long term care may as much as double over the next 25 years;** 7 million in 1994; **14 million by 2020**; and 24 million by 2060."

Let's talk about this for a moment. If 12.8 million Americans are receiving long term care assistance, and "only" 2.4 million are receiving such in institutions, then that would mean that 10.4 million are receiving care at home—the home of a relative, friend, or another arrangement. So, who's giving the care? We'll find out in a minute. But take a look at the statement of **14 million needing care by 2020. That is less than a generation away!** Who's going to be giving care (at home, or in an institution) to this large number? I think by now, we know! Again, *we needn't deceive ourselves about the fact that big time long term care is well on it's way.*

Not only should we be concerned about informal caregiving in the home, but we need to realize that we have valid concerns with caregiving in institutions, *currently*, due to *a shortage of nurses and caregivers of all types.* In February of 2002, a report from the Department of Health and Human Services concluded that *"the vast majority of the nation's nursing homes—about 90 percent—are staffed too thinly to properly provide basic services..."* The report further assessed a cost of $7.6 billion of today's dollars, per year, to achieve proper staffing.

In August, 2002, the Joint Commission on Accreditation of Healthcare Organizations reported that the *nation's nursing shortage* has had "significant consequences during the past five years, *even contributing to patient injuries and deaths."* The report says there are 126,000 nursing positions unfilled in hospitals nationwide, but in addition, to the nursing home shortages addressed in the paragraph above, *some home health care agencies are being forced to refuse new patients!* It was also estimated that unless something changes, as the nation's baby boomers start to require serious care by 2020, "there will be *at least 400,000 fewer nurses available to provide care than will be needed."* The obvious is already here; *we are short of caregivers now*, whether in institutions as professionals, or at home as personal and informal family members.

Now, let's look at some startling statistics developed by the state of California. *California is home to the largest number of age 65 and over people in the United States (3.6 million,)* and has the governmental resources to track informal (home) caregiving, so we find great value in their work. California has published a booklet, "Quickfacts The Elderly," and an article from the Family Caregiver Alliance entitled, "Who's Taking Care?" To develop information of this sort on a national scale, would take the efforts of each state, then a compilation of those efforts. Therefore, we have the state with the largest (nearly 10 percent) population of the nation's age 65+ residents to thank for their significant contribution to this important body of knowledge. The findings, as astonishing as they are, would seem to bear out what happens on a national scale, and even though they are state specific, I find no reason they would not be representative of our nation as a whole.

1) **Families** in California **provide 80 percent** of all long term care **at home**.
2) Nearly 57 percent of caregivers are age 65 and over; 40 percent are 18-64.
3) **One in four households** in California is involved in care giving.
4) Twenty to forty percent of **caregivers also have children under 18.**
5) The average woman spends 17 years caring for children and **18 years caring for an elderly relative.**
6) In California, **53 percent** of caregivers under 65 are **juggling work and care giving.**

The above statistics are certainly discouraging to people who have been involved in informal home caregiving, and "echo" similar statements compiled from serious and severe real life situations. We might call it a sanitized view of very important information. Look again at the above six items, and visualize where you might see yourself currently or in the future, and determine if **LTC insurance policies, which pay for home care of the sort described above would allow you to avoid similar situations for yourself and your family.**

In addition, let's take a hard look at the following four enlightening statistical statements from the article "Who's Taking Care?" developed by the Family Caregiver Alliance, Statewide Resources Consultant to the California Department of Mental Health, which not only discuss the caregivers, but the physical, mental and economic results of their efforts.

1) **Caregivers are predominantly female (76 percent),** and over half are either wives (34 percent) or daughters/daughters-in-law (32 percent)…An average age of 60.5 years. More than one in five (21 percent) is 75 years of age or older. On average, **caregivers have been providing care for nearly 5 years.**

2) **29 percent of caregivers under the age of 65 say they quit their jobs to give care, and another 25 percent reduced their work hours.** Caregivers report providing an **average of 87 hours of care a week**, yet they only **receive an average of 11 hours of help a week** in care giving from their own family and friends.

3) Research has shown that prolonged care giving has **negative effects on the emotional and physical health of caregivers.** The **caregivers** served by California's CRCs are **at risk for experiencing serious emotional and physical health problems of their own.**

4) Two-thirds (66 percent) of the family caregivers report significant health problems and **41 percent say their health is now worse than five years ago.** Well over half **(59 percent)** of California caregivers seeking help and support from a CRC, **show clinical symptoms of depression**. The most common self-reported health problem of family caregivers is depression. Mental health concerns remain a serious and pervasive problem.

If you haven't gotten the full impact of these four statements, read them again, until you do get the full impact. Imagine. There is enough material embodied in these four paragraphs to do an entire book on caregiver's problems in general, and women caregivers in particular. For instance, check out that first paragraph which verifies the "75% lady caregiver" statement. Then tie in the facts that *one in five of the caregivers is over age 75 themselves*, and that on the average, they have been *providing care for nearly 5 years!* These are overwhelming facts.

Not only that, but anyone who has experienced caregiving can testify that it is not easy work.  Paragraphs 3 and 4 above explain the effect that this effort has on the **health** of the caregiver.  As a consequence of this difficult task, the caregivers find themselves "experiencing **serious emotional and physical health problems of their own!"**  I wonder!  Forty one percent say that their health is worse now than five years ago, to the extent that nearly 60 percent of them show clinical symptoms of depression, which seems to be the most common self-reported health problem of caregivers.  I think we've made the point, but I have to wonder **how much of this grief could be avoided with a Long Term Care policy, which would allow professional help to come into the home for even as little as five or six hours a day, to offer some relief for what in reality, may be a twenty-four-hour-a-day job.**

I am reminded of a friend of mine who described the ordeal of taking care of his brother for twelve years.  His simple statement was, "It will change your life, **not just for a few hours a day, but for several hours… every day of your life**."  He told of getting up half and hour earlier each day, coming home at noon, and going to bed half an hour later each evening, seven days a week—for twelve years!  I think I understand.

## SALARIES, FINANCES, AND SOCIAL SECURITY

With that background, and now that we know who really provides about 75% of the care, what can we expect of the women who go off to work, in addition to providing care to an older family member, and see what kind of an impact caregiving has on employees in this country.

Let's start with wages.  Many studies conducted by such organizations as the AFL-CIO, Institute for Women's Policy Research, and The National Council of Women's Organizations (composed of more than one hundred women's organizations), as well as other studies, conclude that **full time working women earn only about 73 to 74 cents for every dollar that their male full time counterparts earn.**  If this information had not been developed by these, and several other highly respected entities, we would consider the results preposterous.  Yes, we've heard these numbers, and in fact, heard that the gap is closing, but in reality **this travesty should not be visiting us now into the 21st century.**

These numbers are **shameful**, and reflect the greater outrage; that **all forms of retirement and its problems are disproportionately out-of-balance towards the needs of women.**  As we have shown, women have a greater and longer need for health care, a greater and longer need for long term care, a greater and longer need for Social Security, and a longer need for day-to-day living than men. But, it appears that women cannot even earn the necessary wages of a full time job **which can help enable them** to prepare for retirement.  Whoa, what's wrong with this picture?  As a **country about to explode with every need I have discussed, we must work on a major overhaul of each issue and correct these problems, before we double the expected number of recipients in the next generation.**  Long Term Care insurance, purchased at a young age, and a satisfactory Medicare Supplement purchased at age 65 can solve two of the problems, *but the problems of Social Security, retirement, and livable wages must get addressed soon.*

Let me make something crystal clear at this point. *Should men be concerned* with these issues—the ones discussed previously, and this issue of women's wages—at this juncture? *The answer is an unarguable and loud yes!* It doesn't take a nuclear scientist to understand that since the female gender is at greater risk for the medical and long term care needs we have discussed; that dollars for payment of these situations becomes something close to critical mass. I'm not saying that men keep women from receiving equal pay for equal work, even though that may be the case, but "the system" seems to have developed just such a scenario. In case any man looks at this chapter and determines that they are immune from the consequences of what appear to be women's problems—think again. A complete brain will easily identify that if women can't receive adequate incomes to deal with disproportionate longevity, caregiving responsibilities, and health concerns, yet pay the bills, who would that responsibility fall back onto? Oh, yeah, the government. Sure. And who pays the government? The taxpayer. And who pays the majority of the taxes, if women's incomes don't compete? Guess!

This is not all that difficult to figure out. And it's not all that difficult to arrive at a solution. Get women's wages up. Redistribute the caregiving workload. Make the total employment picture more sensitive to women's logical and sensible needs, when not do so, results in "radar-screen warnings" that say, "Change the system *so the ladies can pay their own way*, or we're going to be doing it anyway." And, buy Long Term Care Insurance during the working years. Yes, there I go again, and as one of my college professors used to say, "Good ol' Iverson, He never forgets the objective." Now that I've vented, let's get back to the facts.

Lest you think I have the cart before the horse here; in discussing wages before discussing working caregiver problems, let me set the table, and point out why *disproportionate salaries for women and Social Security need to be addressed first.* Simply, Social Security beneficiaries receive benefits in proportion to what they have paid in. That's right, it's just that simple. If you make less money, you pay less in, and *subsequently take less out per year.* Now*, further exacerbate that problem with extended longevity,* and it's pretty easy to see why most elderly women live in poverty. In fact, according to the U.S. Department of Labor, *of the elderly poor, nearly 75 percent are women.*

There are a few other employment factors, which should be included in the male/female disparity. According to the National Council of Women's Organizations, *women are less likely to work full time, thereby reducing* Social Security contributions; and *women are more likely to spend time out of the paid labor force, again, lowering their income and Social Security contributions.* In addition to those problems, *only 38 percent of women receive employer-provided pension benefits* compared to 57 percent of men, according to the National Council of Women's Organizations. So, with this background, let's get to the problems of America's caregivers, who we now know are three-quarters women.

An AARP study conducted in 1997 found that "80 percent of working caregivers reported emotional strain, 50 percent **reported financial strain**, and 40 percent missed work on a regular basis due to the health needs of an elderly loved one*." Is it any wonder that financial strain and missed work (which results in even lower wages) is a serious burden to the day-to-day needs of a worker, and also creates a lower payment into the system which many workers rely on to solve most retirement needs?*

Dozens of corporations have conducted studies regarding *the influence and effect on both the employer and the employee who must provide family caregiving.* The conclusions are pretty similar, and, obviously, affect both parties. The common threads were 1) that employees work fewer hours than desired; 2) that employees must take time off from work without pay; 3) that some employees have to turn down advancements; 4) that the caregiving employees' ability to stay in the work force is overtaxed; 5) that employee vacation time, sick leave, and personal leave time is used up quickly; 6) that the employee's own needs (emotional, physical, financial) go unmet; and 7) that some employees simply have to quit their jobs.

A study by the National Alliance for Care Giving *puts some numbers on the faces of the facts* listed above. 1) The aggregate cost for care giving to U.S. business...exceeds $29 billion per year. 2) 69 percent of caregivers arrive late or leave work early. 3) 67 percent take time off during the day. 4) 64 percent use up their sick days and vacation time. 5) 29 percent resign. 6) 22 percent take a leave of absence.

Then, a report by the National Center for Women and Aging *puts some astonishing dollar amounts to the facts.* Suppose we rely on them for hard numbers which, relate to employee caregiving in general, and *female employee caregiving (since 75% Of caregiving is performed by women) in particular.* "Employees who are forced to care for an aging parent pay a toll in lost income and added stress with the following: 1) *$566,500 in lost lifetime wages.* 2) *$67,000 lost lifetime retirement contributions.* 3) 29 percent pass on promotions or new assignment. 4) 25 percent pass on transfers or relocations."

So there you have it. The problems of caregivers in the workforce, with dollar amounts attached. But, sadly, there's more than the dollar amounts and the physical and mental health concerns we have discussed. There is also a matter of *the ultimate sacrifice* as reported in the Journal of the American Medical Association on December 15, 1999. The Journal cites that, *"elderly people caring for their spouse were 63 percent more likely to die than non-caregivers."* We don't have a female/male ratio breakdown, but the facts are clear—caregiving takes its toll on all involved, and what were once carefree, loving relationships can become *strained, tested, and complicated, if the caregiving must be provided by family members, whether for financial or voluntary reasons.* A large part of the chapter on "The Emotional Issues" in this book, is dedicated to the "sandwich generation," those caught in the middle of raising their own children, sometimes being expected to hold a job or two, and caring for their elders. I wish these conditions were easier to write about, but they are not.

In summary, so many writers say it all so well, that I cannot help but quote a few of them. A brilliant piece, which appears in the Older Women's League (OWL) web page, ties things together quite well. In an article titled, "State of Older Women in America," the writer encapsulates our chapter by writing, "Today in America, the average woman age 65 and over, lives six years longer than the average man. As a result, she is typically widowed and living alone. She struggles to make ends meet on *an annual income of $15,615 (compared with over $29,171 for men).* During her lifetime she probably spent 17 years caring for children and 18 years caring for elderly parents. Her retirement income is also smaller because she probably did not receive a pension, and was paid less than the average man. *As a result, she receives lower Social Security benefits.* She spends a higher proportion of her income on housing costs—leaving less for vital necessities such as utilities, medical costs, food, and transportation. The average older woman spends 20 percent of her income each year on out-of-pocket health care costs." That pretty well sums it up, doesn't it? *The facts are there, now all we need to do is pay attention to them, and do what we can do today to overcome the obstacles of tomorrow—prepare for them.*

Dr. Gary Applebaum, Senior Vice President and Medical Director of Renaissance Gardens, wrote in a December 12, 2001 issue of Long Term Care Provider, "Who would have ever thought that *the baby boomer generation would be the biggest caregiver generation in history?* With the aging of the older generation comes a barrage of challenges. Families and caregivers must learn to understand and care for adult relatives, especially those who are ill or frail. *Businesses must become much more aware of the needs of older adult employees,* as well as of the morale and productivity issues of employees caring for older relatives."

"The perplexing thing about elder caregiving is that most employees suffer in silence, or so they think. For a variety of reasons, stemming from a need for privacy to denial, they usually do not want to discuss their situations with supervisors or coworkers. However, in most cases, their actions speak much louder than words. *These are people who are stressed, conflicted, and frightened*. People who have maxed out their sick, personal and vacation days, get frequent personal phone calls daily, arrive late and leave early, have way too many "family emergencies," and are dependent on the kindness of coworkers…"

"When you consider that by the year 2030 over 25 percent of all Americans will be 60 years or older, and by 2080, there will be one million U.S. centenarians, you can't afford not to take *this silent crisis* seriously."

Well said, Dr. Applebaum, well said. *"The silent crisis."* How true. And how few of us are willing to *expose the silent crisis and start shouting about it? What this silent crisis can do to our citizens if we don't prepare for these painfully obvious problems now, or even better, yesterday, deserves bold front-page headlines.*

As if all of the previous information were not enough somber news, listen to what Peter R. Fisher, Under Secretary of the Treasury, had to say in a press release from the Office of Public Affairs, November 14, 2002. The remarks were made relative to all the Social Security and Medicare and Medicaid promises made by the U. S. Government over the last decade.

"Think of the *federal government as a gigantic insurance company* (with a sideline business in national defense and homeland security) *which only does its accounting on a cash basis—only counting premiums and payouts as they go in and out the door.* An insurance company with cash accounting is not really an insurance company at all. It is an accident waiting to happen."

"This particular insurance company, it turns out, *has made promises to its policyholders that have a current value $20 trillion or so (give or take a few trillion) in excess of the current value of the revenues that it expects to receive.* A real insurance company could try to grow its way out by raising premiums and its earnings on investments faster than its liabilities. *The federal government, however, would have to raise taxes or borrow faster than it increases outlays."*

As for my own conclusion, I hate to be the messenger of bad news, but *I know that at least two of the problems can be solved. Today. Sooner, than later.* I make no apology for offering the solutions of Long Term Care Insurance and Medicare Supplements. If I didn't think there was help available, I wouldn't have written a book about it. I have thirty-two-plus years in the insurance field and I know the value of paper. I have experiences, which I wish I didn't have. Too many times I have seen *personal situations where people denied the facts and delayed purchasing LTC coverage when premium was absolutely no problem. Denial was the problem. "It won't happen to me," was the attitude.*

To explain, let me offer a few personal stories. Not too long ago I became familiar with a family situation where "Mom" just wouldn't buy LTCI coverage, because, as she said, "The five children will take care of me." Less than six months later, she became a person in continual need of care, and she was right—the youngest daughter quit her job and came home to take care of Mom. For one month. Then this. "I've got to back to where I was living and try to get my old job back, because it's far easier than this," was her lament. Then the oldest daughter came to me and asked if we could still write the policy, which I had tried to convince her mother to buy. Sadly, I had to explain that it was too late. (You can't insure the car when it's sitting at the bottom of the lake, and you can't insure the house when the garage is on fire.) But, I couldn't resist telling the daughter why. "I couldn't get your mother to purchase an LTCI policy because *she said that you would take care of her." Brutal, but factual. Delay and denial.* Mom went to the nursing home and paid for it herself.

119

## Chapter 11

More recently, I found out about a personal friend, who had requested a first copy of my book, which I gave to him, and we and his wife spent some time talking about Long Term Care, and their need for a policy. I didn't get the job done. Within six months my friend developed a serious heart problem, and his wife, who was "sharp as a tack," at the time we discussed LTC, was diagnosed with Alzheimer's. We now know that this insidious disease can last a long time, but her case seems to have advanced rather rapidly. So, again, the oldest daughter quit her job in another city, and came to take care of Mom and Dad. Time will tell.

One of my best policyholders, a man in his fifties, looked at things differently, and calmly stated it all so well. After I had delivered the policy, which covered both he and his wife, he stated, "Ron, I just couldn't see my wife having to spend down our assets and eventually lose everything that we have spent years building up, if something were to happen to me. That's why I did this with you."

A lady agent friend of mine, who is very knowledgeable about LTC insurance matters, says that one of her biggest barriers in a "couples" presentation, is convincing the husband that in the long run, with an LTC policy, he will save the money he intended for his wife and family, so that "Mom" will not have to finish her last years in poverty. Funny how "Mom" somehow already knew about that.

Yes, the problems and conditions for women in America are serious, as presented by the evidence I have offered for your consideration. But as severe as all of this is, I am proud that I represent the Long Term Care insurance industry, which finally can solve some of these problems for those who think ahead and prepare. Long Term Care insurance coverage can provide some peace-of-mind for the whole family, for at least part of the problem, even though **the unfairness of it all seems to settle on the backs of the women of this country.**

# CHAPTER 12

# THE INSURANCE ISSUES

## *HOW TO EVALUATE POLICIES AND CHOOSE THE ONE WHICH BEST FITS YOUR NEEDS*

While America abounds with financial publications offering people advice on how to **create** wealth, or assets, only a few have been written offering advice on how to **preserve** those assets. *"Guarding Your Gold II" is one such publication*. Like the old prospector, you found your gold, worked hard to dig it out, and now you'd like to keep it—for yourself, and your family. The **new found family money,** of the last twenty years, **has created new needs for protecting it.**

Preserving assets in the face of **extended longevity** is a factor. Another factor will be nearly **nonexistent availability of social support** created by the demographic imbalance of a much larger group of older Americans versus a significantly smaller work force—never before seen in this country. The incredible **inflationary rate of all health care costs** in America in general, and the long term care needs of retirees in particular, have created the need for **new and unprecedented creative personal protections** of individual family assets.

**Financial peace-of-mind for Americans** in the next four decades will only be achieved by "guarding your gold" **against all forms of normal and natural aging demands. Care—who's going to provide it, and who's going to pay for it**—will be the "voice crying in the wilderness" for many of nearly eighty million Americans as we **approach this aging precipice.** Those that plan ahead will not have to be a crying voice, their family money—**their gold**—so to speak, will be available to them for unexpected—**make that expected**—long term care needs. Here's the roadmap to "guarding your gold." Choose the route that fits you best, and fit the plan to fit your needs.

## A BRIEF BACKGROUND OF LTC INSURANCE

Long Term Care insurance is a somewhat new product brought on by the demands of fairly recent developments and innovations in the nursing home, home health, assisted living, and community health care fields. LTCI policies currently present insurance solutions for each of the new types of care, but **because some types of care are relatively new themselves, insurance products to provide benefits for them, have understandably only recently been developed in the last decade.**

A combination of valuable contributions by the National Association of Insurance Commissioners, state legislatures and Congress, and the industry itself, have improved

Long Term Care insurance solutions in these formative years. As a result, the **LTC insurance industry has "grown up," and finally offers the American public the variety of quality products,** which it has come to demand.

An important note for those of you who have accountants or personal financial planners is in order at the beginning. Since insurance agents cannot give legal advice, and are ill equipped to have inside knowledge of a client's financial affairs—**the agent, accountant, and attorney, or financial planner, along with their client**—may find value in working together in regard to estate planning, Long Term Care Insurance, and asset preservation.

Think of the advantage of simply explaining the tax benefits of the "Tax Qualified Policy" to a corporate or personal attorney or accountant, who may not be aware of the best value for his or her clients' asset preservation goals. The advice of all parties involved creates an advantage for the average client. Remember however, that accountants sometimes are not aware of their clients' interests in LTCI, or may not even know that the client has purchased a policy. Therefore, **it is imperative that the client notify both tax advisors,** if they retain such, and the astute LTCI agent should be sure to mention to the client that he or she is available to visit with the accountant or attorney to inform them of the choice made by the client.

If you do not have an accountant or attorney handling your affairs**, the same accomplishments can be achieved** by using the explanations found in this chapter to help craft your own best solution, **in consultation with your LTCI agent or financial planner.**

It is our duty to help **clients understand the federal and state tax advantages of current LTC insurance products**, which are available to individuals, C-Corporations, S-Corporations, LLC's and sole proprietors. You will find these items in the following chapter, entitled **"The Tax Issues—And The 'Tax Qualified' Policy." You need not be an accountant or an attorney to follow the information.**

## THE CRITICS

We had some critics in the early years. The insurance industry has been attacked, criticized, challenged and regulated since day one. Sometimes with good cause, sometimes without. The general public has a distaste for insurance. I don't enjoy paying premiums for something non-tangible. Nobody does. That's part of human nature. Those who understand it, accept it. Those who have something "at risk" believe in it, and welcome insurance as the solution. The problem comes in understanding insurance. A one sentence snapshot will do. Identify the risk, spread the costs of the risk through a "pool", transfer the risk to the pool, and take from the pool when needed. So, those who have a distaste for insurance do so until the day they need it. Both transactions (putting into the pool, and taking from the pool) take place by the millions daily. Whether it is an automobile risk, property risk, liability risk, homeowner risk, health risk, or death risk, they all spell "pooling of risk,"—or "insurance."

In the 1990's, the industry was challenged with a new criticism. We were called on to address the problems of Long Term Care and Asset Preservation, and as soon as we responded, the "advocates" cried "too much premium!" "Too little, too late" seemed to be the rallying cry. In a way, that's right. People who don't prepare for any event will experience the frustration of too much premium when they've waited years to purchase proper coverage until "just the right moment to buy". We've talked about purchasing coverage at a young enough age for actuary to calculate future claims expectations. People who accept paying $1,000 every six months to protect their $30,000 automobile (and their liability) balk at paying $50 to $200 a month (for a couple age 40-60) to protect $200,000-300,000 of their future, and the assets they are accumulating.

When the insurance industry picks up the ball and says, "Okay, we can present you with an opportunity to insure against those future costs," the advocates react with their "overcharge" drivel. More than once I have had people or their children call me and ask me if I could insure someone after the decision had been made that they needed to go to a nursing home. Waiting until debilitating old age has set in certainly will result in "too much premium" because rates must be calculated for soon to be collected benefits. What goes into the pool must be calculated to cover the costs of those who need to take from the pool. Who's to say, "Who or When?" That's insurance.

## THE FIRST POLICIES

So, let's take the insurance industry from its infancy in **nursing home products,** and discuss the old policies by identifying what was wrong with them.

Basically, there were *three things wrong*. *First, not enough insurance companies were in the market.* The industry did not recognize the need for Long Term Care insurance, because real needs had not yet been defined and most of the new needs—home care/home health care, assisted living, etc.—had not yet been developed. Only a few companies specialized in the market, and those that did, did not have enough nursing home industry data available, to properly assess the insurance needs of the elderly. The policies therefore became a somewhat "hit-and-miss" attempt to half-heartedly understand the real requisites of those in need of total long term care.

*Secondly, policies were sold primarily to the elderly*, who were soon to be in need, and a sound actuarial data base was nonexistent. Therefore, rates were based on the *least needed type of care, that of skilled care,* and policies were developed which had a comparatively low premium. Because the policy was not geared to pay for the most utilized type of care, custodial care, the policies were generally worthless to people facing LTC needs. Policies sold previous to 1987 generally offered a "base" amount of say $50 for Skilled care, and half benefits ($25) for intermediate or custodial care. They were sold exclusively to people over 65, and generated annual premiums of around $300. In addition, a whole spectrum of new types of care such as assisted living, adult day care, hospice care, home and home health care, residential care facilities, Alzheimer's facilities, community care, and several others were *in their infancy as industries themselves, and insurance coverage for these types of care had not been developed.* Keep in mind that this "old" policy series was very limited, and readers and insurance agents alike, should carefully evaluate the worth of any policy issued prior to 1991.

The *third problem arose with inflationary trends in the care industry*. Daily nursing home rates had been somewhat static for several years, but with an ever growing elderly population requiring more utilization, greater regulation and expanded guideline requirements, and a much greater number of services provided, nursing home rates began to climb. These general inflationary trends of higher wages, higher costs of providing care, higher food and medical costs, expanded services, as well as the costs of dealing with government regulation, created an inflationary rate in excess of the national trend in America during the 1980's.

Thus, what had been a $40 per day rate rose to $50, $60, $70 and beyond in a relatively short time. Eastern, Midwestern, Southern and Pacific Coast rates saw an even greater increase to as high as $160 per day, as far back as 1994. With this scenario then, (which developed in a short time along with the rise of general health care costs of the nation,) what good would a $25 per day rate do for a person facing a long term nursing stay? Very little. Again, the old policies met nearly none of the real needs of those facing long term care costs.

Additionally, most of the old policy series had a number of *"gatekeepers."* Although the *insurance industry and the National Association of Insurance Commissioners have made terrific strides in eliminating gatekeepers in LTC policies*, they need to be discussed here.

*"Gatekeepers,"* by their simplest definition, mean policy provisions, which needed to be met for the client to obtain benefits. Stated another way, *they were provisions which allowed the insurance companies to escape payment.* Such terms as "Medically necessary," "following a three day hospital stay," or "following a skilled care stay," in a "Medicare approved facility," and "pre-existing conditions" of an incredible amount were abundant in the old policy series and were in fact, "gatekeepers." Thank goodness most gatekeepers have now been eliminated in the LTCI industry.

Another less subtle form of gatekeeping surfaced in the denial of payment due to a technique known as *"claims made underwriting."* Claims made underwriting allowed policies to be issued with little or no careful underwriting previous to the policy being issued. If a client were to present the company with a claim within the two year "contestability" period, the company refused to pay benefits because of a technicality or determination that a pre-existing condition had not so been noted on the application, and simply refunded the premiums and denied the claim. *In all fairness to the insurance industry, only a few companies followed this technique; most companies abhorred the practice, and with sensible candor, it has been eliminated by most states and most companies.*

All of which adds up to the following advice. Be particularly suspicious of policies issued prior to 1991, (and perhaps as far back as 1995, for home care/home health care,) and seek the advice of counsel, or your state insurance department, or a qualified LTC insurance agent in examination of those policies. Above all, do not deal with an agent who would represent a later series of LTC insurance products, which would include any of the above mentioned "gatekeepers." All policies sold in a state have to be approved by the state insurance department. Since 1987 and previous to 1991, some of these policies were approved and may have been issued, thus causing a "slipping through the cracks" syndrome for the unaware purchaser.

## THE NEWER POLICIES

We are now ready to include some further definitions and provisions which the reader should look for in your LTCI shopping and subsequent purchase.

What to look for....Note: As you are aware, The Long Term Care, Short Term Care, and Home Health Care insurance fields are relatively new, even though they have stabilized. For that reason, much of the terminology and many of the features of the products in this field are constantly changing and being improved. The following represents what has been generally accepted as standardized thinking in the LTC Insurance field, and are important considerations, which you should evaluate in your purchase of an LTC policy.

## THE BASIC FEATURES OF A MODERN COMPREHENSIVE LONG TERM CARE INSURANCE POLICY

1.) *The policy must cover all levels of care in a nursing home*—Skilled, Intermediate and Custodial. The policy *must allow for identical benefits, up to the chosen limit, for each level of care.*

2.) Is the policy an *"indemnity" policy, or an "actual expense/ reimbursement" policy?* Either one is acceptable, but there are some variations. The "indemnity" policy pays the actual benefit amount you have chosen. In other words, if you choose a $120 per day benefit, that is the exact amount you receive as a benefit. If you have included a simple 5% inflation rider, that amount will go up 5% per year. If you have included a compounded inflation rider, that amount will start at the base level, increase at 5% in the second year, and then will be compounded each year in the same way that compound interest works in a bank account.

So, the purchaser of an *indemnity* policy knows before hand that he or she will be receiving an *exact amount* for the particular care at the moment claims begin to be paid. This can be advantageous, particularly if the amount is in excess of the actual charge. However, I have had more than one client state, "I don't want to make money on the policy, I just want the bill paid." The trade off is that the indemnity policy will cost more in premium than the actual expense/reimbursement policy, for obvious reasons.

In addition, overuse of the indemnity policy was one of the reasons that "tax free" benefits were limited in the legislation found in HIPAA '96. Quite simply, some people had found a way to choose high benefit amounts in indemnity policies, perhaps even duplicate policies (buy two or three,) go on claim, and make money living in a nursing home. What a way to make a living! Tax free! At any rate, the indemnity policy has a place in LTC insurance for those that can afford the extra premium, but they must realize that there are limitations to the amount of non-taxable benefits they can receive.

The *"actual expense," or "reimbursement"* policy, on the other hand, **pays only for the actual expense billed by the care providers** (inflation riders may be included,) but a note of caution is in order here. If you buy a $150 per day benefit, and the charge is actually $130 per day, you will receive only the $130 as the "actual expense or reimbursement."

Why a note of caution? There are three reasons. First, the "actual expense" is paid up to the amount chosen, not over the $150. Don't think that a $150 per day "actual expense" policy will pay $150 if the actual amount billed is less.

Second, if the nursing home chooses to use $120 as the actual base, and bills differently for other services, (personal items, etc.) you may be accountable for those services, while the policy may pay only the base rate. Anyone who has seen this technique used in hospital billings will understand the concept. (A hospital will announce a daily *room* rate of, say $800, but when the actual bill is received, an itemization of that bill will disclose myriad additional charges over and above the $800.) An "up-front" check with your nursing home is in order to examine just how they actually do bill.

The final consideration of an "actual expense" policy has to do with the inflation rider. If you have chosen a compounding inflation rider, and that rider outstrips the actual increase of charge from the nursing home, you may not receive the benefits you were counting on. In other words, if your inflation rider compounded to a $150 amount, and the nursing home rate only increased to $140, you would still receive only the $140. This is not a big issue, and in all likelihood will not happen, but it is an item for your consideration.

3)      Familiarize yourself with the phrase *"pool of money."* In the past few years the industry has finally addressed the fact that most people would rather remain at home for their care, if at all possible. But, while most companies, in the early days, only issued policies covering actual **nursing home care costs**, those who wanted to receive benefits for **care at home had to purchase an additional home care/home health care policy**, or hope for the availability of a home health care rider built into their LTC policy. The home care policy also became known as a community care policy, because the company pretty much paid for coverage in the policyholder's home, a friend or relative's home, an adult day care facility, or a variety of places other than a licensed nursing home. Payment for certain "assisted living" facilities also required a specialized policy or rider (option) in order for the policyholder to collect on help with activities of daily living, medical assistance, or cognitive needs, which could be offered, and as well served, in an assisted living facility. Qualifications for receiving benefits were different for each type of care, and gatekeepers were prevalent in nearly all the policies sold prior to 1996. In actuality, most of the policy problems listed in this paragraph were rectified by most of the

companies in the LTC insurance arena in the late '90's, as the Comprehensive Long Term Care policy was developed.

So, finally the industry woke up to the real needs of people in search of care, whether it be in a nursing home, at home, or at an assisted living facility. The true definition of comprehensive Long Term Care became a very liberal interpretation of "care" required by those in need. States began to require that companies market policies which included nursing home care (at any level), care in an assisted living facility, and care at home or in the community. *Finally*, common ground had been found. Gatekeepers for each separate type of care were removed, policies were broadened in their scope of coverage, and in their type of coverage, and the "pool of money" concept became the norm in the true "Long Term Care" definition.

What, then, was the final product like? Very simply, the pool of money concept now enabled people to **collect benefits regardless of where the care was given**. If a person in need of help with activities of daily living, medical assistance (excluding qualification for benefits of Tax-qualified policies), or cognitive disabilities, what difference did it make *where* the care was given? No riders were needed to seek payment for coverage at home, rather than going to a nursing home. The pool of money concept simply says, "pay the premium, and within certain guidelines embodied in the policy, we will pay for your care *wherever* it is delivered, up to the daily maximum you choose."

Where the pool of money concept becomes interesting is found **within the use of the benefit dollars** available to the insured. For instance a client purchases a pool of money policy with a five year benefit period, with a maximum benefit of $150 per day. The client chooses home care/home health care/community care as his or her first option. The cost for this care, on a six-hour basis, is $90. The **remaining $60 stays in the pool of money** to be used as needed at a time the client chooses to go to an assisted living facility, or in turn, to a nursing home. In other words, savings on home health care could result in a five-year policy becoming a five and a half year policy, in reality. Any combination of variants can be calculated, but the important factor is that the consumer is far ahead with the choices offered in a pool of money contract, simply because of the flexibility in where to receive benefits, and the savings enjoyed (and deferred,) by being cared for other than in a nursing home.

Well, what is the trade-off? **Slightly higher premiums for pool of money contracts** than for a simple nursing home policy. But now the coverages combine, allowing the consumer much greater choice than having to purchase more than one policy. When written in combination, such as in the pool of money policy, the premiums of a true comprehensive LTC policy are lower than separate policies for similar coverage.

The industry critics must really be upset with this approach. Giving the people what they want (home care and care in an assisted living facility,) and increasing premiums even more than for a simple nursing home policy must aggravate their viewpoint, since for years they wanted the public to believe that the original approach was unaffordable.

Again this baloney is challenged by an ever increasing percentage of Americans who opt to have their assets protected through LTCI policies, and do not expect that the government is going to provide for their long term care through Medicare and Medicaid. In fact, in 1998, the American Council of Life Insurance performed a study relating to the "affordability" of Long Term Care Insurance. The study found that 81 to 47 percent of the people in the age range 45-64 could afford LTCI coverage. Generally speaking, premiums for a 55-year-old are 50 percent lower than for a 65-year-old, and 70 percent lower (than the 65 age range,) for a 45-year-old. Sorry, critics, **Americans can afford to protect their assets. Government for the last ten years has admitted it cannot afford to take on more than  Medicare and Medicaid can currently offer, and has passed legislation to encourage people to provide for their own LTC costs.**

4.)        **What are elimination periods?** In simple jargon, **the "elimination period" is the deductible.** The deductible, or elimination period, is the number of days you choose to pay for the cost of care yourself, before receiving any benefits from the policy. Each company will offer a variety of elimination periods ranging from first day coverage to 365 days. Not all companies will offer all the deductible periods, but by company they will include usually three or four options ranging from first day coverage (0 day elimination) to 20 day, 30 day, 60 day, 90 day, 100 day, 150 day, 180 day or 365 day.

The reason for such a wide variety of elimination periods (deductibles) **is in consideration of premium**. Obviously, first day coverage will be much more expensive than a thirty day elimination, the thirty day elimination will be more expensive than a 100 day elimination, and so on. Bearing in mind that Medicare will pick up the **first twenty days of skilled nursing home care for medically necessary care**, the first day coverage seems to be possibly redundant. But, remember, that is for skilled care only, and does nothing for custodial care. Whatever elimination period is chosen, the policyholder should make certain that they are comfortable with the premium amount.

The reader must be aware of language in the Federally Tax Qualified Policy, which may be confusing. So, in all fairness to the reader, let's take a run at clearing up the elimination period question, before you do become confused. The language is taken from IRS Notice 97-31, and embodies the definitions of a *"chronically ill individual,"* (which a policyholder must be certified as, in order to receive policy benefits under the "Activities of Daily living" trigger of the TQ policy). The ruling reads as such, "An individual is a chronically ill individual under the ADL trigger only if a licensed health care practitioner has certified that the individual is unable to perform (without substantial assistance from another individual) at least two ADLs for a period of at least 90 days due to a loss of functional capacity. **This 90-day requirement does not establish a waiting period before which benefits may be paid or before which services may constitute qualified long term care services."**

In other words, then, *the 90-day waiting period* **is not a deductible or elimination period**. *It is simply a requirement of the policy that the client must be designated as "chronically ill" to start a plan of care written by the health care practitioner; a definition, or designation, so to speak, for you to become eligible for benefits.* So, if you have a zero day deductible, the benefits will still be paid from the first day forward regardless of the 90-day certification requirement for your plan of care, if you qualify for benefits. I trust this paragraph has eliminated any confusion about the two terms, rather than create questions. Also, please remember that this language is only in reference to the ADL trigger. It does not appear in qualification of benefits for the cognitive trigger, nor does it appear as a condition for obtaining benefits in Non Tax Qualified policies.

Choosing the elimination period simply boils down to what you face with **premium amounts**. One person may wish to purchase first day or twenty day elimination period coverage because the higher premium amount may not be a factor. The next person may find a better value in choosing a higher elimination period (deductible) and save premium dollars. Personally, I believe in sending as little premium as possible to insurance companies, while maintaining some of the risk myself, thus utilizing the higher elimination period to save premium dollars.

Balancing the premium spent with the benefits received, and the ability to shoulder the difference in the amount of the deductible, is a common practice in insurance purchase, such as homeowner's and automobile coverage. Each person's financial abilities are different, and this difference must be weighed when seeking insurance advice. Most consumers are concerned with **protection from a major financial catastrophe** brought on by unforeseen events. The same can be said for purchasers of LTC coverage, who wish to protect their assets from a major invasion, and are willing to accept a smaller blow, by balancing premiums with a combination of higher deductibles, thereby self-insuring for a larger number of days.

5.)    **What are the levels of benefits available?**  This is simple enough. Most companies will offer a benefit ranging from $50 per day to $300 per day. Some companies may offer coverage on a monthly basis, in $100 increments. Thus the $100 per day benefit from Company A, and the $3000 per month benefit from Company B would calculate to the same amount.

The key is to find out what nursing home rates, home health/home care rates, and assisted living rates are in your geographic area, or in a location of your choice, ahead of time. Then you will have some idea what to use as the base benefit amount in the first year of the your policy, and **attach an inflation rider,** which would keep up with the inflationary problems we have discussed. You don't have to assume that you will land on the exact spot, but care given to your own financial considerations will direct you to an amount, which you can find acceptable to your own pocketbook.

Some people may find that an amount somewhat below the going daily rate is more suitable, since they would in fact be **co-insuring** themselves for the excess daily amount, even considering inflation. In other words, if you find a nursing home which appeals to you with a $150 daily rate, you may want to choose a $130 daily benefit with an inflation rider, thus co-insuring yourself for the remaining $20 per day, which would then mean you would pay the remaining $600 per month (and incremental inflationary expectations) yourself, from your retirement income. Again, consideration of premiums paid is the key to this technique. Above all, if you underinsure, as in the example above, **_make certain that you have purchased the inflation rider_** to keep up with the future.

Personally, I advise against this technique. I tell the story of a pair of shoes. Who would buy a pair of shoes that are too small to begin with, and hope that the tightness will wear off over the years. It won't—buy the proper fit at the beginning.

6.) **_What are the benefit periods available,_** or how long do you want the company to pay for your Long Term Care? Since the purpose of this book is to protect people from having to "spenddown" their assets, you will want to consider what you feel is the **_proper length of benefit period to insure preservation of those assets._** True, there will be many options available—they range from as low as 80 days to 360 days for Short Term Care—and as short as one year to lifetime for Long Term Care.

Let's take a moment to discuss **_Short Term Care_** and its relationship to Medicare and Medicare Supplement policies. Remember that Medicare pays for the first 20 days of _Skilled Care_ in a Medicare Approved Skilled Care Facility. Remember also, that _nothing_ is paid on _intermediate_ or _custodial care_ by Medicare. On the 21st day of a skilled care stay, Medicare, in 2003, has a $105 per day deductible, which will apply to days 21 to 100—again, only for Skilled Care. Medicare Supplements in 2003 will pay the amount over $105. **_Sounds like a good deal doesn't it? It's not._** So few people stay on skilled care over 20 days that the benefit is seldom used, and some although Medicare Supplement policies may pay this "skilled care" deductible, again, they are seldom utilized, because of the 20 day Medicare rule.

**_There is, however, an honest need for intermediate and custodial care_** after the 20-day period is used up. That's where **_short term care_** becomes valuable. When doctors transfer their patients from skilled care to intermediate or custodial (convalescent) care, Medicare ceases to pay nursing home benefits and the patient is liable. Since around 66% of nursing home stays are six months or less, Short Term Care policies can be of value. These policies are usually sold for terms of 90, 180 or 360 days and obviously carry a much smaller premium than LTC policies. **_They have their place, but do not consider them as a substitute for Long Term Care, because they are not designed for the same purpose._** Also, when a person is considering purchase of a Long Term Care policy, why duplicate benefits and pay for both policies? If, in fact, you are looking for "first day coverage" simply purchase it in your LTC policy. Again, **_Short Term Care policies are not the proper tool to use in asset preservation, but do have a place for those who want some protection at a smaller premium._**

Normal Long Term Care policy benefit periods start as low as one year and jump in various increments, depending on the company chosen, to 2 year, 3 year, 4 year, 5 year, 6 year, and Lifetime. That's fairly simple. Some people will decide that they can afford only a 1 or 2 year benefit period. On the other hand, some will determine that family longevity indicates that lifetime benefits are their best consideration. As we've noted before, who's to say how long a person will live, let alone how long they will live with long term care needs.

So, for example, is a two-year benefit period enough? **Would it really protect considerable assets against long term care needs? Depending on the asset base, probably not.** Even if we talk Medicaid and refer to their rules, the Medicaid "snapshot" of countable assets (resources) is taken on the date you apply for Medicaid. Further, Medicaid looks at all resource transfers occurring within the 36 months (currently, in most states) prior to the date you apply for Medicaid. The rules are simple. You cannot give resources away for the sole purpose of making yourself eligible for Medicaid. Transferring or selling any resources during this period can result in *ineligibility* or *penalties*, so extreme caution is in order. Again, remember that these rules are **not apropos to the "Partnership" states** of Connecticut, New York, California, and Indiana. All other states will have some variation of the intent of this paragraph, but the basic principle remains the same.

For these reasons, then, **a benefit period of at least three years, or even four years is recommended.** Obviously, the legal transfer processes take time to complete, so the purchaser of LTC insurance should be fully aware of "lag time" and allow enough time in their planning to compensate for sorting and delay, **if transfer is their intent**. In all reality, if a person is admitted to a nursing home or begins to require home health care as the first step toward going to a nursing home, that may be the proper time to begin thinking about asset transfer, but then again, maybe not. **The natural tendency to avoid transfer of assets, until absolutely necessary, is the rule rather than the exception.**

Interestingly enough, many people suffer from two perceptions in their waning years. First, some folks think that they're going to "take it with them." We all know that's not true, but that attitude prevents needed planning from taking place, and **delays what should be an orderly process.** The "younger generation," who in all common sense would like to start the transfer process, is continually rebuffed in their attempt to bring it to fruition. **Unfortunately, many times the process never even gets started**, and what should have been achieved while all parties were able to contribute, becomes a legal maze consuming months, even years, of family, legal and bureaucratic time. Incapacitation, failed health and death have a way of proving this point. Therefore, **choose an LTCI policy with a long enough benefit period to achieve your goals.**

The second problem, and a very serious and realistic one at that, deals with the elder person's faith and trust in his or her children. Circumstances can sometimes dictate delay, and they are very real. Suppose that the "children" are headed for a divorce, or that the "child" is himself in poor health or incapacitated, or that the "child" is a spendthrift or has no sense of financial acumen. What does "Grandma" or "Grandpa" do in that case? **Does transfer of assets sound like a sound solution should the patient recover (or want to return home) and have no home to return to?** These transfer doubts are very logical and omnipresent thoughts in the mind of a troubled elder. They are personal considerations, but by no means are they small. And again, **the longer the LTC policy runs in length of benefit period, the less immediate the financial pressure for all parties.**

7.) **_What are the issue ages?_** Existing actuarial data has affected the thinking of most industry "decision makers" and as the "chain of anticipated use" shortens, the availability of policies for people over 84 in the life and health market is almost nonexistent. This problem highlights the **_need to attend to the LTC matter as soon as possible, because delay may turn into denial._** _Premium consideration is a factor also, as in any age rated policy, premiums actuarially become high in ratio to benefits received._ A further problem arises in the age bracket 84-89, in that most companies limit that group to a one or two year benefit, if the coverage is even available.

I have told the story of the young 94 year-old lady for whom I was able to provide an LTC policy. At that time, I was fortunate to represent a company which had no restrictions on age, dealing with the actual health of the applicant on a face-to-face paramedic interview, and Attending Physicians Statements, as underwriting requirements, rather than age. Most companies have **_age restrictions on underwriting_**, and perhaps we will see that change, but don't expect it anytime soon.

As for the younger ages, many companies are now reducing eligible age from an original forty or fifty age bracket to age eighteen or twenty, and as the demand for earlier purchase of LTC insurance becomes obvious, we may see most of the industry follow suit.

8.) **_Is inflation protection available?_** If you are dealing with a company that does not offer this benefit either automatically or by rider, forget that company. You should have a choice in the matter. More importantly, you need to deal with a company that either **_includes the inflation rider at moment of purchase or guarantees future insurability, without evidence of insurability, at a later date._** What good does it do to purchase LTCI today without an inflation rider, or a guarantee of future additional purchase at a later attained age, when you may not meet underwriting requirements? Inflation riders can be purchased which will raise the base coverage by **_5% per year on a simple schedule or 5% per year on a compounding schedule._** Some companies allow the purchaser to raise his or her base coverage by a certain percentage (usually 10%) every two years. The key is to guarantee that the purchase (which will be calculated at the new attained age,) is allowable regardless of physical condition or insurability.

9.) **_What are the "pre-existing conditions" requirements?_** Probably one of the greatest advancements made by the industry comes in the area of "pre-existing conditions." Since underwriting must be an important factor in considering issuance of an LTC policy, **_many companies have changed the old approach of issuing policies with a "pre-existing condition" exclusion._**

Older policies may have contained total exclusions for any pre-existing problem. That is to say a person may have had an item of medical history which existed before application for a policy. If the client had a medical history of say, diabetes, that condition (and in some cases, anything associated with it,) was not covered (excluded) as a condition of obtaining benefits. About 1989, many companies reduced that to a six month period, i.e. benefits could be awarded after a six-month waiting period.

Many companies, however, have eliminated "pre-existing conditions" altogether. In other words, *if a policy is issued, any pre-existing condition would be covered with no waiting period.* That's the good news. The bad news is that underwriting tightened up and policies were not issued to people with certain maladies in their health histories. That is still the case and always will be the case. Nobody would think of insuring the automobile after the wreck; or the house after the fire; therefore, the same holds true in the health care field. On the other hand, many companies still retain the six-month pre-existing condition period for those conditions exposed on the application or revealed during the underwriting process.

The secret is to find out which companies take certain risks while another company's underwriting rules would be cause for rejection. I don't mean to sound alarming, because the underwriting rules of most companies are fairly easy to satisfy. Except for serious problems, underwriters generally are pretty liberal in their interpretation of the rules. You may have to try more than one or two companies to find out which one will accept your application.

10.) *How does the company underwrite? In other words, how does an applicant qualify for LTC coverage?* All companies use a different set of criteria for underwriting, but one item will always be present. The first thing that happens is for an agent to take an application. The agent will have in his or her possession an Agent's Underwriting Guide, which will enable the agent to tell immediately if a serious pre-existing condition would be cause for denial. The Underwriting Guide of acceptable conditions, or non-acceptable conditions, will shorten the strokes and avoid unnecessary pursuit of coverage if the company's guide indicates that the client has pre-existing ineligible medical problems.

Assuming that the agent's underwriting guide and questions on the application allowed submittal of that risk, the next step will be home office underwriting. This will always include an APS (Attending Physician's Statement) from each doctor you have consulted in at least the last five years.

As the underwriter awaits this information, most companies will conduct a personal telephone interview with you to find out if the information on the application was correctly recorded. This serves two purposes; total disclosure of all underwriting information, and discouragement of unscrupulous agents who incorrectly record information, or worse, leave out important information in order to make a sale. This practice results in a bad relationship for all involved, because a client may have been led to believe that a policy would be issued, when in fact the APS could disclose information which may cause declination. *Be particularly careful to see that the agent accurately records your medical information. You will save yourself a lot of grief, since you must sign the application.*

Will a physical be required? Probably not, but if you have not seen a physician for years (many people haven't) you will probably be visited by a paramedic from your community who can provide the necessary information for the home office underwriter. This is a simple exam usually done by a Registered Nurse, who is affiliated with a national organization specializing in home exams. Nothing more than a telephone call from the paramedic sets up the appointment at your pleasure, and the company pays the paramedic.

Another item, which nearly all LTC companies have implemented is the *"Face-to-Face" interview*. Face-to-Face is an assessment conducted in the applicant's home by a specially trained licensed nurse who will ask a series of questions regarding daily activities, medical histories, medication use, exercise, current living conditions and arrangements, and body measurements (blood pressure, height, weight, etc.) Depending on the age of the applicant, most companies will also conduct a *cognitive assessment*, which evaluates the current cognitive abilities of the prospective client. A part of this assessment will include what is known as the "delayed word recall" test, in which the applicant is shown a series of words and then asked to repeat some of them a few minutes later.

Even if you find that you do not qualify for what the industry calls "standard" or "preferred" rates, many companies are now offering coverage at "sub-standard" rates, which include the same benefits you originally asked for, but the price of the coverage may be higher. The "upside" is that many people, who could not previously obtain policies because of a pre-existing problem, can now at least purchase coverage.

11.)   *What are the requirements for "triggering" (qualifying for) benefits?* This is probably the most important of the items discussed this far, in comparing policies and companies, and what to look (and look out) for in that comparison. As we said before, the old policies required medical necessity as THE requirement for obtaining benefits. Well, that's bad news and another reason to check that old policy and divest yourself of it. The industry quickly recognized that medical necessity—as a sole source of "triggering" benefits—was unfair to the policyholder, and nearly all policies issued since 1988 have expanded the rights of the client to obtain benefits. Those rights to obtain benefits were expanded into what became known as the "triple trigger". The triple trigger of medical necessity, help with activities of daily living, and cognitive impairment, was truly a step forward in providing for the needs of the policyholder. True, *medical necessity still remains as a way to receive policy benefits, with the exception of current* Federally "Tax Qualified" policies.

A drawback with the current version of the "Tax Qualified" LTC policies is that *Medical Necessity was removed as one of the three normal triggers* for qualifying for benefits. Supposedly, the intent was to avoid duplication of the benefits of Medicare, but since Medicare contributes so little to long term care, what was possibly gained by removing medical necessity as a time honored trigger for obtaining benefits? My own thinking is that Congress will revisit this part of the law and reinstate medical necessity as a trigger sometime in the future. In a previous edition of this book I originally predicted that this would come sooner, rather than later, but the specifications written into the "Tax-qualified" policy now seem pretty well entrenched in American LTC insurance thinking.

In the "Definitions of LTC Insurance" chapter, we discuss ADLs. For your benefit, let us review them here. ADLs (Activities of Daily Living) became the second improvement in "triggering" benefits. Activities of daily living are simply those basic functions a person performs for himself or herself each day. Depending on which company you are reviewing, they will number five to six. Also, depending on the state where you live and whether or not you choose the "Tax-qualified" policy or the non-tax qualified policy, there may be a seventh ADL, that of "ambulating." *Usually the six major ADL's are bathing, feeding, dressing, transferring (mobility,) toileting, and continence (bladder and bowel control.)*

Simply, when a person is unable to perform one or two (depending on the company interpretation, and in the case of the "Tax-qualified policy, the definitions of that policy) of these basic human functions they are considered eligible for nursing home admission or home care, and LTC benefits. This definition more accurately describes the conditions under which a majority of people seek benefits for long term care. For this reason, **do not under any circumstances entertain purchase of a policy which does not include ADLs as a "trigger" for benefits. Furthermore, do not entertain a policy which would require that more than two ADL's be met as qualification for benefit.**

Again, it should be mentioned that the ADL's referred to in the "Tax Qualified Policy" are simple, but strict. IRS Notice 97-31 describes them as such: "The six ADLs listed… are eating, toileting, transferring, bathing, dressing, and continence. Section 7702B (c)(2)(B) further provides that a contract is not a qualified long term care insurance contract unless it takes into account at least five of these six activities in determining whether an individual is a chronically ill individual." So, simply, *the TQ policy says that the inability to perform two of six activities without substantial, hands-on, or standby assistance will qualify you for benefits.*

Another major improvement, which "triggers" benefits, fits neither the medically necessary need, nor the ADL need. That is the qualification of ***cognitive needs*** or mental conditions which are caused by a number of diseases. Alzheimer's and Parkinson's are the most commonly known to the public, but there are others. By all means, any policy you purchase should include the above conditions spelled out, and clearly defined. You may also find the wording "other mental conditions of an organically demonstrable nature," in contracts which were, or are, issued under without regard to "Tax Qualified" status.

When evaluating the cognitive trigger benefits of the Tax Qualified policy, we, again, are able to quote IRS Notice 97-31 which says: "Cognitive Impairment Trigger—For purposes of the cognitive impairment trigger, taxpayers may rely on *either or both* of the following safe-harbor definitions:

(1) "Severe Cognitive Impairment" means a loss or deterioration in intellectual capacity that is (a) comparable to (and includes) Alzheimer's disease and similar forms of irreversible dementia, and (b) measured by clinical evidence and standardized tests that reliably measure impairment in the individual's (i) short-

term or long term memory, (ii) orientation as to people, place, or time, and (iii) deductive or abstract reasoning.

(2) "Substantial Supervision" means continual supervision (which may include cuing by verbal prompting, gestures, or other demonstrations) by another person that is necessary to protect the severely cognitively impaired individual from threats to his or her health or safety (such as may result from wandering)."

If you consider any company or policy that has qualifications less liberal than those stated above, you are wasting your money. There is no need to settle for less and a review of what you may have purchased in the past is in order.

12) Is *a Home Health Care provision included, or at least provided by rider?* Because Home Health Care is a completely different ball game, you may be interested in attaching HHC by a rider. Some companies will offer a "stand alone" Home Health Care policy, which may be purchased in addition to the basic nursing home policy, but most people would prefer the savings of having HHC included in the basic policy, or attached via a Home Health Care rider. There was a time, and I'm sure it still exists in some states' code books, when the true definition of Long Term Care required that Home Health Care and Community Care be included in the Nursing Home policy, and not added to the policy by rider.

13) *How does the company treat Home Care or Alternate forms of LTC?* Please be aware that *Home Health Care* and *Home Care* are two different topics. Home *Health* Care is a very valuable part of your Medicare Part B benefits, and some *limited* Home *Health* Care benefits are provided by your purchase of Part B of Medicare. But, a short search of the *"Guide To Health Insurance for People with Medicare"* will familiarize you with the tight requirements needed to qualify you for Medicare Home Health Coverage. It will also point out the gaps in that coverage, including not paying for "services that are primarily to assist you in meeting personal care or housekeeping needs." In other words*, no help is available through Medicare HHC for help with ADL's*.

It is very important that Americans understand this, because *help with ADL's is the number one trigger of Home and Community care needs.* Home Care is different from Home Health Care in that a person may require the assistance of a ***personal care helper for ADL's***, rather than ***a professional helper*** such as an RN, LPN, Physical Therapist, etc., ***for medical or health needs.*** Recent reports of fraud and abuse in Medicare Home Health (estimates have been as high as 25%,) and the resultant limitations on that industry have made Medicare Home Health even tougher to come by. At any rate, the LTC purchaser should understand that the *Home Care Benefits* of a *personal* nature may be more important to them than *Home Health Care* benefits, by a *professional*, because the triggering of benefits under ADL's, or cognitive needs *is much more likely than under medical necessity*, and covers them for the same type of care they would receive under custodial care in a nursing home. It is important that potential policyholders are aware that *both Home Health Care and Home Care* can be purchased in a normal comprehensive LTCI policy, for those cases not covered by Medicare.

Alternate Forms of Care, or Plans of Care, are important to the policyholder because this feature may allow the client to **stay at home, or in the home of a friend or relative, an alternative living center,** or any number of other locations and receive the same benefits that they would receive under custodial care in a nursing home. Plans of Care, or Alternate Forms of Care are evaluated and determined by a specialist in caregiving, a care coordinator, or in the case of a "Tax-qualified" policy, a certified health care practitioner, and can be agreed upon by the client, the doctor and the company. Look for this feature and see if the Alternate Plan of Care is an *automatic provision* before purchasing an LTC policy. **This feature is definitely in the best interest of the policyholder.**

Both the Home Health Care/Home Community Care and Alternate Forms of Care provisions will solve the age old problem of "I'm never going to a nursing home!" Great! Nobody says you have to. If all parties agree on a form of care which can keep you at home or in the community, why go to a nursing home? What could be better? Again, these two features are examples of the LTC industry providing for the demands of the public, thereby increasing the value of the current form of products.

**Studies have shown that most people would prefer to remain at, or return to, their residence if they can receive similar qualified care at home, or with an alternate plan of care.** You should ask this question and find out if this option is available by rider, or if it is included in the LTC policy. If it is not included or available by rider, find a company which has this feature. This will prevent you from having to buy a "stand alone" policy for Home Care.

14) **How does the policy treat "Instrumental Activities of Daily Living"?** I include this question here because it follows and coordinates with all the features of Home Care and Activities of Daily Living. **"Instrumental" Activities of Daily Living go much further in terms of benefit to the policyholder.** "IADL's", allows the personal caregiver to assist the client with normal household chores, which the client may not be physically or emotionally up to. Such simple activities as phone calling, bill paying, grocery shopping, laundry, housekeeping, and a thousand other normal activities, may be, from time-to-time, be a nuisance to a person receiving help with actual ADL's. Most Comprehensive LTCI policies, now allow for such chores to be completed by the caregiver, who is already being paid by a Home Health Care agency, which is in turn being paid under the benefits of Home Care in the Comprehensive LTCI policy. This service availability is no small item to those receiving Home Care benefits, and you should ask to see if IADL's are included in any policy which you seek.

15) **How does the policy treat Assisted Living Facilities Benefits?** Let's face it, America is not building very many new nursing homes in today's business climate. What? Then what's all this talk about the need for nursing home insurance and the coming demographic problems of huge increases in the number of elderly folks? The answer is twofold, but simple. In a word, competition is the first answer; and the second answer

is, the availability of options, which allow a person to **choose where they will receive their care.**

My agents are taught to sell the most modern of policies, which, as we have discussed, **offer care in the home, assisted living facility, or in a nursing home.** Think about this. First, people would rather stay at home for their care, if at all possible. Second, within the past ten years, there has been a great proliferation of what have come to be known as "assisted living facilities." Frankly, while something over 30,000 assisted living facilities exist in the United States, and they offer care similar to all but the most severe of custodial cases, who would not choose to receive their care in an assisted living facility, rather than go to a nursing home?

In addition, a great number of these assisted living facilities are new or nearly new, and many are designed as spacious, first class lodges, with amenities abounding. Most of them are actually retirement homes wherein healthy vibrant retirees choose to live, until such time that they many need assistance with their activities of daily living. At that point, they simply move to another wing, change apartments, and continue on as before, with personal care help given by employees of the assisted living unit. Assisted living then, is the competition for the established nursing home industry.

Nowadays, the typical scenario usually runs something like this. **Stay at home as long as possible. Move to an assisted living facility as the next step. Consider the nursing home as the final alternative.** Having selected the proper LTC policy means that the insurance company has provisions for the policyholder to *receive care in all three locations.* In reality, not many people will choose, or be able, to make a stop at each place, but the point of the "pool of money" policy is that those choices **are available.** *That's where the term "freedom" comes into play. Freedom to choose in what setting the policyholder wishes to receive the benefits of their LTC policy.* Will asset transfer allow this choice? Hardly. Will Medicaid allow this choice? Probably not, unless nursing homes become so crowded, or so expensive, that the state must find alternatives to satisfy the demand.

Will an LTC policy which provides for this option up front, built into the policy, be the answer? Most assuredly, assuming that you have purchased a policy which includes home care and assisted living, with payment for such being made at reasonable levels in comparison with nursing home benefits. **Home care at 50% or assisted living at 50% will not be enough,** but you can easily find policies which will range from those percentages all the way to 100%. The cost of care in an assisted living facility can run from 30% to 40% less than care in a nursing home, and you may have to supplement your care at home, or in the assisted living facility, but maybe not. If so, you will find the tradeoff in lower premiums, but *policies for 100% straight-across-the-board are easily available and to your best advantage.* Yes, you will pay more premium, but the freedom of choice in where to receive the care at 100% of full daily benefit will probably be worth the price.

Incidentally, I have found that *not only the policyholder, but the families of the policyholder* are far more receptive to "placement" in an assisted living facility. We spent a whole chapter on the emotional issues surrounding caregiving, and believe me, the community spouse and the families of the insured do not consider this as a small matter. Just think about it. Which sounds better to you? "We had to put Grandma in a nursing home," or "Grandma just moved into one of those new assisted living facilities."

## ADDITIONAL FEATURES

Let us now address additional features. The following items are somewhat less important than the "basic fifteen" outlined above, but collectively they are of significance and should be reviewed for your care in selection of companies and policies. You will find that most of the features are embodied in most current Long Term Care policies sold today.

1)   *Is a hospital stay required prior to long term care benefits being paid?* In most of today's policies, this language will not appear. If it is included in a policy or company brochure, avoid purchase of that policy. In view of the expanded benefits described above, *this policy is not in your best interests* and you should not purchase a policy with this limitation. If you do have such a policy in your possession, you would be well advised to seek a replacement policy which does not have this language. A note of caution however, is in order. In the health insurance business, you should *never drop any existing coverage until a new improved policy is in your hands.* Pre-existing conditions may have developed which make you ineligible for new coverage, and your new attained age (since the purchase of your original policy) will have a bearing on the rates. *Some coverage may be better than no coverage.*

2)   *Is the product guaranteed renewable?* If it is not, do not purchase. All companies have by now included language which allows the policy series to be guaranteed renewable by state. In other words, a policy series may be dropped by a company, (usually in favor of a more beneficial policy,) but you *retain the right to renew your existing policy by paying the premium. The company cannot exclude you, or drop your coverage, because of a claims history you may develop.*

3)   *Does the policy include a "Waiver of Premium" clause?* Today, most companies include waiver of premium in their policy. This is an important feature for you. "Waiver of premium" means that if you are admitted to a nursing home and are receiving benefits for that admission, or receiving home care or assisted living care, *you can stop paying the premium on your policy after a certain number of days, usually 90 to 180.* This is a takeoff from the benefits included in most life insurance policies, which say that after ninety days of a disability, the premiums will be waived for the period of the insured's disability. Some LTC policies go so far as to allow the waiver of premium benefit to apply to the remaining "at home" spouse, after premiums have been paid for a certain time. Remember, however, that after the benefit period is interrupted by your dismissal from the nursing home, and you go "off claim," premium payments may or may not resume, depending on the company you have chosen. As you can see, the "waiver of premium" clause is an important feature for you.

Chapter 12

4) **How does the policy treat "restoration of benefits?"** Most policies on the market today contain this feature, which can be very valuable to you. Following a long term care confinement, 100% of any benefits paid are restored once you have returned home, and have not been confined to any convalescent care facility (or received home care) for a period of six consecutive months. In other words, if you are confined to a nursing home for eleven months and have a three year benefit policy, then recover to the point where you do not need care and are able to return home for six or more consecutive months without benefits, the original three year **benefit period will be restored** *and your benefit "clock" starts again.* Be sure to look for this benefit when shopping your companies.

5) **How does the company treat "spousal discounts"?** Since assets are normally held in joint ownership, both spouses are equally at risk should LTC become a necessity. Therefore, LTC coverage is obviously recommended for each spouse. Studies have proven that married couples are more interested in caring for each other (for as long as is physically possible,) than in admitting one or the other to a nursing home. For that reason, many companies offer a spousal discount for couples that purchase the policy together. Check to see that your total premiums would or would not be affected by purchasing from a company which will offer the spousal discount. Most do.

6) **How does the company treat what are known as "survivorship benefits" and "spousal waiver of premium benefits?"** This is a somewhat confusing item, because most companies, which offer survivorship benefits and spousal waiver of premium benefits, have different definitions, interpretations, and limitations regarding the two features. So, let's try to find some common ground which will keep somewhat within the basic meanings of these two separate features.

First of all, the company will require that both spouses were insured, either at the same time if purchased individually, or on the same policy if jointly issued by the company. Secondly, **"survivorship" means that one of the spouses died.** In that case, the *company will waive the premium for the remaining spouse* if the policy has been in force for at least ten years, and the remaining spouse's policy will be considered "paid up". If the policy has not been in force for ten years, the remaining spouse may, depending on the company, be considered as "paid up" at the end of ten years. Limitations will apply depending on the company.

Spousal waiver of premium on the other hand, **does not require a death,** but does *allow the premium of the "at home" spouse to be waived* after a certain number of days of confinement and benefit payments to the spouse confined to the nursing home. In fact, this is not a very common feature, and if offered by a company, it will normally be as a rider which will require additional premium, but some companies do extend waiver of premium to the at home spouse.

7) **Does the company offer a "Shared Benefits" Rider?** The Shared Benefits Rider is a very innovative feature that allows each spouse the opportunity to utilize some or all of the benefits of the other spouse, should the need arise. For instance, let's say that

each spouse on a policy has chosen a five year benefit. What happens if the need for benefits for one spouse becomes seven years, and the "at home" spouse has not needed to utilize any of the benefits? The Shared Benefits rider, which of course requires a small additional premium, *allows each spouse to utilize the benefits of the other, should such a situation occur. So, essentially, the five year policy, now becomes a seven year policy for the spouse requiring care, while three years remains for the spouse not needing care.* A very simple and useful feature found with recent policy offerings.

8) *How does the company treat the "elimination period"?* This factor is important if you are to be admitted to a nursing home for a short time, then released, then readmitted. *Does the elimination period start all over again, or does it accumulate?* Some companies will allow the elimination period to accumulate during the lifetime of an insured. As an example, you have a policy with a 100-day elimination period. You are admitted to a nursing home for two months, then released. You have used up 60 days of your 100- day deductible. Ten months later you are readmitted to the nursing facility. Does the 100-day deductible start over again, or did your policy allow the 60-day previous stay to be applied to the 100-day elimination period? This feature is not uncommon with today's policies, but you should check to make sure if the *Cumulative Elimination Period benefit* is available.

9) *How does the company treat care given to an insured by a family member, or friend—in other words, an "informal caregiver"?* One of the companies which I chose to represent for LTC coverage in the early '90's included a feature which I had never seen before in *any health policy. The feature allowed a family member (spouse, son, daughter, grandchild, etc.) to administer help with ADL's to the policy-holder (under the home care provisions of the policy) and the company would pay for the service.* I was absolutely amazed. Remember that needing help with ADL's is a trigger for receiving benefits in an LTC policy, and the caregiver need not be a professional healthcare practitioner.

I'll never forget one seminar attendee who exclaimed, "You mean that I can quit my job, take care of my mother, and get paid for it?" The answer was a very affirmative yes—with one stipulation. The family member would simply have to go to a *Home Health Care Agency and be trained as any other personal care trainee would.* The training would take about ten days, the insurance company would pay up to $300 for the training, and the family member would then become an employee of that agency, and be paid as a personal caregiver to her mother. Likewise, the insurance company would pay the agency for the benefits received under the policy.

Sounds too logical? Could be. Some companies have caught on to the value of this approach, but many others still drag their feet and deny coverage if a family member is involved in the caregiving. *Why should a complete stranger be regarded as a qualified caregiver, when a family member, particularly a spouse, could very well qualify to perform even better and more satisfying service.* Even perhaps as a "live-in," for a more balanced caregiving effort. At any rate, this may not be an important factor to you, but anyone who purchases an LTC policy with any form of Home Care or Alternate

Plan of Care options should not be restricted from using a family member as a candidate for their personal care needs, in this day and age.

10) **_Will your company allow for reinstatement if the policy lapses due to cognitive impairment?_** In other words, if you are paying your premiums on an annual basis, (or any other mode) and you forget to pay the premiums due to cognitive loss, will you be allowed at least five months in which to pay the premium and reinstate the policy? Most companies have gone to a five or six month **_cognitive impairment reinstatement feature, which says you can be reinstated, without evidence of insurability,_** by showing that your doctor verifies that you have suffered a loss of functional capacity, and pay the back premium amounts due.

Better yet, most companies have also gone to what is known as a **_third party notification system._** This system allows the policyholder to choose one or more people who would receive notification from the company should the above described situation develop, within thirty days of a lapse notice. **_This allows the son or daughter or whomever was chosen, to look into the issue and see why the premium was not paid._** Problems of this nature have even developed into a service industry that tracks the obligations of forgetful people and sees to it that the power bill is paid, premiums are paid, and taxes as well as other legal matters, which could become cumbersome problems for the elderly, are efficiently handled.

11)    **_How does the policy treat Respite Care?_** Respite care is a type of personal care normally offered by non-medical personnel. It is more of a companion type of care, **_which allows the usual caregiver to take a "respite" (vacation) from the daily chores of caregiving._** Respite care is short term in that it will involve only a few hours or few days on an irregular or regular (once a week or once a month) basis. Respite care is normally performed on a volunteer basis, to provide companionship or monitoring, can be accomplished at home, an adult day care center, or church, and serves both the caregiver and receiver with a "change of pace" for a short time. This feature is included in most current policies.

12)    **_How does the policy treat Adult Day Care?_** Adult Day Care centers have become a normal part of every urbanized community, and have become a very important part of the care-giving industry. **_The growth of Adult Day Care centers has been a "Godsend" to those who are burdened with taking care of an adult who needs constant attention._** Although the issue of Adult Day Care is more important in Home Health Care or Home Care policies or riders, we should discuss it here because you may have need of an Adult Day Care facility. The key point with insurance companies seems to be **_whether or not the facility is licensed by the state as such._** Obviously, the states are concerned with the quality of care given at Adult Day Care Centers and have developed sensible standards, which must be met for licensure. Keep this state licensing requirement in mind, because most companies will pay only for care in a licensed facility.

13)    *How does the policy treat Hospice Care?*  Hospice care is a type of care normally provided by registered nurses in hospitals or nursing homes who administer to the needs of the *terminally ill.*  These highly qualified "angels" serve in a very unique fashion.  Their purpose is to provide dignity and comfort to those people and their families who face imminent death, usually in the face of prolonged suffering.  My family used their services in the untimely death of my nineteen-year-old son, and I cannot say enough about them.  The Hospice people help immeasurably in preparing for the inevitable and counseling after the fact.  For purposes of our discussion, however, I must point out three important matters.  First, Medicare will pay for some allowable Hospice services, provided certain criteria are met.  Second, some Medicare Supplement policies will supplement those expenses.  Third, *most LTC policies now contain provisions for Hospice benefits.*  Therefore, you may wish to know how your LTC policy can be of value here.

14)    *How does the policy treat nursing home "Bed Reservation"?*  Bed reservation has become a valuable item, in that a nursing home patient may need to leave their nursing home bed and go to a hospital for any number of days, thereby leaving a bed unoccupied in the nursing home.  Most policies now *pay the nursing home for reservation of that bed for up to fourteen, twenty one, or thirty days, thereby satisfying the policyholder's charges for that space, through the "bed reservation" benefits paid by the insurance company to* the nursing home.

15)    *How does the company treat "Non-licensed care"?*  This is a serious question when considering nursing homes.  Most states have a number of "Personal Care" facilities, which do not qualify as "Licensed Skilled Care" facilities. They are not licensed to provide Skilled Care, but in essence, do *provide custodial care* on a twenty-four hour basis.  Most policies require your admittance to a "Licensed Skilled Care Facility," as a criteria for nursing home benefit for LTC.  With some companies *you may need to request an alternate care facility (Personal Care), after your initial admittance to a "Skilled Care Facility,"* and they may allow benefits to be paid to the alternate facility, or home care arrangements made, after agreement between the policyholder, the doctor, and the company.  Most companies currently, however, will pay only for "Licensed Skilled Care Facilities" and will not allow "non-licensed" care as an alternate, unless you choose to have care given in a licensed assisted living facility, or would receive "at home" care from a licensed Home Health/Home Care Agency.  You should check both the policy and facility in terms of licensing.

16)    *Does the policy offer Prescription Drug Benefits?*  Some do, most don't, and then with severe restrictions and limitations.  However, this benefit could become one of the "whistles and bells" over the years, depending on the scope of yet-to-be determined legislation regarding the prescription drug picture in America.  Prescription drugs are a very big item in America, both in cost and utilization, and a policy, which might offer some payment toward them is an obvious advantage to you.  Remember, however, the phrase "in consideration of premium," and consider whether or not you may be paying too much for this benefit.

17)     ***Does the policy include an Accidental Death Benefit?*** A rather unusual item, but nevertheless, one which a few companies offer. This should by no means be considered an important item in view of the real issues of LTC, but some companies have offered it in their total package.

18)     ***Does the company offer a "Return of Premium Benefit"?*** To the untrained eye, this may seem like a real feature, and some bureaucratic minds would incorporate this into all policies. However, most people in the insurance industry view this concept simply as an overcharge. All insurance rates are set actuarially, that is to say, the premium charged is designed to pay benefits and company expenses, and contribute to company reserves and solvency. If you add return of premium benefits to what is actuarially determined to be the "needed" rate, you simply have to overcharge for that service.

Consumer groups, in their zeal to "protect" the consumer, clamored for this measure to the extent that they nearly had the NAIC believing it. Okay, we'll charge you twice as much as we should, so that we can return the premiums after ten years if you don't use them. Big deal. Absurdity runs amuck when consumerism rears its head. Did you ever get your automobile premiums back after a lifetime of payment? Does the homeowner policy pay back the premiums you paid on it for thirty years?

Of course not. ***The purchaser bought insurance for transference of risk, not to use it as a bank account.*** So your house didn't catch on fire. Your premiums went into a pool that allowed the company to pay for somebody's house in Florida, who had suffered a hurricane, or a hailstorm in Kansas, or an explosion down the street.

Only life insurance policies work as cash value builders, not property, casualty, or health policies. Overcharging in an already "high dollar" field like health insurance is ridiculous. Beware of this concept. Yes, it's there with many companies, perhaps even by some mandate, but look out for it, keep your discretionary money where it belongs, in your investments, at your discretion, not someone else's.

An item of concern here is the financial condition of a company, which offers high dollar return of premiums after ten years. Many companies in the LTC arena guarantee the rates for three years. Remember when we said that, for several years, the entire industry did not have a time-tested formula for accurately determining rates based on decades old factual actuarial data? With those two factors given, how is a company supposed to pay claims ten years down the road, return premiums through return of premium provisions, and not raise rates when they see the calamity coming in four or five years? When company corporate officers see a potential drain on reserves through normal loss experience a few years after a series of policy issues, you will see already high LTCI rates go out of sight. Not only that, but the policyholder may have experienced some serious medical conditions and, obviously, will have gained age and be forced to go shopping at a time when attained age and pre-existing conditions will force him or her regrettably out of existing markets. As a matter of fact, you won't find too many companies which are outright sold on this return of premium concept, except that they were forced into it by consumerism or perhaps, mandated "do-gooderism."

**19)** *How does the company treat the mandated Non-Forfeiture Provision offer?* By now most states at the urging of the NAIC have mandated that the companies *offer Non-Forfeiture Benefits in lieu of the return of premium benefit.* This concept of Non-Forfeiture is a better solution, and the point the NAIC made was that companies should at least *offer* Non-Forfeiture as a way to find some relief for people who had started paying premiums on LTC policies only to find that through some misfortune, or incorrect original purchasing (or more likely, incorrect sales) techniques, found that they could no longer afford to pay the premiums.

The question then became, "How can I get some of my money back after I paid $3,200 a year in premium for four years and can no longer afford the policy premium?" Well, if the people purchase the non-forfeiture benefit, they will not get money back, but will be credited with a paid-up amount of their premiums being used to satisfy the benefits of their policy according to the provisions of their policy. This concept is fine and good, but even though the overcharge is less than for return of premium, by 15% to 20%, there is *still an additional charge* for the added non-forfeiture benefit. Some states still allow companies to offer the return of premium rider in lieu of the non-forfeiture benefit, but the original problems, those of overcharge and future rate increases, do not go away.

Non-Forfeiture riders generally work like this. First of all, you must pay the total premium for three years. By total premium, I mean the basic policy premiums for the product you have chosen, and the *additional charge for the non-forfeiture benefit rider.* Depending on your age, and the company, that *additional* amount may vary from 13% to 40%. After three years (or more), if your policy lapses due to non-payment of premium, you will have *the amount of premium paid (in some cases the non-forfeiture premium is excluded) convert to a paid up policy equal to 30 times the daily nursing home benefit at time of lapse, or an amount equal to all the premiums paid, whichever is greater.*

So, for instance, if you paid $2,000 per year in premium for three years, and failed to make the premium payment in the fourth year, you would be awarded a Lifetime Maximum Benefit (paid up) policy of $6,000. If you had chosen a $100 per day benefit, with no inflation rider, you would be able to receive 60 days of LTC coverage. My own preference is for agents to not oversell policies, and above all, take great care in selling only to those who have a need, and can afford to fund that need. That is why most states have adopted *"suitability" forms, which must be filled in by the prospective insured, indicating that the premiums, affordability and product are suitable for that client. Nobody ever does anybody any good in a sale which is not well thought out in terms of need and affordability.* Above all, the client should not be pressured into thinking that an LTC policy is needed, when the basic essentials of shelter, food, and transportation may have to go wanting.

One more thing regarding non-forfeiture. Some companies have developed a phrase called *"Full Non-Forfeiture."* Please do not confuse "Full Non-Forfeiture" with anything in reference to "non-forfeiture" in the paragraphs above. *Full Non-Forfeiture offers the client the opportunity to have premiums passed on to children or grandchildren upon the death of the insured(s). It is not a return of premium to the policyholder(s)* after so many years of premium payment. Full Non-Forfeiture is a feature much like a life insurance policy, and the client pays an additional premium for the rider. It is a **death benefit**, and in reality, some companies will pass the full amount of all premiums paid to the beneficiary, regardless of claims; and others will pass on a portion of the premium, and may reduce the amount of any claims paid from the portion received by the beneficiary. *This benefit, obviously, will be of interest to some people who would like their estate to receive as much value as possible.* **The tax considerations, and estate factors of this rider, should be reviewed by an accountant.**

20)     **Does the company offer a "Single Premium," "Ten-pay," "Twenty-pay," or "Paid-Up at 65" policy,** or a variation of that sort on premium payments? Many companies currently offer Single Premium, Ten-pay (ten year payment), or Twenty-pay premium modes. With the advent of HIPAA '96, and the federal tax deductibility features of the Tax-Qualified plans, more agents began to search for this product.

A word of caution is in order here regarding a single pay policy. *If* a certain type of Corporation can handle this legally, and *if* all the tax advisors and attorneys agree that this make good fiscal sense, then go for it. *If* all the "ducks are not in a row" don't allow yourself to be fooled into what may turn into a major headache.

I see Single, Ten, or Twenty-pay premiums as an attractive tool for certain, select individuals, *who can afford to pay greater amounts of premium ahead for themselves and save considerably on premiums which would otherwise have been spread out for years.* **I also see Ten-pay plans, or Paid-Up at 65 plans, as an ideal fit for clients in their early '50's who would like to have the premium payments cease at about the same age as they decide to retire.** Thus, putting in more premium in their final (and usually higher salaried) working years, in anticipation of a lower income at age 65, may be a great way to quickly solve any future LTC asset preservation problems, far in advance of possible needed care.

*Single premium or Ten-pay premium payment plans will undoubtedly save people a great amount of money* **over the years**, and **in effect create a paid up LTCI policy years in advance of the children worrying what to do about estate settlement, or a loss of a portion of the inheritance to lengthy nursing home stays.** If you are in a position to consider Single, or Ten-pay, or Paid-Up at 65 plans, to create a paid up policy for yourself, by all means, I suggest that you search out the market and utilize the savings.

So, the above items are of importance to you, and should help guide your efforts to secure the best of coverage in your purchase of LTC insurance. While no company will have all the features mentioned in our criteria, you will be able to sort out which features are of **major importance to you**, and enable you to seek and select the coverage which best fits your personal needs.

My job is to present the picture in as broad a scope as possible, *but keep in mind not all items are essential to a "perfect purchase." **In reality, there is no such thing as a "perfect purchase,"** and you won't, in all probability, see all these criteria captured in one policy, but paying attention to these items will make you a wise shopper and improve your chances of purchasing the best policy your money can buy.

## GROUP LONG TERM CARE INSURANCE

As the LTC insurance industry matures and **the value of purchasing at a younger age becomes more commonly understood,** both the industry and America's workplace owners will have to recognize the value of **group LTC coverage as an employee benefit,** or at least the opportunity for **voluntary purchase of group LTC coverage.** Nearly ten years ago I prognosticated that by the end of the century, group LTC would be the third most sought after employee benefit (behind group health insurance and retirement plans) by the end of the century. Whoops. Not yet. Credible sources indicate that by the year 2000, less than 5,000 companies had made group LTC coverage available for their employees, citing other more important factors, such as staying profitable, as the main reason for not including it in their benefit package. But the concept is gaining steam rapidly, and it **behooves you to enquire of your employer, assuming you are still working, to see if at least a voluntary group product is available through your worksite.**

This picture will change, although not as rapidly as I envisioned. Even though there does not seem to be a great price break for group purchase (due to the real factors of utilization and inflation) the underwriting of younger people on a group basis does present a very affirmative picture for employers and employees alike.

If you are interested in group LTC coverage, and you are an employer who would like to add this benefit, a note of caution is in order for those who currently utilize a Section 125 Cafeteria Plan. **According to current IRS regulation, LTC will not be allowed to fit into a 125 plan** because it is currently regarded as a form of deferred compensation. This ruling could change, assuming the "Long Term Care and Retirement Security Act of 2003" passes as federal legislation, but it behooves the employer and his Cafeteria Plan administrator to stay updated until, or, if in fact, the ruling does change, and then within the parameters of Section 125 qualifications.

## RECENT LEGISLATION REGARDING LTCI

One more item must be considered. Legislation on Long Term Care Insurance will be an ongoing endeavor during at least the next decade. The last significant legislation regarding LTC insurance was embodied in HIPAA '96. **On May 14, 2003, Representative Nancy Johnson of Connecticut introduced into the House, and Senator Charles Grassley of Iowa introduced into the Senate,** companion bills which would have further modified LTC law in America. **"The Long-Term Care and Retirement Security Act of 2003,"** offered several features, which would have included "above-the-line" tax deductibility for purchase of LTCI, would have permitted 125

Cafeteria and Flexible Spending arrangements, and would have provided tax credits for eligible caregivers. As the bills work their way through Congress during the summer and fall of 2003, *Americans concerned about the issues in this book can hope that the legislation will pass.* If they don't, be prepared for similar legislation sometime in the next decade, which will alter current law and tax considerations for the future. We can't say how, nor when, or in what fashion, but only that it will happen.

## A WORD ABOUT RATING THE COMPANIES

Before we close this chapter, an issue of major importance must be addressed—*that of company solvency.* As in all your insurance dealings, you want the company to be there when you need them. While the industry as a whole has been on solid financial ground, events over the years have caused some, but very few, companies to fall into receivership, bankruptcy and takeover. Nobody is more upset than the policyholder who finds his company has "gone under."

There are ways you can help yourself with this problem before it occurs. First, ask a potential agent to give you the current A.M. Best guide on the company he or she is representing. It will be a small "tract sized" handout. If they can't provide one at the moment, they certainly have access to one from the company. If that doesn't do the trick, a trip (or maybe even a call) to the library or insurance commissioner is in order. You should look for the current rating for that company. You will find it in the guide, or perhaps the librarian will look it up for you, or a letter to the company will secure one.

There will be a number of independent financial rating services, and they will each have certain criteria, but you would be well advised to see that the major letter is at least "A+", "A", "A-", or "B+". If the company does not meet these standards or better, ask if the company is owned by another company which is rated that highly. Many huge financial organizations are "holding companies" for a number of insurance companies, which, when combined, represent great strength in assets and reserves. I say use A. M. Best first, because it is the most oft quoted when insurance company stability is discussed. There are other excellent references besides A.M. Best, including Weiss Research, which traditionally has done very thorough research and very accurate ratings of not only the insurance industry, but of nearly all of the significant financial institutions in America. Both A.M. Best and Weiss Research virtually rate all companies.

Three others, Standard and Poor's, Duff and Phelps, and Moody's Investors Service rate only the companies with which they contract in return for a fee.

I make no recommendations for any rating service or its ratings, but *after 33 years in the insurance industry, I have come to have great respect for companies which carry ratings (each rating company will have a variation of a somewhat generic system) of "A+", "A", "A-", or "B+".* In terms of your money, its a good place to start when considering *whether or not your policy is as good as "the paper it's printed on."*

# CHAPTER 13

# THE "SHORT" LIST

## WHAT TO LOOK FOR IN LTC POLICIES AND COMPANIES— HOW TO ANALYZE YOUR OWN NEEDS

AUTHOR'S NOTE: *Remember that you do not need,* and will not find, *all* of the provisions listed below with any one company. There is no such *thing as a "perfect purchase."* Much of the terminology and many of the features of the products in this field are constantly changing and being improved. The following items represent current accepted and standardized thinking in the LTCI field and are important considerations available for your use in evaluating your purchase of an LTCI policy. Following the reading in the previous pages of this chapter, you can use this list as a "short" list for making policy comparisons for either new or existing policies. Do not be afraid to ask an agent to use these criteria when evaluating, recommending, and comparing various policies and companies. *Please remember that no company will offer all the features. There is no need to duplicate them, and each company will have it's own variation.*

1. Policy must cover all levels of care in a nursing home—Skilled, Intermediate, Custodial. _____

2. Are benefits paid on an indemnity basis, or "actual charge/reimbursement"? _____

3. Is the "pool of money" concept available? _____

4. What elimination periods (deductibles) are available? First day—20 day—30 day—60 day— 90 day—100 day—180 day—365 day. _____

5. What are the levels of Benefits available? Minimum—Maximum— _____ _____

6. What are the benefit periods available? 80 day—180 day—1 year—2 year—3 year— 4 year—5 year—6 year—Lifetime. _____

7. What are the issue ages? Lower and Upper. _____

8.  Is inflation protection to increase daily benefits available?  Simple—Compound—Rider?  _____

9.  What are the pre-existing condition requirements?  _____

9A.  (old policies)  Is a hospital stay required prior to nursing home benefits being paid?  _____

9B.  (old policies)  Is a nursing home stay required prior to receiving home care benefits?  _____

10.  How does the company underwrite?
APS?____
Physical—Paramedic?____
Face-to-Face?____
Telephone interview?____
Substandard available?____

11.  What are the requirements for "triggering" (qualifying for) benefits?
Doctor's Certification____
RN or care agency Certification____
Functional incapacity____
Cognitive impairment____
Medically Necessary____
ADL's (Activities of Daily Living)_____
How many Defined_____
How many Necessary_____

12.  Is the policy federally "Tax Qualified?"  _____
Is the policy federally "Non-Tax-Qualified?"  _____
Does your state allow for a state deduction?  _____

13.  (old policies) Does the policy cover Alzheimer's, Parkinson's and other mental conditions of an organically demonstrable nature? _____

14.  Is Home Health Care included, or at least provided by rider?  What percentage is paid?  _____

15.  How does the policy treat Home Care or Alternate Forms of Care?  What percentage?  _____

16.  How does the policy treat Instrumental Activities of Daily Living?  _____

17. How does the policy treat Assisted Living Facility Benefits?  What percentage?  _____

18. Is the product Guaranteed Renewable?  _____

19. Does the policy include a "Waiver of Premium Clause?  _____

20. How does the policy treat "Restoration of Benefits?  _____

21. How does the policy treat "spousal discounts"?  _____

22. How does the policy treat "Survivorship benefits"?  _____
    How does the policy treat "Spousal Waiver of Premium Benefits"?  _____

23. Does the company offer "Shared Benefits"  _____

24. How does the company treat the "elimination period"?  Accumulative?  _____

25. How does the company treat care given to an insured by a family member?  _____

26. Will the company allow for reinstatement if the policy lapses due to cognitive impairment?  _____
    Does the policy have third party notification?  _____

27. How does the policy treat Respite Care?  _____

28. How does the policy treat Hospice Care?  _____

29. How does the policy treat Nursing Home Bed Reservation Benefits?  _____

30. How does the company treat "non-licensed" care?  _____

31. Does the company offer a Return of Premium Benefit?  _____

32. How does the company treat Non-Forfeiture provisions?  _____

33. Does the company offer Single Premium, Ten-Pay, Twenty-Pay, or Paid up at 65 payments? _____

34. Does the policy pay 100% of the daily benefit for Assisted Living Facilities? _____

35. Does the client have to go to a nursing home first before qualifying for Alternate Plans of Care? _____

36. Does the policy provide for a Personal Care Advocate? _____

37. Does the company offer group rates and underwriting? _____

38. What are the company's financial ratings?
A.M. Best's_____
Affiliation_____
Affiliation's Best's rating_____
Company's Assets_____
Affiliation's Assets_____
Company's years in business_____
Company's years in the LTC, STC, HHC business _____

# CHAPTER 14

# THE TAX ISSUES

## *AND THE "TAX QUALIFIED" POLICY*

The Health Insurance Portability and Accountability Act of 1996 (HIPAA '96), which embodied hundreds of pages of health care legislation in general, *had a great deal to do with Long Term Care insurance in particular, and provided a variety of regulations, mandates, tax breaks, and tax implications.* The term "Federally Tax Qualified Long Term Care Insurance policy," which was designed and enacted into the major legislation of HIPAA '96, became the standard which most of the LTC insurance industry has embraced. Read on.

In the chapter on "Insurance Issues", under the requirements for triggering of benefits, I used the quote, "What the Lord giveth, the Lord taketh away," when, in all reality, I probably should have said "What the Federal government giveth, the Federal government taketh away." Simply, HIPAA '96 has *given most of the individual purchasers of Long Term Care insurance* in the United States a "tax break" for the *purchase of their own* LTCI policies. Yes, the Federal government now allows a tax break for citizens to purchase LTCI policies, and depending on how you can apply its value to your adjusted gross income, the break may, or may not be, much of a benefit.

But, the legislation also *removed one of the three triggers* for benefits—*that of "Medical Necessity*—as a means of qualifying for benefits under its "Tax Qualified" policy definitions. This is strange. Under the first nursing home policies issued*, medical necessity (skilled nursing care)* was about *the only way to qualify* for benefits. During the '90's, the LTC insurance industry responded to the real needs of the public by adding "activities of daily living" and cognitive impairment as triggers, leveling benefit payments for all three triggers, adding Home Care, Alternate Care and Assisted Living as additional forms of benefits, removing separate gatekeepers, and adding a host of other improvements to policies, by the mid '90's.

Then with HIPAA '96, the Federal government formulated a plan that removed a part of that foundation—that of medical necessity—in order for policyholders to be guaranteed a tax break under its "tax qualified" policy. In the time since, most companies have endorsed the concept of the "tax qualified" policy, and have directed their major marketing efforts to the policy which offers at least a *guarantee of tax deductions up front, and a guarantee that benefits received will not be taxable to the policyholder.* In addition, and in fairness to the "TQ" policy, *premiums are generally less when purchasing the "TQ" policy*, than when purchasing the non-tax qualified policy, because of the removal of the "medical necessity" trigger.

The interpretations of the tax qualified policy require some skill, particularly as to how each taxpayer can utilize the deductions, but let's discuss them after we find out what the tax "advantages" are, how they are realized, and the limitations for collecting benefits. Keep in mind that the following information applies to LTCI policies sold after Jan 1, 1997. Policies sold prior to that time are considered "grandfathered" and are eligible for tax qualified treatment if the policy qualified as an approved LTCI policy by the state in which it was purchased.

So, with the background of "TQ" and "Non-TQ, and how it all came about, let's help you gain knowledge in the basics of Federal Tax-Qualified policies and their requirements and limitations; differences found in the TQ policy and the Non-TQ policy; application of tax law and IRS codes, to individuals, Partnerships, C-Corps, S-Corps, and LLC's; and Tax Benefits as they apply to purchasers of Tax Qualified LTCI.

Simply, HIPAA '96 has given most of the individual purchasers of Long Term Care insurance in the United States a "tax break" for the purchase of their own LTCI policies. In addition, **business purchasers of LTC policies were given tax consideration, although the makeup of the business (C-Corp, S-Corp, Sole Proprietorship, LLC, or Partnership) will determine which set of rules must be followed** in order to utilize the tax benefits of the TQ (Tax Qualified) policy.

## A NOTE OF CAUTION TO THOSE WHO WOULD PRACTICE "MEDICAID PLANNING"

For many years, some attorneys recommended the use of "Medicaid Planning" for their clients, a **practice wherein transfers of property through various techniques would qualify people of means for the benefits of Welfare, or Medicaid.** Since Medicaid funded nursing home payments have become a serious financial problem for both state and federal government budgets, OBRA '93 (the Omnibus Reconciliation Act of 1993) and HIPAA '96 each instituted measures, which required each state to implement laws and recovery enforcement of Medicaid recipients, who may have received taxpayer paid nursing home payments for their care.

Most states will have enacted laws with individual variations of the following:

1) A *"Lien Law,"* which allows Medicaid to place a lien on the home of a Medicaid Recipient, with several provisions regarding eligibility and recovery.

2) An *"Estate Recovery Act,"* which looks to the estate for repayment.

3) An effective, aggressive *"Medicaid Recovery Unit,"* whose purpose is to investigate transactions made before Medicaid eligibility and *possibly* recover funds paid on behalf of the Medicaid recipient.

In view of these laws, and as discussed in several parts of this book, particularly the chapter on "Medicaid Issues," it would seem, that attorneys will be further ahead to understand and recommend the advantages of the "Tax Qualified Policy" for their clients, than to risk the questionable benefits of recommending Welfare to their clients.

## TAX TREATMENT OF PREMIUMS FOR "FEDERALLY TAX QUALIFIED" POLICIES

### PREMIUM DEDUCTIONS FOR INDIVIDUALS:
1) *First*, the taxpayer(s) must itemize on *Schedule A of federal income tax form 1040.*
2) LTCI premiums qualify for the *medical expense deduction.*
3) *Limits on the amount of premium qualifying for deductibility:*

*Premium Deduction Limit—Per Person—*2003-2004 Tax Years
(*attained age* before the close of the taxable year)
(this amount is restructured each year for inflation)

|  | 2003 | 2004 |
|---|---|---|
| Age 40 and younger | $ 250 | $ 260 |
| 41 – 50 | $ 470 | $ 490 |
| 51 – 60 | $ 940 | $ 980 |
| 61 – 70 | $2,510 | $2,600 |
| 71 and over | $3,130 | $3,250 |

4) The premium limitation for the taxpayer(s) age is the amount that *can be* added to other itemized and unreimbursed medical expenses.
5) The *amount over 7.5%* of the Adjusted Gross Income is the amount of the Net Schedule A deduction.
6) The amount of this deduction is to be added to other itemized deductions, such as state tax deductions, real estate tax deductions, home interest, donations, etc.
7) *Multiply* this amount *by the taxpayer(s) marginal* tax rate.

## PREMIUM DEDUCTIONS FOR BUSINESS:

## FOR THE SELF EMPLOYED:

1) The Omnibus Appropriations Conference Agreement of 1999 included a provision to accelerate the phase-in of the 100% deductions for health insurance, including premiums for qualified

long term care insurance, purchased by self-employed individuals under section 162 (1) of the Internal Revenue Code. Under this provision, self-employed individuals are permitted to deduct a percentage of health insurance premiums for coverage for themselves, their individual spouses and their dependents, up to the maximum limits described for individuals above. ***The TQ LTCI deduction allowable to the business, for premiums paid by the business, is the lesser of the premium, or the dollar limit as stated above for individuals. Any amount in excess can then be brought over to the self-employed's personal returns and eligible for medical expense deduction***. The acceleration of the phase-in is as follows:

| *Taxable year* | *Conference Agreement Percentage Deductible* |
|---|---|
| 2002 | 70% (per person) |
| 2003 | 100% (per person) |

## FOR C-CORPORATIONS:

1) The C-Corporation can generally deduct as a medical business expense, ***all premiums*** paid for employees (including owners), their spouses and dependents, and "W-2" retirees and their spouses with the tax qualified LTCI policy. The employer's contributions to the employee's policy purchase are ***not included as income to the employee.*** In addition, the C-Corp can pay for selected classes of employees only.

## FOR S-CORPORATIONS, LLCs, AND PARTNERSHIPS:

1) For participating employees who ***own more than 2% interest in the partnership, LLC, or S-Corp,*** the rules are the ***same as for self employed individuals, as cited above.***

2) For employees who are ***not as described in the paragraph above***, the employer may generally deduct as a business expense all premiums for covering "W-2" employees, their spouses and dependents, with the tax qualified LTCI policy.

## THE ADVANTAGES OF THE DEDUCTIONS

Now, let's evaluate the ***advantages of the deduction*** for individuals, self-employed, members of an LLC, partnership, or S-corp, who hold more than 2% of the stock in any of these entities, for the tax year 2003. If the client(s) is under 65 years of age, the main deductions will probably be in various itemized deductions, with a small amount of unreimbursed medical expense. That scenario, would then make it difficult for the client to reach an amount over 7½ percent of adjusted gross income, thereby enabling the client to take advantage of the "medical expense deduction" of the TQ Long Term Care insurance premium. *But remember, in most cases, we will be talking "joint policies," whereby both spouses each enjoy the deduction,* and the total premium allowable would be greater.

If the client is over 65, they probably have little or no mortgage deduction, and *medical expenses may be rather high*—again—particularly in the cases of joint policies on both spouses. In this case, the Long Term Care insurance premium, when added to their other unreimbursed medical expenses, *could provide a considerable tax deduction.*

There are other advantages to the TQ policy. The most common and immediate are:
1) *Greater rate stability,* as actuary has calculated expected losses on two triggers.
2) The client knows two factors in advance—*how much the tax advantage will be,* and that *the benefits will be received tax free.*
3) The advantage of the *business being able to deduct premiums* and the employer's contributions to the employee's premium *not being included as income to the employee.*

Above all, taxpayers and business owners should consult their accountant or attorney and see what the advantages *to federal tax deductibility and state deductibility* would be.

## BE AWARE OF THE DIFFERENCES BETWEEN THE "TQ" POLICY AND THE "NON-TQ" POLICY. LET'S COMPARE THEM.

1)      The policy sold with the identification of a "Tax Qualified" policy (most companies offer "TQ" currently, but the astute LTCI agent will have both to offer) has certain limitations. For instance, as previously discussed, the *triggers for benefits under the TQ policy have been limited to two options—cognitive impairment,* i.e., Alzheimer's, Parkinson's, etc.; and necessity for *help with activities of daily living.* This product excludes medical necessity as a criterion for nursing home benefit eligibility. This is in opposition to most *"non-tax-qualified" policies that do have this "third trigger"— medical necessity—;* which enables a policyholder to qualify for benefits. As previously mentioned, the trade-off in the TQ policy is usually the requirement of less premium.

2)      The tax qualified policy has a provision which says that a policyholder must be designated as a *"Chronically Ill Individual"* to be eligible for benefits under the two remaining triggers—ADL's and cognitive. The policyholder must be *certified as such* within the previous twelve months by a *"certified health care practitioner,"* (physician, registered nurse, or licensed social worker), and certified that he or she will a) be *unable to perform two ADL's for a period of at least 90 days* due to functional capacity; or

b) has *severe cognitive impairment which means "requiring substantial supervision"* to protect such individual from harm to self or others and from threats to health and safety, before any benefits of the policy can be paid. *This certification is not needed with "non qualified" policies.*

3)     *Benefits paid to the policyholder* under the "tax qualified policy" have been *ruled as non-taxable income* (limited to the greater of: actual expenses or $220 per day for TY 2003 and $230 per day for TY 2004).

4)     The Department of Treasury and IRS have not ruled (as of December, 2003) on the taxable status of benefits received under *the non qualified policy*, and probably never will.  Simply, this non-ruling, has left policyholders and producers both, wondering why nothing is being said.  (My own personal opinion is that under indemnity policies, any amount received by a policyholder over and above the actual expense of care, may come to be regarded as income.  But with the "pool of money" or actual expense policy, I cannot imagine a court in the land that would allow *reimbursement* of nursing home or home health care/home/community care expenses to be considered taxable.)  No ruling has been issued during the six year period since OBRA 96, so don't hold your breath on this one.  As a solution, should a ruling be made, most companies are offering a one year window for replacement of either type of policy upon news of a less favorable incentive for either plan.

Some additional notes of interest regarding the "TQ" policy are in order.  First, there is *currently no limitation on the amount, which a C-Corp can expend as premium for a "TQ" LTCI policy*.  In other words, a "10-pay," "20-pay," "Paid Up at 65," or Single premium (Paid-up) policy would be of benefit to a middle-aged client who would like to have premiums cease near time of retirement.  Secondly, though few have been set up, the premium for any entity is deductible through utilization of an MSA (Medical Savings Account.)

In addition, true LTCI policies (policies which were defined as LTCI policies by the Insurance Department of the state in which they were issued) *written before Jan 1, 1996, are considered "grandfathered" and receive "Tax qualified" status.*

## Important note regarding current LTCI tax law and possible expected changes:

*Two identical bills effecting changes to LTC tax laws were introduced in the Senate and House in 2003, which looked as though we could expect an "above the line" 100 per cent tax deduction for all taxpayers, and inclusion into Section 125 Cafeteria, or "Flex" plans.  On May 14, 2003, Representative Nancy Johnson of Connecticut introduced into the House, and Senator Charles Grassley of Iowa introduced into the Senate, companion bills which would further modify LTCI law in America.  "The Long-Term Care and Retirement Security Act of 2003," offered several features, which would include "above-the-line" tax deductibility for any purchase of LTCI, would permit 125 Cafeteria and Flexible Spending arrangements, and would provide tax credits for eligible caregivers. As the bills work their way through Congress during the summer and fall of 2003, Americans concerned about the issues in this book can hope that the legislation passes. If the bills don't pass, be prepared for similar legislation sometime in the next decade, which will alter current tax law and tax considerations for the future. We can't say how or when, nor in what fashion, but only that it will happen. Should the 2003 legislation pass, it will outdate the tax deductibility techniques described above. However, at the time of this writing, we must refer to laws and codes currently in place, and assume that no changes will take place until further legislation is enacted.*

One more item. Purchasers of LTCI insurance, "qualified" or "non-qualified", should not overlook the opportunity to address **state tax deductions** which several states (those with income tax laws) have allowed. In several instances, the states were far ahead of the federal government in reducing their own budgets for Medicaid nursing home assistance, by allowing the premiums for purchase of Long Term Care to be state income tax deductible. Some even went so far as to allow **anyone** who purchased LTCI on a family **member, to receive the deduction on their own tax bill.** In other words, some states allow the "child", who presumably is in a superior financial position, to purchase LTCI on parents or grandparents, and receive the deduction on their own personal income tax.

Obviously there are additional considerations when contemplating the issues of longevity, hospitalization, asset preservation, long term care and long term care insurance. Insurance agents don't have the authority to provide for these accounting and legal issues, and in fact should highly recommend the use of an accountant or attorney for them, rather than trying to do this with just a simple explanation or form.

**When inheritance of assets** is an important part of the potential beneficiary's planning, it behooves the receiving party or parties to **protect the asset for themselves**—purchasing LTC on the grantor and receiving a tax deduction on their own income for doing so, is both possible and prudent. Personally, I would recommend looking into this solution as opposed to embarking on the risks and tribulations of Medicaid planning.

In conclusion, it must be remembered that **tax considerations, either Federal or state, no matter how large or small they may be, should not be a major consideration in a decision to purchase LTC. The most important factors have been and always will be asset preservation, proper transfer timing, and the freedom of the policyholder to receive benefits in the setting of their choosing**—at home, in an assisted living facility, or in an alternate setting, as well as in a nursing home.

# CHAPTER 15

# THE FINANCIAL ISSUES

*WHO'S BEEN PAYING FOR WHAT!?*
*Also*
*THE VALUE OF THE REVERSE MORTGAGE*

Probably the greatest concern addressed in the hundreds of articles and booklets written during the past few years, regarding Nursing Home Costs and Long term Care, has been the financial concern. *"Who pays for What?"* could be a single title of America's elderly studies.

People who have spent their entire lives building a "Nest Egg for the Golden Years" have probably **had little time to devote to the preservation of those assets.** Unless they were guided in this matter by a very astute long term care insurance agent, life insurance agent, financial advisor, accountant, or lawyer, the **likelihood of addressing conservation of those assets has probably escaped them.**

Along with the normal financial influences of up-and-down interest rates, taxation, market disarray, etc., the American investor has also constantly faced uncertainty in the area of inflation. Let me explain. No matter what we invest today, it is influenced by the general national economic climate. Suppose you have $100,000 to set aside in any manner of investment. **No matter where you place the asset, and no matter how much you diversify it, outside influences will affect not only your principal, but also your return.** Tax considerations **further** affect your returns and reassess them within a phrase we call "net return."

In other words, if your $100,000 was invested in a number of diverse areas and at the end of one year returned (or grew) $10,000, you would consider this a 10% return on your investment. However, depending on your personal tax situation, if that $10,000 was subject to 28% taxes, your *"net return"* would be only $7,200.

Unfortunately, another factor must be introduced. Allow me to interject the word *"inflation" into this equation.* Remember that you invested your $100,000, and that your "net return" was $7,200. If, during the year, the rate of inflation was 4%, you can further depreciate the real earnings, in terms of inflation adjusted dollars, to $3,200. **Not a very pretty picture, but one, which constantly faces America's elderly investor.**

In addition, the recent "bear" market, the uncertainty of the market in general, and the havoc created with some pension plans, during the last ten years, has made the average investor more than a little nervous. The problem of comparatively low interest rates on Certificates of Deposit over the last five years adds to this grief. The person who is **counting on bank savings or investment income, as a great many of the retired** *elderly are, to supplement retirement income,* (social security, pensions, etc.) *is faced with a pretty grim income sustaining scenario.*

Why do I regard inflation as an all-important factor here? Simply put, the cost of nursing home care has been on the increase since the inception of the first home for the aged. While you thought your investment was growing at a satisfactory rate, inflation in the nursing home industry has grown at a 4% to 7% annual rate (depending on location) over the last twelve years. And, it isn't slowing down. According to a major study completed by the MetLife Mature Market Institute, during the summer of 2003, *"the nationwide average of nursing home inflation, had jumped 8% over the year 2002." Also, health care inflation is expected to reach from 12 to 17 percent from 2002 to 2004.* Hardly welcome news for millions of citizens about to embark on their most health care and long term care dependent years—and hoping that their income, investments, and investment income will be enough to keep up with this craziness.

This trend, in all reality, will continue. No matter what government programs are put in place, if any, to control our out-of-balance health care picture, *you can expect nursing home costs to rise at a greater rate than the rest of our nation's inflationary rates.* Don't be fooled into thinking that some magic governmental program will be made available for those who have assets to protect, while forgetting to consider inflation of nursing home, home care and assisted living costs.

Certain areas of investment such as the stock market, mutual funds, and real estate (in most parts of the nation), have performed well over the past few decades, or at least until the first few years of the Twenty-first Century, as far as the stock market is concerned. A severe downturn in the stock market during the early 2000's caused many an investor to reevaluate their "hole card" in market investment, whether as an individual, pensioner, or mutual fund player. Home values have generally gone up, which makes a nice entry on the asset side of the average senior's portfolio. Farm and ranch real estate remains stable depending on where it is located and the value of that property as an income producer.

Commercial real estate, REITs, etc., have seen dramatic "ups and downs" as evidenced by the Savings and Loans debacle of the late '80's and early '90's. That little fiasco came to haunt American taxpayers (and millions of savers) to the tune of a 200 billion dollar bailout, and will not soon be forgotten by America's elderly. But, *all in all, most investment plans have increased and "appreciated" the senior American's personal ledger during the time they were constructing their retirement plans.* I dwell on the above factors, because they are the foundation of the normal senior *investment* picture.

## THE "SECRET" OF THE REVERSE MORTGAGE

While a satisfactory *investment* picture is common for many retired people, there are those who face a problem, which is quite different. That problem is found in mortgage-free home ownership. How could that be a problem? Suppose that the family home is the *only real asset*, beyond a moderate savings account and checking account. The problem is that the *family home* is a *non-income producing asset.* Yes, it is paid for—is probably *appreciating in value*—and, in fact most retired elderly may not have a mortgage on this property. However, the "fixed income" from Social Security and perhaps a pension or other retirement plan, pretty much limits what these people can do to protect the family home as a transferable asset in case of an extended nursing home stay, since it is not income producing and is, in fact, *an illiquid asset.*

The family home then, has become vulnerable, since welfare reform laws enacted in the mid-1990's (state lien laws) make home ownership a target of Medicaid recovery. Suppose you *qualify* for Medicaid because you have no *investment type* assets, or have spent down what you had, to pay for your own nursing home care. Now you qualify because the personal residence is considered by Medicaid to be an "exempt" asset. At the time you qualify, the home is considered "exempt" from eligible resources. However, in most states, since OBRA '93, laws have been enacted which say a lien can be placed on the property, and, with very limited and very few exceptions, will be collectable upon the death of the second spouse. In other words, the state will now recover, via the lien law, the amount of money used on your behalf to pay for your nursing home stay. *In my opinion, that amounts to little more than a loan.*

So, if in fact, you are borrowing from Medicaid to pay your long term care costs, why not borrow from a bank to pay long term care insurance premiums, and protect the entire value of the home from a Medicaid lien? Doesn't seem possible? Well, until a few years ago, the idea sounded a little absurd, and was not well understood or utilized. But the banking industry, as well as the insurance industry, has had to mature in its thinking, and face the realities of today's economic climate. *The secret is in the innovation of the "reverse mortgage," an idea whose time has definitely arrived.*

The reverse mortgage has literally become a solution for those who might face loss of a family home, as an inheritable item, through either personally paying for nursing home costs, or "borrowing" from Medicaid. Your lending institution or your state housing program will deal in depth with the particulars of this concept, but a few sentences here will help people understand how to utilize this little known concept to transfer more of the *"who pays for what"* from the "personal pay" and "Medicaid pay" slices of nursing home costs to the "insurance paid" portion of the pie.

Suppose you have a fixed income, and a non-income producing illiquid asset (the family home) paid for. How can you find the *extra dollars to pay Long Term Care Insurance premiums?* Very simply, contact your local mortgage company and ask for *a "line-of-credit" reverse mortgage*. With the line-of-credit reverse mortgage, you simply *borrow, each year, the amount needed to pay an LTC premium.* Sounds too hard? Not at all. The *premium amount is simply borrowed and paid each year*, and the entire asset is protected from nursing home, or home care costs, because the insurance policy is in place should you need your benefits. True, the amount borrowed each year, and the interest due, accumulates, so that at the time of death, *there is a mortgage due and owing on the property, but certainly not of the magnitude that a recoverable debt to Medicaid would incur.*

Another factor for your consideration is that most homes appreciate in value. So, **while it is true that a line-of-credit mortgage is building up, so usually will the value of the residence, perhaps to a greater extent than the mortgage.** Since the amount of the insurance premium is dependent on such factors as age, length of benefits, amount of benefits, etc., care should be taken to keep the premium as low as possible, yet assure that the coverage will allow for high enough benefits (including an inflation rider) to make the transaction sensible. The reverse mortgage has its place, and as with most banking and insurance solutions, when properly used, can be a very effective tool in protecting the home as an asset until normal transfer techniques can be put in place.

Valuable information about reverse mortgages is available from the National Reverse Mortgage Lenders Association. This organization has several free publications regarding all types of reverse mortgages. Refer to Chapter 25 "Where to Go..." to find contact information.

With the above investment picture addressed then, let us move forward on the issue of finances, namely **"Who pays for What?"—or at least who has been paying for what.**

Depending on where you live, you can count on current nursing home expenses to run at least $42,000 per year, with home care (on an eight hour basis) and assisted living costs not far behind. Some areas of our country have a much higher rate, and the facility you choose can have an even higher rate due to amenities, the quality of the facility, and the care given. **Remember that I said AT LEAST $42,000.** (A facility which requires a $120 per day rate, will equate to $43,000 per year, and that amount will undoubtedly rise in the face of 4%-7% annual inflation!)

Whatever, don't count on that amount going down, it just isn't in the picture. New requirements regarding quality of care and service are continually mandated by governmental authorities and passed down to nursing home administrators for compliance. The licensing and compliance requirements in this field are bulky to say the least, and create a continual flow of paperwork, which further drives the costs of the nursing home expense itself.

While I warn people that no less than $120 per day should be the underline of proper protection, that figure should in no way be considered as sufficient in many parts of America. In most metropolitan areas, particularly the Eastern seaboard, Midwest, and Southern Sunbelt, a more accurate amount will be in the $150-$250 per day range. **These numbers, while seeming outlandish to the uninformed, are not manufactured by insurance company people. They are indeed real.** It behooves the reader to research potential costs in any given neighborhood well in advance of a possible nursing home entry. Always remember to include the **inflationary factor** in your thinking. What is true today will definitely be different tomorrow.

## SO, WHO'S BEEN PAYING FOR WHAT?

When addressing *"Who pays for What?"* a brief picture of the current history relating to national figures is in order. Depending on who is "slicing the pie chart" we find minor differences in a big picture.. The important point is to look at a national composite and see how the breakout of payment can affect you and your family.

One important item—*private insurance has paid very little in the past, because insurance as a solution was not asked to relieve these costs until very recently.* As I said in the "Q and A" chapter, the problem of rising Nursing Home costs is a somewhat new phenomenon created by a general national surge in health care costs. Because a problem must exist, and be identified and defined, and before insurance companies can offer solutions, the historical payment information will reflect only small contributions from insurance payments towards data collected as few as five years in the past. As private individuals are alerted to the needs for insurance solutions, either through the purchase of individual or group policies, *we are seeing this part of the "pie" divide into a larger contribution from private insurance and, hopefully, a smaller portion for direct pay by individuals and families.*

So, in the few sentences listed below, let's condense the "who pays for what" portion of the nation's long term care bill. I dislike statistics, because they all come from sources with different interpretations, dates, methodologies, and goals; and generally you can get lost in them to the point of the numbers being meaningless. Depending on whom you listen to, and depending on whether or not the statistics are related to *nursing home figures only*, *or the total long term care bill (nursing homes, assisted living, home care, home health care, non-professional care, etc.)* you will get a terrific variation of "just the facts, ma'm." But for the basics, the following will suffice.

Let's use the numbers *David M. Walker, Comptroller General of the United States, quoted before the Senate Special Committee on Aging on March 21, 2002.* They are simple, to the point and even though they are derived from government statistics for the year 2000, they are relevant as fairly recent information.

1) "Long term care spending from all public and private sources…was *about $137 billion for persons of all ages in 2000."*

2) "Over *60 percent of expenditures for long term care services are paid for by public programs, primarily Medicaid and Medicare. Individuals finance almost one-fourth of these expenditures out-of-pocket* and, less often, private insurers pay for long term care."

3) "In 2000, *Medicaid paid 45 percent (about $62 billion)* of total long term care expenditures."

4) "In 2000, *nursing home expenditures dominated Medicaid long term care expenditures,* accounting for 57 percent of its long term care spending."

5) "Expenditures for **Medicaid home-and-community-based services** grew tenfold from 1990 to 2000—from $1.2 billion to $12 billion."

6) "**Individuals' out-of-pocket payments**, the second largest payer of long term care services, accounted for 23 percent **(about $31 billion of total expenditures in 2000.)**"

7) "The vast majority (80 percent) of these payments were used for nursing home care."

8) "**Medicare spending accounted for 14 percent (about $19 billion)** of total long term care expenditures in 2000."

9) "**Private insurance...accounted for 11 percent (about $15 billion)** of long term care expenditures in 2000."

So there you are, now you know, if in fact, you take the time to make sense of it all. Don't dwell on the figures too much, but let's talk about a few of them.

As you can see from the above statements, there are a number of significant and even dramatic revelations for people who had no idea of *"who pays for what"* portion of the nation's long term care bill. Perhaps the biggest surprise is found where people incorrectly assumed that **"Medicare will take care of it"! As indicated above, this is not true.** Early on, Medicare paid only about 2%-5%. That percentage **has increased in recent years, to as much as 12-14%,** due to a combination of the increase in utilization of hospital facilities covered by Medicare (and that utilization being followed by the twenty days of skilled care coverage) and an ever-increasing elderly demographic spread.

But, why does Medicare pay so little? Let me explain. Medicare is a health "cure" program. Medicare was designed to give its recipients quality health care by providing part A hospitalization "free", and by purchase of a part B physician payment. **Medicare was never intended to pay nursing home costs in any proportion. It's that simple.** In a nutshell, Medicare pays for sickness. That is what the program was designed for, and should be recognized for its terrific contribution to America's "sickness" and "curing" needs. **Medicare works—but not for something it was not intended for.**

Why then, does Medicare pay **anything** towards Nursing Home costs? Again, the answer is very simple, although not very commonly understood. Medicare operates under what is known as the Prospective Payment System, commonly referred to as "DRG's". By way of simple explanation, DRG means Diagnostic Related Grouping. There are roughly 500 reasons you can go to a hospital. Each reason (DRG) is assigned a code number, which specifies a certain number of days allotted for **acute (hospital) care**.

After the initial hospital care is received, the patient is deemed either to be in need of recovery, or, able to return home. If the patient is deemed not recovered, and if RECOVERY is not complete, Medicare has already paid for the allotted DRG expense of hospital care, **and recovery, recuperation, and convalescence needs are**

***transferred to a licensed and approved Skilled Care Facility (Nursing Home).*** This care is received in facilities known as "swing units," "aftercare," or "extended care", and whatever your facility chooses to call itself, they all mean the same thing—a recovery facility in a licensed and Medicare approved Nursing Home setting, and a ***prescription from the doctor to receive "Skilled Care" only.***

Knowing that many people are not fully recovered and able to return home (i.e. stroke, broken hip, heart problem, etc.) Medicare has chosen to allow an extra 20-day ***recovery period in a Skilled Nursing facility under Skilled Nursing Care. That is the only type of a nursing home stay that Medicare currently pays for.*** Since that care allows up to twenty days, Medicare payment (for all practical purposes) stops on the twenty-first day. Alas, this is the reason that Medicare pays only about 12-14% of the nation's nursing home bill. Remember that Medicare was intended to provide basic *health* care to its recipients, and *medical recovery* is a prerequisite for Medicare payment. Although 95% of the people in nursing homes are there because of a necessity for help with Activities of Daily Living or Cognitive reasons, ***ADL's and Cognitive needs are not identified or considered as medical reasons.***

Who pays the remaining 88-86% then? The next "shocker" is that personal payment (the patient or patient's family) paid roughly 23% of the total picture. But, what about Medicaid? That issue is repeatedly addressed elsewhere, but at this point we should discuss the combination of the two, since totaled together***, personal payment and Medicaid payments comprise around 88% of the payment structure.*** Remember that Medicaid requires asset spenddown and therein lies the problem for the average "middle American."

Simply stated, if you have eligible resources (assets) you will be expected to pay for a nursing home stay of any duration. (This is as it should be. Medicaid was designed to aid the country's truly poor, not as a "catchall" for families to hide or illegally transfer assets in order to artificially qualify for some government program.) The Omnibus Reconciliation Act of 1993 (OBRA 93), and the Health Insurance Portability and Accountability Act of 1996 (HIPAA 96) rectified most of the "loopholes" that people of substantial means used to qualify for taxpayer supported nursing home payment.

***So, either you, or your family, or your Long Term Care Nursing Home policy, fit into the privately paid category.*** That means, of the nation's total 2000 nursing home *and* home health care bill of $137 billion, over 23% was paid by people with the assets (means) to support that payment. ***What percentage of those people who used their own money would have preferred to have insurance money pay the bill? I would suspect a very high percentage,*** but keep in mind that many of these patients did not have proper access to the value and techniques of LTCI before the first date of their needs. If insurance companies had not been called upon to focus on this problem, and increasing government budgeting problems caused havoc for states and the nation as a whole, ***who's left to pay the bill? Those that can "afford" it.***

Chapter 15

To "afford it" means that ***people will either pay the nursing home and home health care bill themselves or pay insurance premiums, which, in turn, will pay the bills.*** As more and more Americans are becoming aware of the possibility of risk transference to insurance companies, the ***"out of pocket" slice of the tax pie is beginning to grow through the "private health insurance" slice.*** Though the 2000 numbers reflect $15 billion (about 8 percent) in private health insurance payments for the total bill, we will see this number grow as more people take advantage of the asset preservation, freedom of where to receive care, better quality care, inheritance, and peace-of-mind features of the LTC insurance policy.

If Americans are to continue shouldering this bill, the structure of payment must continue to change with ***insurance eventually paying the largest portion of the private slice.*** That's what this book is all about. Those who have no assets, or have accumulated very little by way of financial acumen in their lifetime, have little to worry about. They will qualify for Medicaid with relative ease. ***However, for those who have something to lose, or will have something to lose, the picture is quite different.*** With rights come responsibility, and ***any sensible person has not only the right, but also the responsibility to protect what they have.*** At least now, people can provide for themselves, transfer the risks to an insurance company, and make legal preparations to protect their future, without facing "spenddown" and impoverishment. And ***the slice of "Who Pays For What?" will ultimately become a much larger "insurance pay" piece of the equation.***

# CHAPTER 16

# THE CAREGIVERS ISSUE

## *BE THANKFUL FOR THE "SAINTS" AND "ANGELS" WE DO HAVE*

It could be, in this country—in this great land of plenty—that we've had things too good, for too long a time. Maybe we take some important things for granted. Maybe we overlook many of the valuable contributions that others provide for us, and to us—the efforts of others, which make our lives more comfortable. I'm saying that, we, as a nation, **have overlooked the contributions of caregivers as being necessary elements** to the **total** way of life in this country. I know of no national "Caregivers" holiday, or a "National Caregivers Week," and in fact, must admit that the word "caregiver" was not a part of my vocabulary until a decade ago.

The word caregiver is not your average household word, and most people in the United States would be hard pressed to provide a comfortable definition of the word. The software in my computer, in fact, will not identify the word *"caregiving"* without running a squiggly red line underneath it, which indicates that out of about 40,000 words, "caregiving" has not yet been included as a normal, acceptable, English language word, at least by my software maker. Strange. The software wants two words—"care giving." Sorry, computer, I win on this one. The word deserves—and the caregivers themselves, deserve—more recognition.

So let's do it here. **Let's make an issue of thanking these "Saints" and "Angels," and look into what makes them such a valuable part of the fabric of our society.** Let's talk about their (and our) problems and see what we can do to improve the working conditions of the caregiver in our society. Let's develop an attitude and impetus that will allow young people searching for their place in a future work force contribution, **to view the job as a satisfactory lifelong career, not just an occupation.**

I prefer to take a positive approach to the total issue of caregiving, even though there are those who would criticize and disrupt the efforts of a portion of our nation's caregiving effort. I would like to think that, within the system in which they are forced to function, **caregivers by-and-large, are doing a fantastic job. Unfortunately, there are a few parts of the system that work against them.**

First of all, we spend a lot of time in the "Elder Abuse" chapter talking about the problems of Medicaid dependent nursing homes. Throughout the nation, the media has exposed evidence of nursing home problems, and we discuss the issue in depth in that chapter. The criticism always seems to develop one main theme—the lack of quality care, or worse, evidence of neglect, and even, "criminal" abuse. My thinking is that the **system of Medicaid dependent nursing homes creates this situation**, because of two main problems—*less than satisfactory working conditions, and the lack of a decent salary for the caregivers.* When the nursing home itself must operate within a *"barebones" budget, how could conditions and pay possibly be any better for the workers in the trenches—the caregivers?*

Now, let's make the situation even worse. As the need for care is about to explode across the nation, due to the demographics of a baby boomer generation, we see the *number of people available to give care*, in fact, *going down!* Yes, the number of workers seeking careers in the health care industry is "heading south." Current studies indicate that we are on our way to being short from 400,000 to 800,000 nurses *(professional care)* by the end of the decade. In addition, the number of available workers *is less for personal, or nursing assistant care, in comparison to the number of bodies in need of care.*

In fact, The American Health Care Association completed a 2002 survey of 6,155 nursing homes, which *should bring the severity of two situations* to the attention of Americans—that of *recruitment* of workers to nursing home careers, and the *turnover of help and corresponding vacancy rates* in nursing home jobs. The report states:

"In 2002, nursing homes had numerous nursing staff related vacancies. Overall, **nearly 96,0000 full-time equivalent health care professionals were needed** to fill vacant nursing positions at nursing homes across the United States. The majority of the vacancies were **for Certified Nurse Assistant positions.** ...Overall, **nearly 52,000 CNA positions were estimated to be vacant.** In addition, about **13,900 Staff RN and 25,100 LPN positions were estimated to be vacant." "CNA turnover rates** exceed 60% in 65 percent of states, exceeded 80% in 37 percent of the states, and **were above 100% in 20 percent of the states."—(to as high as 135% in one state.)** ..."Recruiting new direct care staff remains a challenge for nursing facilities."**

This information tracks identically with what the President of the National Association for Home Care and Hospice, Mr. Val Halamandaris says, when he states that *"good people (executives, nurses, and home care aides) have left the field of home care in droves."*

Unless we train teen-agers and the very youngest of the "Echo boomers" to become care providers, we're short of folks, folks. Not a very comforting thought to those who see themselves in a position of needing care in twenty or thirty years.

The second part of "our system" addresses the problems of non-institutional, or informal home caregiving. What system? *We have no system* in place to provide even the most minute amount of help to people who prefer to care for their own loved ones in their own homes. Yes, the feds are looking at some mediocre offerings of help, some of the states are *starting to address* the issue (probably because some of the older lawmakers are beginning to wonder about their own well-being), and employers are *seriously starting to evaluate* the effect that elder caregiving is having on their work forces. But that's about it.

The Family Caregiver Alliance and *some* other elder organizations are paying serious attention to the problems, by offering what they can. But *who knows how to turn to them for help? Awareness needs to become "A SHOUT,"* especially now that the baby boomers, who have redefined every demographic strata they have moved through, are beginning to understand the problem. This, like so many other elderly issues, seems to be *an issue that people ignore UNTIL IT AFFECTS THEM!* One solution will be forthcoming—count on it—*tax breaks for informal home caregiving are on their way.* They won't amount to much, but they are going to happen and they are going to help to a certain extent.

Now it's soapbox time. The astute reader will put some thought into these situations, and look for a way out of the quandary for themselves. Where can you go to find a solution to the *Medicaid reliant nursing home problems* of underpaid staff, challenged to the max to deliver high quality care? Where can you go to ensure that you don't have to count on family members to deliver home caregiving to you, should the situation arise? Obviously, home caregiving by loved ones, may be the preferred choice, but *should it have to be the only choice?* Where can you go to find a solution as to where you would want to receive care, and know that the money is available to pay for the best care your money will buy? The answers are all contained in one phrase—Long Term Care insurance. After all, *the message of this book is to insure yourself against the costs associated with long term needs, but also to insulate yourself against the coming problems of caregiving in general, for all Americans.*

## SO WHAT CAN WE DO FOR THE SAINTS AND ANGELS?

We could probably develop a list of fifty different problems in the caregiving industry, just as we could do in any other industry, but the effort would simply be an exercise, a duplication of several other chapters in this book, and we really don't need to bang that drum anymore. *Let's just settle on the two main problems—initiating an attractive wage for caregivers, and doing something about improving working conditions.*

We need to address the issue of raising wages for the *caregivers currently employed*, and see to it that the salaries of future nursing home employees, home care employees and general caregivers *are raised to a level where people will view this occupation as a career.* The level of quality caregiving is directly proportional to the opportunity for a livable wage. *We cannot expect to pay little more than minimum wage and encourage people to seek employment in the current system.* Many nursing homes and home care agencies have been less than successful in *recruiting and retaining conscientious health care workers* for two reasons. The first is *salary consideration,* and the second is *working conditions.* We certainly know by now that the "wages of Medicaid" is not death, (though maybe not much more—a living wage comes to mind), and that *Medicaid and Medicare are not going to solve this problem.*

While it may be easy to criticize the system for allowing some less than desirable personnel to be employed in such an important role, we need to remember that costs (two out of three dollars of nursing home budgets goes to wages), have been a major detriment to upscaling wages. ***Perhaps three of every four dollars*** has to become the norm. Or ***maybe even four of five.*** More of the expense burden being picked up by Long Term Care insurance company dollars will help. But where do we find high quality people who are willing to work with the conditions that the job requires, for a salary less than livable? This will be our challenge over the next twenty to thirty years—***not twenty to thirty years from now—starting now!*** America must simply find a way to recruit and retain better employees for its caregiving industries. ***Higher salaries for the "real trench workers" is one way.***

The second reason has to do with the type of work required. ***"Burnout" is easy to come by in the care industry,*** and a person who fully anticipates job satisfaction in this arena can very easily find themselves despondent or depressed with the daily routine and requirements of caregiving. Simply, ***it takes a special person to cope with, what would seem to many of us, far less than desirable working conditions***. Looking forward to a job shift of changing bed pans, lifting nearly helpless people, preventing and curing bed sores, dealing with the heartbreak and embarrassment of incontinence, bathing, and feeding and medicating frail and helpless people requires a disposition bordering on Sainthood. We should be thankful that ***anyone*** wants a job of this nature, and especially thankful that nationwide, ***we do have a legion of dedicated, serious caregivers, who are able to do high quality work and who genuinely care for their patients.***

The working conditions problem may have to be ***addressed by improved medical technology, and entirely new innovations in caregiving equipment.*** Perhaps the picture has changed, but I can remember a few years ago when one of the biggest problems facing nursing homes was that of obtaining worker's compensation insurance at a reasonable rate. How can we expect a 125 pound caregiver to lift and help a 185 pound patient perhaps several times a day, and then repeat that routine with a number of other patients, without sooner or later injuring themselves? This is but an example of the need for completely new technological innovations in caregiving, and science and industry need to be called upon to lead the way, ***not as an afterthought, but as a specific targeted mission.***

These two items alone, increased career type compensation, and technologically improved working conditions, will help ***attract and retain workers who have a genuine predilection for caregiving.*** The result would be a ***greater assurance of quality caregiving,*** and help remove the perception of some people, that caregiving in many situations is simply "warehousing." In addition, a concerted program to seek out and prosecute Senior fraud and elder abuse (through a single purpose agency, as suggested in the Elder Abuse chapter) will go a long way toward ensuring that America's retirees and elderly can expect a greater degree of protection against what already ***may be on its way to becoming a national disgrace***. We can do better. And ***with the coming increase in care needs, we'd better be getting better, at doing better, NOW!***

# Chapter 17

# Elder Abuse

## *A DISGUSTING ISSUE— BUT WE MUST TALK ABOUT IT*

## ELDER ABUSE—BAD ENOUGH AND SURE TO GET WORSE (UNTIL WE DECIDE TO DO SOMETHING ABOUT IT)

I need a word. A word which will accurately describe why I delayed writing this portion of the book until the very last. I'm sure there's one out there, but it would have to be a word which could combine the feelings of disgust, dismay, disheartenment, sympathy and empathy. Perhaps "consternation" comes the closest. Why, in America, with the greatest systems for social justice in the world lying within our grasp, do we have to discuss this issue*? Why does such an issue even exist?* And why do I find elder abuse so tasteless and repulsive that I have an aversion to addressing the issue, as important as it is.

Am I just an example of what is flowing through our society? Do we all feel a little bit like turning our heads, hoping this problem will go away if we avoid taking it head on? *Or are we just deceiving ourselves* at a time when millions of people are perched on the edge of longevity—and hope that what has gone on in the past, will be corrected in the future, in time for us to land in a featherbed of genuinely sympathetic care in our old age?

Abuse of any nature is unacceptable. As a society we have only recently begun to pay attention to the many different forms of abuse, with child abuse and spousal abuse gaining the most attention. *Only occasionally do we hear of elder abuse.* When we do, we *view it with shock, and regard it with disbelief, contempt and disdain.* We don't seem to understand that there are those who would mistreat and actually harm elderly people, especially on a frequent and perpetual basis. Why? Because we would *like to believe that such atrocities could not take place,* and perhaps we even take a viewpoint of "out of sight, out of mind." "Let them take care of themselves" might be an uneducated observation. But elder abuse does exist, and like so many other crimes, *much of it simply goes unreported.*

Imagine the misery of an older person who is abused day after day and is afraid to report it to anyone because, after all, "I have a roof over my head." The problem is that the abuse can take many forms, *none of which the frail and sick person can defend themselves against.* We would like to think that nursing homes are able to prevent what would seem like abuse to those within, and to those who visit them. But in reality, several forms of abuse occur within care centers of all types, and not just on an occasional personal basis. Although all states have some statutes that supposedly protect patients,

173

several instances have occurred where mass abuse of residents has taken place. Unfortunately, these instances are *discovered well after the fact,* well after the patients have suffered physical and/or emotional abuse, and many times, well after the perpetrators are gone.

Remember that we said only about twenty percent of the people needing long-term care receive it in institutionalized settings? Well, if that number is representative, then about eighty percent are receiving care in what we would consider the safety of their own homes; the homes of family, friends, relatives or in-laws; or at least within the community on a part-time basis. This *would seem to imply that these people are far less likely to be subject to abuse,* and would indicate that we need not worry about an abuse factor, let alone the quality of care they receive. But too many cases surface from time-to-time to allow us to be complacent and to have secure feelings in this regard.

So let's look at the total picture, whether the older person is institutionalized, or receiving care at home or in the community. *Will either scenario make a difference? Not on our best day.* We see "numbers" in newspapers declaring that violent crime over the last few years is supposedly on the decline. I suspect that in reality, that information is simply a matter of reporting, and how the numbers are gathered. *But what about the "numbers" for elder abuse?* Do they even exist? I doubt it. Yes, I've heard the reports of anywhere from half a million to one million cases per year, but those figures, even though they include reported cases, cannot begin to approach what is really happening, because too many actual incidents simply go unreported. I submit that any agency concerned with elder abuse in the United States could only develop theories and conjecture about the number of abuses actually occurring daily, versus the number of cases reported. For instance, *who does the abused elder report to? How, in most cases, could they report abuse? How many millions of cases go unreported out of the fear of retaliation after the authorities have gone?*

I'm not saying that the problem of elder abuse is overlooked. *I'm saying that not enough seems to be going on to prevent the abuse.* In February of 2002, the General Accounting Office, the investigative arm of Congress, conducted hearings regarding the abuse of elders in nursing homes, assisted living facilities and other institutions. Among the findings, was *the repulsive fact that physical and yes, even sexual abuse, of the elderly often goes unreported, or is reported so late that convictions are unlikely.* The report also cited insufficient legal and regulatory safeguards against hiring nursing home workers who have a record of abuse. Neither, Medicaid or Medicare, require criminal background checks of nursing home employees, according to the report. "Crimes are crimes no matter where they are committed," said Sen. John Breaux, D-La., the panel's chairman. "Crimes that would normally be prosecuted if they occurred on a street corner are shoved under the bed if they occur in a nursing home." In addition, local law enforcement officials complain that they are seldom summoned to nursing homes to investigate allegations of physical or sexual abuse, and that, when they are, by the time they are able to respond, the evidence has often been compromised.

On August 2, 2002, Long Term Care Provider, a particularly good reference to weekly news items regarding Senior issues, delivered an Associated Press story discussing a U.S. Administration on Aging study of elder abuse. Some quotes are just too important to be overlooked in this chapter, and basically confirm what I have said about how much of this activity goes unreported or overlooked.

1) The study estimates that up to *1 million elderly are physically abused, neglected, or financially exploited each year.* But officials acknowledge that is only a guess.

2) "We don't have a true grasp of it because it's such a big social problem—it's unreported, unrecognized—*it's hard to get a good idea of how much of it is out there,"* said Linda Hildreth, state elder abuse coordinator at the Iowa Department of Elder Affairs.

3) "Unfortunately, it also showed that only one in five comes to the attention of people who can do something to help," said Sara Aravanis, director of the National Center on Elder Abuse in Washington, D.C. *"It's only the tiny tip of the iceberg that we know about. The rest remain hidden well below the surface."*

4) Kathleen Quinn of the Illinois Department on Aging, believes *the detection rate could be as low as 1 in 14.* "There's never been a national random population survey on elder abuse," she said, noting that it's difficult to gauge its scope because *victims often are housebound or isolated by those who prey on them.*

5) The aging administration study completed in 1997 showed *that 84 percent of* elder abuse comes at the hands of a relative, most often the older person's grown child.

6) In New Mexico, a 75-year-old nursing home resident died in January of an infection caused by 22 bed sores, including "one so large you could put your fist into it and bone was visible," said Katrina Hotrum of the state's long-term care ombudsman's program. *"She was unable to scream or ask for help and was left rotting to death,"* Hotrum said.

7) Michelle Grisham, the director of the New Mexico Agency on Aging, verified that her group receives about *8,000 abuse complaints each year* concerning state-licensed nursing centers. "Reporting is low because you have residents who *aren't competent and can't communicate, and they are afraid of retaliation by staff,"* Grisham said.

8) Only eight states have laws specifically addressing abuse of the elderly: Connecticut, Illinois, Massachusetts, Montana, Nevada, Pennsylvania, Rhode Island and Wisconsin, according to the National Center on Elder Abuse.

Of all these depressing statements, I find Number 5, which indicates that "84 percent of elder abuse comes at the hands of a relative, most often the older person's grown child," to be the most disgusting. Even though I report these facts to you, I cannot fathom the sadness of that statement. However, it does confirm my contention that *we need to worry a lot more about the 80 percent of the people who are not receiving care in institutions, and supposedly are safe at home in their care of their "loved" ones.*

## DON'T BLAME THE NURSING HOMES—BLAME THE CURRENT SYSTEM

While it may appear that I am ranting about nursing homes and Medicaid, I am not. The job for the institutions and the Medicaid authorities is hard enough. I am concerned about one hundred percent of the care patients, some of which may be in the system through Medicare and Medicaid home health, and the millions more who are not in the system at all. Newspapers and journals report case after case of home health aides who abuse their patients through a whole host of mistreatment techniques, most of which are illegal, let alone downright sad. *"Manhandling" (or "womanhandling" I suppose) is the most common form of complaint, but other instances; those of robbing, stealing, depleting assets, and check forgery come to mind.* Purposely administering incorrect dosages or even incorrect combinations of prescription drugs, (which personal care people are supposedly not allowed to do) in order to induce confusion or lethargy in the patient, seems to work for the criminally intent home "care provider."

There is no need to submit examples of the thousands of disgusting elder abuse cases which occur in the nation's 16,500 nursing homes and ten thousand or so home health care agencies each year. True, *about 58% of the reported cases seem to be of neglect, either by the professional and personal staff, or by the families of those neglected, or by the older person themselves.* Uncared for bed sores, malnutrition, medication problems, and mental abuse seem to far outweigh the physical abuse; and mental abuse seems to be a matter of degree. But any abuse needs to be addressed, and *as a nation, we do not focus on a determined effort to limit and eliminate* as much of this problem as we can.

I am sure that somewhere in the United States, at least weekly, some major newspaper or television channel does an expose' of a local or statewide nursing home problem. I have no doubt that the problems need to be exposed, because any shortcomings in a nursing home have to be identified before they can be solved. But, *I am not one to lay all the blame on the nursing home, its administrators, or its care staff. I think we need to lay the blame where the problem starts—the Medicaid system—and realize that, as it is currently structured—it cannot work. The "Medicare Issues" chapter of this book deals with the system, the problems, and offers solutions—which in turn should help to eliminate some of the heartbreak of Elder Abuse.*

## CENTER FOR LONG TERM CARE FINANCING

Every now and then, I am blessed with meeting an authority, who understands the true scope of events on the national scene. One such person is Steve Moses, president of the Center for Long Term Care Financing in Seattle. I have known Steve for roughly seven years and refer to him as a "high-octane" man when it comes to his knowledge of Medicaid, nursing homes, nursing home financing, and Long Term Care insurance. The Center publishes one or two weekly bulletins regarding these and other related issues. I have the highest regard for the content, and Mr. Moses' comments. The main theme of Steve's message is the dependency of nursing homes, and to a large part our entire health care financing system, on a government program, that of Medicaid, and it's inability to deliver what is supposed to be quality health care. He does not dwell on the problems of elder abuse that seem to get reported somewhere in the nation weekly, but instead, points out the reasons behind the problems, and why and how we better get them fixed. He and his organization are well worth listening to, so I have included information on how to reach The Center in the chapter entitled "Where to Go…" *Check it out, you'll get an eyeful of significant information regarding the nation's nursing home inadequacies and the background behind what causes them.*

## ELDER ANGELS—HELP FOR THOSE WHO SUSPECT FINANCIAL ABUSE OR "SWEETHEART SCAMS"

No discussion of elder abuse could be complete without including *financial abuse, or more specifically, financial elder abuse.* Yes, physical and emotional abuse seem to naturally come to the top of the table when discussing elder abuse, but few people either know about, or want to admit that they know about, *the big-time serious issue of financial elder abuse. "Sweetheart scams" are the normal entre'* to this type of sophisticated crime, but other more subtle techniques are practiced upon the elderly, as well as the general public. Sure, we've all heard stories of how some trusting and unsuspecting elderly person was bilked out of their money by a totally unknown stranger, who one day decided to target the victim as their best friend, or their closest companion, *or even their lover.*

Most of what I have learned regarding financial elder abuse comes from a small organization called *"Elder Angels, Inc."* Even though the organization is small (and needs the help and encouragement of Americans to develop into a strong national organization), they are by no means ineffective. The story of their origin is the stuff of mystery books, and in fact their story has been recounted in print and television several times. The founders of Elder Angels have been involved in super sleuthing dozens of cases of "Sweetheart scams," wherein a fancy young lady tantalizes an older gentleman of means, or a fine-looking young man captures the heart of an older lady with financial resources, *solely for the purposes of separating the victim from their assets.* The work of Elder Angels is truly intriguing, but the *value* of their work is unbelievable. They have saved millions of dollars for people who would have lost out to financial abusers.

Not only have Fay Faron, a private investigator and founder of Elder Angels, and Ann Flaherty, Executive Director and Chief Investigator, made a *career out of investigating senior fraud, they have been able to do their work well enough to obtain prosecution of criminals in this important area of abuse.* Their efforts are well known and highly respected in the jurisdictions in which they have served. Having met them and personally seen some of what they do in their San Francisco office, I have only the highest regard for their mission, and the role it *could* play across the nation. *As $40-120 trillion in elderly assets becomes the target of the "scam of choice" for the nation's con artists during the next four decades, the people of this country need to give serious consideration to backing an organization of this nature.*

You will be pleased to know that you have access to Elder Angels! If you have concerns in the area of financial elder abuse or suspect scamming of yourself or a parent, you can refer to the chapter "Where To Go…" and find the address, phone number, web page and e-mail address of Elder Angels, Inc. Their mission statement says it all: *"Elder Angels assist elderly victims of financial abuse.* We strive to prosecute the abuser, obtain restitution for the victim and educate the public about such crimes. This organization is seeking funds from contributions and grants. These funds will be used for unrestricted operating expenses and special projects. Our organization is based in the Bay Area—however, cases are accepted nationwide."

## SO WHAT DO WE DO ABOUT ELDER ABUSE?

We seem "Hell bent" on developing information on abused children and then seeking "proper" home placement for them after proving criminal, or at least bad civil behavior, or incompetence. We seem pretty locked into a system that approaches "child worship," with billions of dollars spent on programs designed to protect, coddle, reprogram conditions, and even "spoil" children in this country. But who looks after the elderly, many of whom *may well be entrapped in far worse conditions and can linger for years in deplorable, even criminal, situations, with no way out?* Who goes to bat to raise billions to see that the elderly are protected, as well as receiving proper care? *My guess is that the expense ratio would be highly embarrassing to our national conscience.* After all, why spend government money on the emotional and physical well being of the elderly frail when they won't be around to vote very much longer anyway? Who wants to create "funding" for programs that would have no value toward promising future political dividends? "What's the big deal, they've lived their lives, now let us get on with ours!" seems to be the attitude. Certainly, future political dividends can be gained from "protecting" the children, while the elderly, as they age and their condition worsens, cannot offer future political promises.

But this could and should change. When we have a Medicare system that is charged with providing retired people with decent health care, and that system has "checks and balances" to detect fraud, abuse and overpayment, and then that system simply can't keep up with corruption—to what the system itself estimated in 1996 to be twenty-three billion in fraud and overpayment, with double digit losses every year along the way to twenty billion in 2002—*we can forget Medicare as a watchdog for elder abuse.* That leaves Medicaid. Yes, the states are responsible for gathering information on elder abuse through their licensing and Medicaid structures. But. again, the states must simply rely on their "reporting" systems. The state's ability to prevent abuse through routine inspections, many of which are not "on the spot," (and many of which the various Medicaid providers are informed of in advance), reduces the chances of finding out what really goes on when no one is looking.

There are some things that **could be done**, however. You have spent a great deal of time studying the Senior issues in this book, and you have seen me make predictions regarding nearly all of them. Now we have an opportunity to present a plan, albeit, not as a panacea for the entire scope of problems presented herein, but at least, as a recommendation for America to get its elder abuse problem under control. As you have been able to discern, I am not a "government cure-all" proponent. But we have an area here, where I can see no other answer. *That would be to call for a new government program whose sole purpose would be to police elder abuse.* We spend billions on the children. What would be so bad about spending five percent of a like amount on the *abuse problems of the elderly?* I do not call for a federal bureau which would eventually be no more than another bureaucracy. I would call for a *completely new federal plan in funding only*, administered by the states, *with one purpose only— that of fighting elder abuse*. A completely new division designed to work with Medicare and its abuses, Medicaid and its abuses, and those who fall outside the system. *Investigators, detectives, accountants, attorneys, and judges whose sole job would be to detect, prosecute, and convict those caught up in the ugly perpetration of elder abuse.*

We may have no choice in this matter to do anything other than what I suggest. Present regulatory forces are not getting the job done (how could they?) and with 76 MILLION baby boomers about to swell the numbers, the problems associated with elder abuse and senior fraud could well be rampant by the time our aged society reaches 50 to 60 to 70 million elderly. With 15 trillion dollars precariously poised to be passed on, *would you suspect that Sweetheart scams alone could evolve into mega operations of gigantic proportion? America needs to start preparing a totally new and different approach to solving this problem NOW,* before the situation manifests itself even more and is compounded by additional demographic numbers. In short, we'd better *start preparing before a national disgrace becomes an epidemic. When the "boomers" wake up one day and find themselves with no mechanism in place to help defend them from these problems, they may find themselves being reminded of what "Pogo" said years ago, "We have met the enemy and he is us!"*

# CHAPTER 18

# SENIOR FRAUD

## *INCLUDING SOME WAYS TO PROTECT YOURSELF*

## SENIOR FRAUD—AN IMPORTANT CONTEMPORARY ISSUE

What? A chapter concerning Senior Fraud and another regarding Elder Abuse in a book about Long Term Care? Would an insurance agent wear a "black hat?" Unfortunately, some would, and **no matter what, there will always be a number of "foul balls" in our industry, or in any other industry for that matter.** Some insurance agents may be guilty of unethical or even illegal tactics to some degree perhaps, but certainly not to any greater extent than any unscrupulous representative of any industry, and **to a far lesser degree than you may have been led to believe.** That's quite a mouthful, but in reality, the statement is true. Why is it true? Simply, because the insurance industry has implemented a great number of checks and balances, which eliminate many of the temptations that appealed to some agents.

We shall see at *the end of this chapter* how this is so, and the reader would be well advised to pay particular attention to the information, because it could very well be useful should you find yourself dealing with an agent about whom you have some serious doubts. Again, all states have different laws and requirements, but, by and large, the guidelines set up by the various insurance departments and the National Association of Insurance Commissioners, as well as the industry itself, have created many safe-guards for the public at large. **But, for the moment,** let us forget the insurance industry and its representatives, because, as I said before, we will address insurance agents at the end of the chapter.

## SENIOR FRAUD—HOW IT DEVELOPS

For now, let us discuss the issue of **Senior Fraud** and why it has become such a contemporary problem. In short, **for retirees, and the public in general we have "bigger fish to fry." Real big fish.**

What comes to your mind when you hear the word **"Con-man?"** What is meant by the word **"Con-game?"** What is a **"Con artist?"** Simply, the "Con" portion of each terminology is short for "Confidence." Yes, **"Confidence."** Remember that word each time you listen to some fast-talking dude who tries to convince you that your Social Security number, credit-card numbers, bank account or checking account numbers are any of his or her business. Will they all be fast-talking? No. Will they all be very good at giving you their pitch? Yes. Will they all contact you by phone? No. **Will they all try to gain your...confidence? YES**. That's what their game is all about. Confidence.

*And "greed."* "Greed?" you question. Yes, greed. **Greed by both parties. The greed of con artists who prey on the greed of simple people.** More than a few normally clear thinking people lose their wits when what seems like an innocuous offer for a "small fee" against making thousands, or hundreds of thousands of dollars, raises its serpentine head. Greed enters in, and hundreds of people daily loose thousands of dollars *(and their own self respect)* when what seemed like "such a sweet deal" turns sour. So the basis for Senior fraud, and fraud in general, can really be identified then in two words, *"confidence" and "greed." That sets the table for the con artist, and the meal begins.*

A few years ago I heard a radio ad in which a former con artist makes the statement that his "clients" were either poorly educated, or couldn't think very fast. I imagine there are other criteria that allow people to be bilked out of their money, but the second factor mentioned by the crook is certainly *the most important factor* to the success of any con artist. **The ability of people to "think on their feet" is the single greatest deterrent to the scammer.** All sorts of fraud could be avoided if the potential target is able to outwit and outthink the perpetrator.

For some, the ability to think on their feet is natural, others need to work on this talent. Why should a complete stranger invite themselves into your life with no invitation from you, then be allowed to proceed to "display their wares" with little or no objection from you? It seems that the first indication of a telephone call or an unsolicited visit, should raise alarms, whistles, and bells and create an immediate instinctive signal, or at least a "gut feeling," that **danger may be present.** Thinking on your feet **has to begin at the outset of the conversation, (which could include a hang-up)** but if you so choose to continue the conversation, hard thinking, readiness, and preparedness *must* be your guide.

**Now, really, why would anyone listen to a sales pitch from an unknown source,** calling from an unknown location, unless they thought there was something it for themselves? Does greed enter into this scenario a little bit? Does the sound of that free car, free boat, free vacation, or free cash sound a little too good to pass up? Do things really come this easy, either by telephone or by mail, or even by e-mail? I recently received one of the millions of mailings sent on a regular basis that *guaranteed* a check already made out in my name, and which was simply awaiting my response. Twice in the *fine print* I found out that my name *had to be selected*, but *if it was*, I was a guaranteed winner. Big deal. I could hardly wait...to throw the thing in the round file.

What are the reasons that the Senior market seems to be a target for any type of scam? How does the con artist know that this group is especially vulnerable and "easy to work." The reasons are abundant. **First, most older people are considerate and courteous to anyone they talk with, so seeming to be inconsiderate or discourteous is not their normal way.** Scammers know this and can detect in a moment if they have a possible hit because of the pleasantness of the target. Secondly, many elderly people are **lonely and will talk to anybody who will take a few minutes to visit with them, regardless of the outcome.** And, unfortunately, as the con artist on the radio said, they might "just not be very smart" to start with.  Believe it or not,  another factor is that *some people just don't care about their money*.  They feel that a small loss here or there won't hurt them, and besides, *"He sounded like such a good man, and I really trusted him."*

Any random list of Seniors can be used as "target marketing" for *scam organizations (who are well trained in their work)* and even a short list of elderly will enable the con artist to find someone on whom to work their art.  Phone numbers are no harder to find than a phone book, and mailboxes no harder to find than your local post office.  Door-to-door swindlers are few and far between, but they still feel *the risk of being caught is far less than the "rewards" they reap, if they can work their charm in person.*  Television and infomercial scammers are just a push button away.

So, just as legitimate businesses, including insurance companies, "target" their market, so do the bandits.  *"Target marketing" as a phrase, is simply selecting a demographic group of people to which a sales organization would like to appeal.*  In other words, selecting the most desirable market to penetrate.  There is nothing wrong with target marketing, and it makes good sense.  A baby food manufacturer would offer products and discounts to the younger age market.  Expensive automobile manufacturers would not waste time and advertising money trying to sell to a young market, and so on.

On the other hand, since we already know that older people possess most of the wealth in the United States, the senior market is afloat with products designed to appeal to retirees and target marketing is the tool of choice for advertisers.  *All too sadly, this same market is the target of choice for fraud,* and just as legitimate enterprise seeks to court this group, *so do the scammers.*  There is a bit of a difference, however.  When con men target their client, they become *"prey," and the word "target" takes on very serious meaning.*  The scammer knows no bounds, has no regard for weakness; exploiting it to the fullest, and has an immunized total disregard for the feelings or finances of the elderly.

It sometimes seems that no matter how hard local law enforcement officers, national interest groups, and various consumer oriented entities try to educate retireds and the public in general about various contemporary con games, *many people simply fail to listen and fall victim.  There are thousands of schemes going at all times,* and I suspect that in this day and age, for every crook removed from the streets and "boiler rooms," there are at least three new recruits ready, willing and well trained to take his or her place in the con-artists "Hell of Fame."

## SOME TIPS ON WHAT TO EXPECT—AND HOW TO PROTECT YOURSELF

What then, are some of the more popular scams and how should we encourage people to identify them.  I would suggest that *this list will look far differently ten years down the road,* when con artists will have "milked the crowd" with existing schemes, and found ways to create newer, even more effective methods of cheating people out of even greater amounts of money—**particularly with technology related endeavors, such as credit card fraud and identity theft.**

I recognize that while the majority of the techniques listed here are used by legitimate businesses and are entirely legal, and ethical, the reader should take extra precautions to check out that legitimacy if they insist on "playing the game," and subjecting themselves to a possible scam.

Listed below are some of the more popular techniques, which have lent themselves to the scammer's creative innovations.

1) Prize offers.
2) Travel packages.
3) Free or discounted merchandise.
4) Vitamins and supplements.
5) Water treatment systems.
6) Investments.
7) Non-existent charities, or charities who never receive your gifts.
8) Money recovery scams.
9) Roofing, driveway, siding and other home repair or improvements.
10) Work-at-home offers and scams (new twists in the early 2000's.)
11) 900-number and 809-number scams.
12) Infommercial scams.
13) "No money down" and "We'll put up the money" scams.
14) Instant wealth scams.
15) "Money-back" guarantees.
16) Some multi-level operations.
17) Internet scams (an example of new scamming adaptations).
18) Lottery scams.
19) Sweetheart scams—both male and female.
20) Credit Card fraud and theft.
21) Identity theft (reported at up to 700,000 cases per year in 2003)

**While most of the above techniques could be legitimate, do not be surprised to find that a huckster is trying to become your best friend.** In fairness to business in general, it should be remembered that most of the above items were innovations of bona fide marketers, advertisers, and sellers, and are still in use by legitimate merchandisers. Like anything else that is successful, **bad people adopt proven techniques for their own scandalous benefit.**

In the chapter on "Elder Abuse" we have a discussion of an organization which has **great value to the elderly in America—Elder Angels, Inc.** However, I feel Elder Angels should be mentioned here because of the role it has played in Senior Fraud as well as Elder **Financial,** (and sometimes physical and emotional) Abuse. So, read the section on Elder Angels—and their location information in the chapter "Where to Go..."—and see how they may be of value to you, if some of the items addressed in the previous list have happened to you.

Listed below are a number of common-sense observations, *a "super-list" so to speak, that should be regarded as the ally of quick thinking people who do not wish to become prey.* When confronted with what you as a consumer might consider a questionable deal, get the message out quickly that you're not interested, and *don't feel like you're offending the marketer. Far better that someone you don't even know thinks you're "a stick in the mud," than for you to have to lose your own self-respect and beat up on yourself because you fell into the trap.*

1) *NEVER give out your personal financial information; credit* Card numbers, bank account and checking account numbers, Social Security numbers, names of friends, family, or creditor information.

2) *Hang up your telephone if you don't like what you're hearing. You may wish to hang up even if you like what you're hearing. You owe nobody an apology. A simple, "Not interested" will do, if you feel you must say something.*

3) If the calls persist, tell the caller to remove your name from their phone bank. *Simply say, "Put me on your do not call list."* You are supported by The Telephone Consumer Protection Act which makes it illegal for companies to call again if you've asked to be taken off their lists.

4) Better yet, as of July, 2003, the U. S. government has improved this technique for you. It is a *national "do-not-call" list, a registry maintained by the Federal Trade Commission, and is a free service.* Even though in 2003, twenty-seven states maintained do-not-call registries for intrastate telemarketing, most of them transferred the numbers on their list to the federal registry to block *interstate* calls. You can register at: www.donotcall.gov. You must give an e-mail address to which confirmation will be sent, and can you enter up to three phone numbers. You can also call toll free to*: 1-888-382-1222 and register your phone number.* If you sign up by phone, you must make the call from the number you want to register.

5) The *Direct Marketing Association* (in its effort to help consumers and *protect the rights of legitimate telephone solicitors and direct mailers)* for years has had a Telephone Preference Service list. You may call them and request that you be put on a list, *which their members will honor* in not calling or mailing unsolicited communications to you. Write them at: DMA, PO Box 9014, Farmingdale, NY 11735-9014.

6) *Never make a purchase over the phone.* If you are interested in a caller's pitch, ask them to send you more information. *If you do purchase over the phone, you may well have made yourself a target from that point forward, because many of the "phone buyer" lists are traded or sold to other phone solicitors.*

7)  Believe it or don't, but ***the major credit bureaus sell information (mostly lists)*** to telemarketing companies and direct mail marketing  companies.  Unless you live in a state where it is illegal, ***Departments of Motor Vehicles do the same thing***. *If you want your name removed from any possible solicitation list, call your state's DMV, and each of the major credit bureaus.*  The major credit bureaus are Equifax (1-800-556-4711); Experian (1-800-353-0809); and Trans-Union (1-800-680-7293).

8)  ***You also have the Federal Trade Commission on your side*** to assist in enforcing federal laws which have been put in place to protect you.  According to Federal Trade Commission regulations:

A)  At the beginning of a call, the caller must identify the company's name and, if it is a sales call, what is being sold.
B)  If a prize is offered, you have to be told immediately that no purchase or payment is necessary.  Don't pay for a "free prize."  If the caller tells you that the payment is for "taxes" on the prize, they have violated federal law.
C)  You must not be asked to pay in advance for services.  Pay  for services only after they are delivered.
D)  You must not be called before 8 AM and after 9 PM, your  local time.
E)  You must not be called repeatedly or be intimidated.
F)  You must be told the costs and restrictions before you pay for products or services.

9)  ***Remember to think on your feet if you have not chosen to hang up. Do not be pressured into buying or giving donations immediately.  Refuse to be rushed***.  Many scammers are now aware that you have been getting educated.  When they say they will call back, either tell them not to, or take time to prepare yourself in making your decision.  Ask more questions than they have answers.  If the caller is not legitimate, they will become disinterested, realize you're a tough customer, lose interest and hang up on you.  You can antagonize them with such questions as *their* own name, where *they* live, who *they* work for, how old *they* are, are *they* married, what number could you return a call to them, etc. until they realize they are wasting their own valuable time, and move on to the next victim.

***If you ask for their name and a number to call them back, legitimate solicitors will have no problem.***  If you are asked to call back ***a 900 number or the area code 809 number, remember that you will be billed for the call,*** may be calling "offshore," where US laws do not prevail, and may be presented with a phone bill as high as ***$25 per minute*** for the pleasure of finding out their "***urgent***" message.  The 809 area code is in the British Virgin Islands, and will usually be originated with a call to you requesting that you urgently call a number in the 809 area code for important information.  My advice is to ***call your state's attorney general and local sheriff's office and report such a call to them.***

10) ***Remember the old adage that "If a deal sounds to good to be true, it probably is."*** If the caller says that you can collect on gifts and prizes only if you act right away, accept the fact that this is bad news for you and great news for the caller. Avoid this pressure.

11) ***Be particularly aware*** of a caller who says that you do not have to check out his or her deal, whether or not the "deal" is a prize, "free" offer, investment, or insurance.

12***) Avoid talking to telemarketers or sales people when you are feeling lonely, or are not feeling your best physically.*** People representing illegitimate businesses are very skilled at sounding believable and friendly, while detecting signs of weakness in your voice.

13) ***If you are contacted regarding home improvements***, ask to see proof of bonding, insurance, worker's compensation and a business license. Look at the solicitor's automobiles to see if they bear out-of-state license plates. Always insist on local references, and never honor requests for cash payments "to get the materials, and get the work started."

14) When you receive requests from what you may ***suspect is a bogus charity, ask for more information, call the charity,*** ask to talk to a person in charge of the charity, and try to identify as much of the entity as possible. Then report to your state's attorney general or your sheriff's office. If the charity is legitimate, they won't mind. Also, if the charity is legitimate, call them and ask how much of the money they actually receive and, how much of it in fact goes to its intended use.

15) Even though people expect that government "is there" to protect them with various laws and enforcement procedures, ***seldom are any real perpetrators caught and punished.*** This is true at both the state and federal level, and probably the greatest failure is in Medicare fraud, where the government itself believes that as much as $23 Billion per year of taxpayer money is fraudulently spent or wasted. However, every now and then, a ray of hope surfaces. In December of 1998, Attorney General Janet Reno revealed that a two and one-half year investigation of ***fraudulent telemarketers*** (named Operation Double Barrel) had been conducted by both state and federal agents and had produced criminal charges against nearly 1,000 telemarketers.

16) Most ***states are now requiring registration of telemarketing entities*** and implementing tougher enforcement of laws already in place. This is a step in the right direction, perhaps too long delayed, but nevertheless, any relief that the public in general and retirees in particular can receive in this regard will be most welcome and very much appreciated.

These may only be the beginning steps, but the important benefit to you as a consumer, is that without the help of consumers like yourself, there would be no leads to even begin investigating these crooks. For that reason, you need to be aware, that if you are targeted by someone you believe is operating a scam, **you should report to local, state and federal authorities what you suspect is taking place.** Let them check things out. If the company and its techniques are legitimate, they will not have a problem with authorities. If not, **you may have helped to put an end to a con artist's career.**

Remember that your local sheriff's department **needs to know** about this type of suspected activity, and by whatever name they are called in your state, the attorney general, department of commerce, criminal hot-lines, insurance commissioner's office, state auditor's office, fraud protection networks, and securities departments, **are all sources for reporting.** A look through the state governmental pages of your telephone book will direct you to the proper agency. The same can be done at the federal level, with additional agencies such as the FBI and Departments of Transportation and Communication becoming involved. **Use these resources.**

## THE LONG TERM CARE INSURANCE AGENT'S ROLE

As I promised at the beginning, let's take a look at how your retired market insurance agent fits into the picture of Senior Fraud. I am not naive enough to think that abuses have not taken place. They have. When several of the nation's largest insurance companies (and their agents) appear on the front pages with news of class action suits, multi-million dollar fines, and deceptive practice accusations, it gets the public's attention. Let me point out however, that these schemes normally come as ruses in two areas; deceptive practices in the sale of *life insurance* products and highly questionable techniques employed in the sale of *investments* and *annuities*. **Seldom were the products themselves called into question, but the methods employed to sell the products were subject to less than honorable, and sometimes downright fraudulent and deceptive means.** Does the word "greed" on both the part of the consumer and the agent ring a bell here? In any event, at least the "alarms, whistles, and bells" on the part of the purchaser, regarding his or her "investments," should have triggered a concern.

Having admitted that abuses do occur, I wish I were brilliant enough to figure out how to keep these events from evolving, either within the insurance industry, or within the realm of individual producers and agents who choose to deceive and defraud. Keep in mind that there are honest and conscientious agents who may be led into believing that what they are doing is honest and correct, only to find out later that they themselves were misled and deceived. But, believe me, **regulators and companies work daily, and hand-in-hand, to curb these possibilities.** In the arena of Long Term Care Insurance marketing, they have made **great strides toward ruling out company and agent temptation, and have implemented innovative and valuable techniques (sometimes legislating them), which protect the public in general and the retired market in particular.**

First, let's discuss the ways in which consumers can protect themselves from what may be an unscrupulous scoundrel agent. Be aware that in all insurance or investment matters, **three common threads** tie into the mind of the agent who deals in illegal or deceptive practices. These ways for brevity's sake are:

1) "Foolin' with the people."
2) "Foolin' with the money."
3) "Foolin' with the paper."

That's about it. Sounds simple, and it is, but let's diagnose what we mean, by example.

1) ***Agent pockets the premium***. Large or small, the amount seems to make no difference to those caught up in dishonesty.

2) ***Agent writes improper coverage, secretly adds extra coverage, coverage not requested,*** or made known to the applicant.

3) ***Agent "twists," or uses high pressure sales techniques*** in order to collect higher commissions (usually first year.)

4) ***Agent "clean-sheets,"*** which means that he or she does not properly ask or record accurate information on an application, thus giving the client the impression that a policy will be issued and "everything is okay."

5) ***Agent tells the client that he or she is authorized*** to give paramedic exams, or that the client should ***not be bothered by*** further questions from company underwriters or telephone interviews.

Now that you know some of the more common techniques employed by the dishonest agent, what can you do to protect yourself?

1) ***Never make out a check in the agent's name*** in the life and health insurance business. ***Always*** execute the check payable to the company. If the agent has what is called "netting authority" the check is still made out to the company and the company will have made arrangements with the agent and his or her bank to deposit the check in what is called a "Premium Fund (or Trust) Account."

2) ***Never pay in cash.*** Temptation can be rampant, and the agent may be using your money to cover other transactions of a similar nature, until they can "catch up." Your application may be delayed for weeks, or even months, or never be submitted at all.

3) ***Always get a receipt.*** Always. Every application from every company in the land has what is known as a ***"Conditional Receipt"*** included in the application papers. Conditional receipt in its short definition means that you have submitted a certain amount of premium with your application, and, if after the company has underwritten your application, according to all the conditions of the

189

application, and the correct answers have been given, and company underwriting has been satisfied, you will be issued a policy, and your submitted premium will be credited.

4) If you are **promised a high return on your "investment,"** and the business is legitimate, **be aware that the risk is probably high.** If the business is not legitimate, know that you may have just **committed yourself to a "Ponzi scheme" or worse, and you may have entrapped yourself in a never ending nightmare.**

5) It is easy to say **"Never lend money to an agent,"** because if you do, you may be opening yourself up to an entirely unhappy transaction. However, some people allow themselves to be "befriended" by agents who seem okay at first, and after several months or years of trust, allow themselves to be approached about a "new and exciting deal that you should know about," or "a business deal that you just can't afford to overlook." Just remember this (and just say no.) If your agent is truly as successful and as capable as you seem to think, he or she will not need your money.

6) **Do not be pressured into buying anything**, including insurance policies or investments, on the spot, if you do not feel comfortable with all aspects of the presentation. "I won't be back in this area for awhile" is not an acceptable reason for you to buy from anyone.

7) **Make sure the policy is delivered.** Don't just forget about it and hope or trust that you have coverage. On the other hand, depending on the product, **allow a somewhat reasonable time for underwriting and policy issue.** Medicare supplements should be a rather fast issue, but Long Term Care, Short Term Care, and Home Health Care policy issue time **might take from four to eight weeks.** Don't get anxious, remember that the company wants to get the business on the books, if it is to be, as badly as you do, but some communication with your agent or company is certainly within your rights.

8) **Thoroughly read all presentations, agreements and policies.** If you feel uncomfortable with this yourself, have an attorney, friend or relative, who is comfortable with insurance contracts, help you with this.

9) **Do not accept a photocopy of a policy.** The bandits have found ways to make copy machines their most intimate tool.

10) Depending on your state, you will probably have a 10 day or *30 day "free-look" period* to read, question, or change anything in the policy you do not need or did not request and, if need be, to cancel a policy. The free-look period starts the day you receive the policy.

11) *Call your state's Insurance Department* if you feel any of the above recommendations are not sufficient, or if you feel any improprieties have occurred.

Now, as I promised, let's take a look at the *measures initiated* by the industry, regulators in insurance departments, and the National Association of Insurance Commissioners; which have taken the sale of Long Term Care, Short Term Care, Home Health Care and Medicare Supplements *to higher standards of competency, confidence, and agent reliability.*

First of all, some states have gone beyond the traditional *"Continuing Education" requirements* (which nearly all states now require) and have required certification of basic and continued education in the senior market, and more specifically in Long Term Care Insurance, to somewhat ensure that at least the agents and producers have been certified to represent a particular mission. Proper education and resulting certification is the first step towards assisting the agent in proper, honest and ethical treatment of people in the retired market.

Second, many companies are now a part of the *Insurance Marketplace Standards Association (IMSA.)* IMSA has devised a set of codes and standards known as Principles of Ethical Market Conduct, and *many companies are requiring that their representatives complete additional studies and agree to sign a "Code of Conduct" form.*

Obviously, any agent who signs such a document and agrees to its provisions can later ignore the principles described, but the degree of awareness which the industry is helping to establish by *reminding agents of these "common sense" rules* is a positive reinforcement.

As a third measure, there are now *nationwide associations which recognize the specialized field of Long Term Care and the retired market in general.* Specialized courses have been developed and offered in the LTC insurance field, which lead to "alphabet" designations, and which recognize the *additional education and knowledge required by the LTCI and retired market producer.* I list some of them here for your reference, but remember that a lack of professional designation does not diminish the abilities of any agent, but that the pursuit of obtaining and continuing education in the LTC insurance market, and a willingness to spend money and complete several hours of education to further one's knowledge, indicates a better proficiency in the area which you are exploring. Listed below are the major associations, and their designations.

1) Society of Certified Senior Advisors—CSA

2)  American Council of Life Insurers—ACLI
3)  Health Insurance Association of America—HIAA
4)  American Association for Long-Term Care Insurance—LTCP
5)  Corporation for Long-Term Care Certification—CLTC

***As an example of improved consumer protection,*** the companies have responded to a problem, which existed early on in LTC production; that of irresponsible and unethical agents "cleansheeting" in order to get policies issued.  Remember that we said this could occur, should any unethical agent not correctly ask the proper questions on the application, or fail to record truthful, accurate answers.  The industry solution to this problem has been a ***personal telephone interview from home office underwriting to the prospective client to repeat application questions and verify the answers.***

This practice has all but eliminated what became known as "claims made underwriting," wherein a company would issue a policy based on little, or incomplete information, and use the two year contestability period as a reason to deny claims, thus completing serious underwriting only after a claim had been made.  Insurance Commissioners are to be thanked for their input regarding elimination of this practice, but in reality, most reputable companies do not take shortcuts, such as "claims made" underwriting, to appropriately evaluate a risk.

***A number of laws, both national and state, have been legislated which protect the LTCI consumer***.  We will list them in a moment, but there is one idea, mandated in some states, overlooked in others, which should become a ***necessary part of all*** LTC sales processes.  Some states require a ***"Suitability Form," known as a "Long Term Care Insurance Personal Worksheet."*** This is a terrific idea and a step in the right direction.  When this form was first developed, some agents, for a variety of reasons, rebelled against asking clients to indicate a rough idea of their net worth and annual income projections.  But I see the form (which we include at the end of this chapter for your own observation), as a very helpful tool in ***accurately measuring the need*** for Long Term Care Insurance.

I believe that the agent cannot properly assess the need for LTCI unless they have taken the time and care to see that their ***client is (or is not) truly a candidate for Long Term Care.***  The most important part of the Disclosure Statement (Suitability Form) is the "Savings and Investment" area, wherein the candidate checks off the amount of assets in their inventory.  The boxes read in ascending order; "under $20,000; $20,000-30,000; $30,000-50,000; and over $50,000."  This is a pretty innocuous request, which allows the agent not to get too personal or too tied up in the client's affairs, and yet develop whether or not they should proceed with a Long Term Care Insurance presentation.

Personally, I would rather know up front if my potential client's interests lie in LTCI, or in a much more sensible need for Short Term Care.  Then, again, some people may prefer to simply purchase Home Health Care, and in each case, ***the Suitability Form directs the agent to the proper presentation***.  What good does an LTC policy do for someone 82 years old living on a fixed income of $11,000 per year, and an asset base of $20,000?

LTCI should be considered as an asset preservation tool, purchased only by people *who can afford the premiums without impairing themselves financially*. The Suitability Form discloses the information needed to properly assess and evaluate the client's needs, and should be mandated in every sale. Those states that require the use of the form certainly have an edge up on maintaining credibility and honesty in their agents' treatment of potential clients.

Now for the *requirements, that collectively have taken much of the risk out of impropriety*, in the retired market sales arena. Some of the requirements are federal mandates, others are state requirements, and still others are required by the various companies. Your state may not require all of the items listed below, but the general picture is as follows:

At point of sale:

1) The agent *must deliver a "Guide to Health Insurance for People with Medicare."* The Purpose is to compare coverages and shortcomings of Medicare in regard to Home Health and Skilled Care.

2) The agent *must deliver "A shoppers Guide to Long Term Care."* The purpose is to allow the client to read the guide, and choose for themselves whether or not LTC insurance is needed.

3) The agent *must deliver "Things you should know before you Buy Long Term Care Insurance."* The purpose is the same as 2) above.

4) The agent *(in some states) must complete*, *along with the client, the Suitability Form, "Long Term Care Insurance Personal Worksheet."* The purpose, obviously, is to determine if the prospect is a suitable client for LTCI, or should be directed to other products; i.e. Short Term Care, or Home Health Care, or no purchase at all.

5) The agent *must offer a Nonforfeiture benefit.* The purpose is to let people know that they can pay a higher premium for some benefits, which they would receive should they choose to drop the policy after a certain period.

6) Since January 1, 1999, the agent *must offer a compound inflation benefit.* The purpose is to let the prospect know that they can pay a higher premium for compounded inflationary benefits, rather than choose a level benefit, or a simple 5% inflationary benefit, or a guaranteed insurability option.

7) If replacing an existing Long Term Care policy, *the agent and the client must complete a Long Term Care Replacement Form*. The purpose is to allow the client an opportunity to evaluate if replacement is truly in their best interests. Age and insurability are the two major concerns. Above all, *never cancel a policy until a new one is in the hands of the policyholder.*

8) In some states, and to comply with some company guidelines, an agent **must complete a "side-by-side" comparison form,** of existing policy features and benefits, with the proposed policy. This sounds like an easy thing to do, but until LTC policies become standardized (if they ever do) this is a somewhat difficult exercise for both the agent and the client. Newer policies will normally far outweigh the benefits of older policies, due to the nature of newer policy forms covering a broader scope of benefits and removing old "gatekeepers" to qualifying for benefits. But additional premium, due to increased age may be a consideration. (Within the last few years, many companies have reduced premiums, in comparison to older policies, and that factor, in turn may be of great *benefit*, even in light of new attained age.)

9) The agent **must deliver the company sales materials** relative to the product being sold. The purpose is obvious. People need to know what they are buying. **Do not accept agent written side agreements or items stricken by the agent from company materials. This is illegal.** Agents highlighting items in a brochure, or pointing out important features with "bullets" is legal, beneficial, and reasonable.

10) Some states will require that **upon policy delivery** you are to be informed through a Disclaimer that your policy may not be included under the **state Guarantee Association's** criteria for receiving benefits should your company go into receivership. This is a company duty and is to be included in the policy in states that have a Guarantee Association and the above requirement. Why is this important in reference to consumer protection? Because agents are prohibited by law from using the existence of a Guarantee Association to advise you to purchase any kind of an insurance policy. In other words, if you should ask an agent about the reliability and stability of a company, no agent is allowed to say, "Don't worry about the company, because the state Guarantee Association will see to it that your claims are covered."

There are certainly other requirements that companies have to meet and want to meet in their normal course of business. **But the above ten items are intended to inform you that, in the sale of Long Term Care Insurance, and retired market sales, the "deck is stacked" as well as can be, to curb the efforts of dishonest agents to cheat the public.** In addition to numerous general laws regarding illegal transactions by any agent in any state, the insurance industry and more definitively, the **Long Term Care insurance industry, has designed these safeguards to prevent the injustices of Senior fraud being played out on the nation's LTC clients**. I think they work, but as P.T. Barnum said, "There's a sucker born every minute." Just make sure that you know what you're doing, and take confidence in the fact that you have been made aware of some of the most common contemporary examples of Senior fraud, and can **recognize, ahead of time, many of the problems associated with, and leading to, Senior fraud. We all need your help.**

# Things You Should Know Before You Buy
# Long-Term Care Insurance

**Long-Term Care Insurance**

- A long-term care insurance policy may pay most of the costs for your care in a nursing home. Many policies also pay for care at home or other community settings. Since policies can vary in coverage, you should read this policy and make sure you understand what it covers before you buy it.

- You should **not** buy this insurance policy unless you can afford to pay the premiums every year. Remember that the company can increase premiums in the future.

- The personal worksheet includes questions designed to help you and the company determine whether this policy is suitable for your needs.

**Medicare**

- Medicare does not pay for most long-term care.

**Medicaid**

- Medicaid will generally pay for long-term care if you have very little income and few assets. You probably should **not** buy this policy if you are now eligible for Medicaid.

- Many people become eligible for Medicaid after they have used up their own financial resources by paying for long-term care services.

- When Medicaid pays your spouses' nursing home bills, you are allowed to keep your house and furniture, a living allowance, and some of your joint assets.

- Your choice of long-term care services may be limited if you are receiving Medicaid. To learn more about Medicaid, contact your local or state Medicaid agency.

**Shopper's Guide**

- Make sure the insurance company or agent gives you a copy of a book called the National Association of Insurance Commissioners' "Shopper's Guide to Long-Term Care Insurance". Read it carefully. If you have decided to apply for long-term care insurance, you have the right to return the policy within 30 days and get back any premium you have paid if you are dissatisfied for any reason or choose not to purchase the policy.

**Counseling**

- Free counseling and additional information about long-term care insurance are available through your state's insurance counseling program. Contact your state insurance department or department on aging for more information about the senior health insurance program in your state.

LEAVE WITH APPLICANT

# Long-Term Care Insurance Personal Worksheet

People buy Long-Term Care Insurance for a variety of reasons. These reasons include to avoid spending assets for long-term care, to make sure there are choices regarding the type of care received, to protect family members from having to pay for care, or to decrease the chances of going on Medicaid. However, Long-Term Care Insurance can be expensive, and is not appropriate for everyone. State law requires the insurance company to ask you to complete this worksheet to help you and the insurance company determine whether you should buy this policy.

## Premium

The premium for the coverage you are considering will be $_____ per month, or $_____ per year.

The company has a right to increase premiums in the future. The company has sold long-term care insurance since 1985 and has sold this policy since 1998. The company has not raised its rates for this policy.

☐ Have you considered whether you could afford to keep this policy if the premiums were raised, for example, by 20%?

## Income

Where will you get the money to pay each year's premiums?
☐ Income     ☐ Savings     ☐ Family Members

What is your annual income? (check one)

☐ Under $10,000      ☐ $16-29,999        ☐ Over $50,000
☐ $10-15,999         ☐ $30-50,000

How do you expect your income to change over the next 10 years?  (check one)
☐ No change     ☐ Increase     ☐ Decrease

*If you will be paying premiums with money received only from your own income, a rule of thumb is that you may not be able to afford this policy if the premiums will be more than 7% of your income.*

(over)

## Savings and Investments

Not counting your home, what is the approximate value of all your assets (savings and investments)? (check one)

☐ Under $20,000    ☐ $20-29,999    ☐ $30-49,999    ☐ $50,000 or over

How do you expect your assets to change over the next ten years? (check one)

☐ Stay about the same    ☐ Increase    ☐ Decrease

*If you are buying this policy to protect your assets and your assets are less than $30,000, you may wish to consider other options for financing your long-term care.*

## Disclosure Statement

| ☐ The information provided above accurately describes my financial situation. | ☐ I choose not to complete this information. |
|---|---|

Signed: _____    _____
                      (Applicant)    (Date)

☐ I explained to the applicant the importance of completing this information.

Signed: _____    _____
                  (Agent/Producer)    (Date)

Agent's Printed Name: _____

My agent/producer has advised me that this policy does not appear to be suitable for me. However, I still want the company to consider my application.

Signed: _____    _____
                      (Applicant)    (Date)

*The company may contact you to verify your answers.*

# CHAPTER **19**

# OVERCOMING YOUR OWN OBJECTIONS

## *(TO LONG TERM CARE INSURANCE)*

I've been in the insurance industry for over three decades, and just about the time I think I've heard it all, I find I haven't. Something new is either just around the corner or right in my lap. Over the last thirteen years I've been presented with a variety of objections, delays, deferrals and downright excuses for not purchasing, either Long Term Care, Nursing Home Care, Short Term Care, or Home Health Care. **Most of the objections were honest and just needed to be listened to, understood, then answered with a simple dose of reality**. Some were humorous, some absurd, and some downright nasty. Let's get the "nasty" out of the way first—I have some responses to the "theme," in the next paragraph, (which I'm not going to share) but overcoming this type of mentality is not humorous.

In my line of work and teaching, objections are to be expected—comes with the territory. Perhaps it's because I live in rural country, but one statement which sometimes rears its ugly head is "I'm never going to a nursing home. *'Smith and Wesson'* will take care of that," or some rendition of the suicide theme. An equally ridiculous response generated over the last few years seems to be bent on the *"Kevorkian"* approach to life and its finality. While both comments are sad to hear in the midst of a spousal or family discussion, they always seem to be followed by a little giggle or laugh on the part of the elicitor, **and a rather blank stare on the face of the spouse.** Flip remarks—off the cuff—intended to be humorous, just don't work, and should not work.

At any rate, I would like to share many of the **more common objections with you, since your consideration of the purchase of Long Term Care is at least a part of the reason for your purchase of this book.** I offer these discussions as first person presentations since many of them will probably be on your mind, and **you may find yourself thinking some of the same things** that others have discussed with me. So, in no particular order, let me offer **solutions to your questions and objections.** At the very least I may be able to help with **legitimate concerns** you may have developed during the reading of this book. Since we're role-playing, please allow me the liberty of a visit with *"Bill and Mary,"* people just like yourselves with honest concerns, questions, and objections. Listen in.

1)    **"WE'LL LISTEN TO YOUR TALK, BUT WE'RE NOT GOING TO BUY ANY MORE INSURANCE."**

"Well, Bill, I can certainly accept that, but a lot of my friends said the same thing until we talked about how they were going to keep their assets in the family. *We're talking about a lot of money here—yours—and your family's—and ways to keep it yours."*

**2)** **"WE DON'T WANT ANY MORE INSURANCE. WE'RE INSURANCE POOR NOW."**

"I hear what you're saying Mary, the costs of all types of medical care and long term care continuing to go out of sight, *I'd like to show you a way to keep from BECOMING poor.* Most people have no idea what the costs of home health care, assisted living, and nursing home care are today, or what they will be at an age when you need to utilize the benefits. I'm actually glad to hear you say that, and I hear it often, because I hear it from people who have something to protect. They know that the premiums they pay are small in comparison to the risk of self-insuring. *If you had nothing to protect, you wouldn't buy ANY insurance."*

**3)** **"I'VE ALREADY DECIDED, I'M NEVER GOING TO A NURSING HOME."**

"Well, Bill, I hear you, but *one hundred percent of the people in nursing homes today said the same thing!* Nobody ever planned on writing checks to a nursing home. The problem is that a stroke, or Alzheimer's, a sudden event and accident, or even just getting old, can create a situation over which you have no control. At that point, you wouldn't get to make the decision, and it would probably be impossible for Mary or the kids to be of help. The facts are, that more than one-half of the women and one-third of the men turning 65 this year will spend time in a nursing home. After that the odds just go up. *The question really seems to be when and for how long."*

*"BUT, the BEST thing about policies sold today is that you DON'T HAVE TO GO to a nursing home. You can utilize benefits right here in your own home,* or in one of the new, beautiful assisted living facilities that are being built today. That's the beauty of our policies, freedom—freedom to choose where you would want to receive care—at home, in an assisted living facility, or if need be, as a last choice, in a nursing home. *Again, YOU KEEP the freedom to choose where you would want to receive your benefits, and WE PAY the bill."*

**4)** **"WE'RE ALREADY COVERED UNDER MEDICARE. MEDICARE WILL TAKE CARE OF ME, WON'T IT?"**

*"Sure, Bill, for twenty days, and even that has to be Skilled Care in a Medicare approved facility.* Most people in nursing homes are there for custodial care, help with activities of daily living or for cognitive needs. That's not covered under Medicare, and that's why Medicare pays only a small percentage of the nation's nursing home bill."

*"Medicare was not designed to cover nursing home bills except for short stays of medically necessary care.* MediCAID has a plan for poor people, or for

those who have to impoverish themselves to qualify. And **with your assets, I doubt if you could qualify**. Let me get to a page, which will tell us whether or not your assets would let you qualify for Medicaid. I'm still concerned about that twenty days."

**5)** **"THE GOVERNMENT WILL TAKE CARE OF US! WE'VE PAID TAXES ALL THESE YEARS AND SHOULD GET SOMETHING BACK."**

"Well, Mary, I would like to think so, everybody would, except for the fact that government has gone the other way, and finally realizes that it can't pay for all the things people want. After we take a look at your assets, maybe they will. **But the truth is, that people with assets must pay their own way, or spend down their assets to a poverty level** before Medicaid will participate in nursing home assistance. In the case of a single person this amount is about $2,000, give or take some change. For married people the non-exempt assets will STILL HAVE TO BE SPENT DOWN to about $80,000, of which the remaining-at-home spouse will be allowed to retain one half. **What I'm saying is, the government WILL TAKE CARE OF YOU AFTER you've spent the money you saved for your retirement years.** But it will be of no help as long as you have money in the bank."

**6)** **"WE'VE GOT MONEY IN THE BANK AND STOCK MARKET. WE DON'T NEED TO WORRY."**

"That's great, Mary! Shows very good thinking and planning on your part, **but let's complete the planning.** We need more Americans who are able to achieve good, sound financial prudence. But let me point something out. Just as you worked hard and prepared ahead for yourself, **why not take a part of the interest on those investments and protect the whole nest egg?** Since you will have to spend your own money to pay for long term care costs, no matter where you receive them, let me show you a way to protect the entire investment by using only a part of the interest it is creating. I don't know what your principle amount is, and I don't even know what your interest rate is, or what your dividends amount to. However, let's say you've got a hundred thousand in CD's, or whatever. Would that be in the ballpark? At your young and tender age, I'd bet that I can guarantee you that we can make the premiums fit into **a program that will take only two to four percent of the principle, and protect the whole investment forever."**

"I can see where you're coming from, but let me give you a thought. Bankers tell me that no matter what, **when somebody retires, they want at least as much money in their account, if not more, during their entire retirement, as they started with. Least of all, they don't want to watch it go down.** As you can see, at no less than $42,000 per year, paying for your own Long Term Care needs, whether in a facility, or at home, you will erode these savings rather quickly."

**7)** **"THE CHILDREN WILL TAKE CARE OF US.  WE'VE TALKED ABOUT IT, THEY'RE GOOD PEOPLE, AND THEY FEEL THEY OWE IT TO US."**

"That's great, Mary.  I've got kids and I hope they'll feel the same way about me. *However, we're finding that may not be realistic.  Do they live in the same city as you do now?  Same county?  Or even in the same state?*  We're finding out that in most situations what we would like to have happen, living with the children, or them with us, is not a reality.  They seem to have their own lives, their own jobs and their own families.  I'm not saying it's right, but I am saying it may be the real world. *We've seen people who said the same thing, tried it for a short time, but it doesn't seem to work very long.  On the other hand, there are people who don't want to be a burden to their children.*  They want to maintain their freedom and independence as long as they can.  Pride and integrity go a long way with people who have been self-reliant and made their own way in the world.  I like your idea, but if things can't be the way we would like them, you still need to protect what is rightfully yours—and someday will be theirs—your assets." *Family money has taken on new meaning in the last twenty years.*  Could we call them—I would be willing to bet that *they've thought about this too, and just didn't feel comfortable bringing it up with you.*  Sometimes they even think about helping with the premium. *Whatever, they should be part of the planning*.

**8)** **"MARY WILL TAKE CARE OF ME AND I'LL TAKE CARE OF HER.  WE'VE ALREADY DECIDED."**

"A great plan, and the right thing to do.  And one which I hear more and more all the time.  We can go either way.  We can offer you a plan whereby you don't have to spend time in a nursing home, *but Mary can have both Professional and Personal help if she should need to take care of you at home.  And you for her, should the need be.*  In addition to that, we can 'tailor make' a plan that will allow you to take care of each other when such a time that lifting, bathing, eating, walking or toileting become a problem.  An interesting thing—we are finding that *more people would prefer to remain at home and care for each other than go to a nursing home.*  A great concept and one that works.  We even have companies that allow a family member such as a spouse or child to take care of you and get paid by a Home Health care agency for doing it. *At any rate, with your assets, we can do both—protect your nest egg, and cover the costs of care in any location.*  But allow me to take this one step further.  Bill, what do you weigh?  What do you weigh, Mary? *Okay Bill, you lay down on the floor and Mary you start moving Bill around."*

**9)** **"I'M NOT GOING TO LIVE LONG ENOUGH TO BE A BURDEN TO ANY-BODY."**

"Well, Bill, you've hit on a point that neither you, nor Mary, nor I have control of, but one thing I can tell you is that *national statistics now tell us that if you live to age 65, you'll make it to about 84.* That's right. We've developed lifestyles, medicine and health care, particularly in the heart, stroke, and cancer areas to the point where *people are living far longer than they did even a generation ago. Who's going to take care of the costs of that longevity? You or me? If you've got assets, certainly not the government."*

**10)** **"AREN'T THERE ANY OTHER WAYS TO PROTECT OUR ASSETS WITH-OUT BUYING INSURANCE?"**

"Yes, Bill and Mary, there used to be, and they were fairly easy to do. And there still are ways, but after legislation like OBRA '93 and HIPAA '96, over the past few years *the ways have become more difficult and speculative, at best.* Why? Because the only alternative to Long Term Care insurance left, or paying the nursing home or health care bills yourself, is transfer of assets. *When done in combination with an LTC policy, this can work out quite well.* Whatever the reason for transferring assets, perhaps in an attempt to qualify for Medicaid, most people are reluctant to do so until the very last moment. Now, I'm not an attorney, so I wouldn't even attempt to advise you on the legal work. But one thing I can tell you, most of the techniques that used to work in order for people to qualify themselves for welfare are now illegal and *certainly not worth the hassle or legal jeopardy that would exist between the people, the state, and attorneys for all parties involved, including the children."*

"Unless people are very sure of the stability of their children's marriages, emotions, finances, health etc., they have a natural and deserved reluctance to divest themselves of their assets simply because someone told them to do so. Numerous articles have been written on the battles that go on when one of the sons or daughters, or more likely their attorney, either encourages transfer too early, or is unhappy with what seemed at the beginning like an amenable agreement, after the transactions have been made. *I would recommend very carefully and cautiously approaching any of these alternatives if you are so inclined to explore them, but in any case, you would need to self insure, or get at least an interim LTC policy for the three-year or five-year transfer "look-back" period, whichever the case may become.* If you are thinking of "going bare" and hoping Medicaid will be the answer, you should rethink that, because with the way *government spending and budgeting has been going, and Medicaid recovery units wanting their money back, using Medicaid may just turn out to be a loan, and a bad one at that."*

**11)** **"I'M A VETERAN.  DOESN'T UNCLE SAM HAVE SOME NURSING HOME HELP FOR US?"**

"Yes, Bill, the Veteran's Administration does have nursing homes around the country, and fortunately, more are being built all the time.  I don't have all the details, but I do know that *you can use up to six months lifetime care at no cost.*  We should consider that when we work on a plan for you.  However, remember, there are four considerations.  First, *in most cases, there are waiting lists*.  Second, *the VA does no good for Mary where a policy would*.  Third*, there is no help for home health or home care, and that is what most people are interested in.*  And fourth, *the VA home may be hundreds of miles from Mary or your family, which compounds the problem and creates a great deal of inconvenience for both of you.*  Also VA nursing homes are really designed for the veteran who can't afford to pay for his or her own nursing home stay."

**12)** **"WE WANT TO WAIT AND THINK ABOUT IT."**

"OK, Bill, I can honor that.  I can accept and understand your request to wait a few days.  *It's a lot of money we're talking about, and its yours.  Remember that's why I'm talking to you—to keep it yours.  I wouldn't live very well with myself if I got a call from Mary or the kids asking me why I didn't persist while she is writing out checks to pay for nursing home costs from your retirement fund."*

"Bill and Mary, you've done pretty well in your lifetimes.  You've watched your dollars and seen to it that you could do the best for yourselves and your family.  Let me put it this way.  What if you had just won the lottery or a big jackpot for, say $100,000.  What would you do with it?  I bet you'd get it to the bank right away.  Why?  *Obviously, to protect it.*  But the truth is, *you've already been big winners over a lifetime, so why not protect what you already have the same way you would a windfall?  Remember, that delay often turns into denial."*

"At any rate, while you're thinking about us, we need to think about you, to see if you can qualify for this coverage.  I'll be thinking about you, but you seem to be in good health now.  Now is the time to remove any doubt about losing the things we've talked about."

"Here's something to think about.  I'm going to write down five reasons not to wait too long.  The first is *AWARENESS*—We are both aware of the need right now.  We will never be more aware than we are now.  Number two is *PROTECTION*—We buy protection today for tomorrow, because we never know what tomorrow will hold—a stroke, heart attack, auto accident, etc. are examples.  Third is *INSURABILITY*—We think we have a chance with your insurability today, we never know about tomorrow.  Fourth is *INFLATION*—We know what the price will be today, we also know that the longer you wait, the higher the price of the insurance and the cost of the care itself. Let's look at some of the math on these sheets I have. Fifth is the **COST**—I can't imagine costs for either nursing home fees or LTC insurance going down. In short, the problem doesn't go away, I go away."

"So, let's not wait too long. Think about it tonight and tomorrow, and let me give you a call late tomorrow, while everything is fresh in your mind. This will give you a chance to think of some more questions you may have. Is that fair enough? Let me leave you with a final thought. *You can't plan your future in the future, you've got to plan it now. I'll call you tomorrow."*

13) **"WE DON'T WANT TO TALK ABOUT IT NOW, WE'RE IN GREAT HEALTH AND FEELING GOOD."**

"I'm glad to hear that Bill, in fact, *that is THE proper time to do something about LTC.* Just as you took measures to build your assets, you probably were in good health while you were building. You're still in good health, and that's why we should do something now*. I've got too many examples of people that were in good health and wanted to wait, only to have something happen that made them uninsurable.* The biggest problem facing Americans today, no matter what the need, is outliving their good health. Think about it. *What happens if YOU, YOUR FAMILY AND YOUR ASSETS outlive your good health? Remember, delay often turns into denial. In addition, do any of us ever find the perfect time to do anything?"*

"Purchasing LTC insurance is like buying life insurance. The younger the age, and the better the health, the lower the premiums. Also, Bill and Mary, remember this. Purchasing LTC coverage won't make you go to the nursing home, *it only provides peace-of-mind for you and your family SHOULD the need arise, perhaps even for at-home care.* Remember the old saying that talking about life insurance won't make you die one day sooner, or live one day longer? Well, the same is true in providing for your living needs*. I'm sure you wouldn't want to wait until your health was affected to make a financial decision of such an important nature."*

14) **"WE CAN'T AFFORD LONG TERM CARE. WE DON'T HAVE THE MONEY BECAUSE OUR ASSETS ARE TIED UP. WE HAVE THE HOUSE, BUT OUR INCOME IS TOO LOW."**

"Mary, *we already established the need when we totaled your assets for the suitability form.* Now, you know your finances better than I, but when we established that need, and according to those ledger sheets, you have over $200,000 tied up in illiquid assets, so I can see where you're coming from. But let me ask you this. *If I can show you a way to pay these premiums without upsetting your monthly income, cash flow and living expenses, would you be interested?*

Okay? Now, do we have any asset that is accumulating interest or paying dividends, such as CD's, securities, or annuities? No."

"So how about this? Banks in this country have finally realized the situation that thousands of fixed income people are in, and have made available a *LINE-OF-CREDIT reverse mortgage on property, which you own and is paid for.* I'm sure you may have read about them in some of the recent newspaper or magazine articles. The federal government and some state governments are even in this business. *These plans are designed for this type of situation. You borrow only enough each year just to pay the premiums to protect the entire asset.* I can recommend such a bank, or you can call your lending institution and see what they have to offer. Remember, you only want a line-of-credit reverse mortgage, and while we know that the mortgage is accumulating to the amount of the premium, and the interest owed, so should your property be appreciating. Therefore, *if the need for long term care or home health care arises, you will not have to spend down from your own assets, or sell them for far less than they are worth to pay those costs.* This concept is a fairly new idea that has come about simply because of situations like yours. Americans are living longer, and the costs of that longevity were relatively unheard of even a decade ago. We should take some time in the next few days and look into this. Would you like me to help?"

"Also, Bill and Mary, your son and daughter probably understand that they won't be able to move from another state and come home to take care of you. *And since they also have something at stake here with their inheritance, perhaps we should let them know that an adequate LTC policy can help solve both problems. I bet they'd be more than happy to split the premiums.* Many states even make the purchase tax deductible for them. *Shouldn't we allow them the opportunity to help make this decision?"*

15) **"WE LIKE THE IDEAS YOU'VE DISCUSSED HERE, BUT WE WANT TO TALK TO THE KIDS."**

"That's a great idea, and one which I heartily endorse. *I recommend the same to many clients, because then your children, who have probably thought about broaching this issue themselves, will be aware of just what your thinking is.* A thought occurs to me here. 'Inheritance' is not a four-letter word, but 'lose' is. I can think of no better way to get some of these things out in the open than getting the possible inheritors involved in your planning. Would it be possible for one or more of them to sit in on a meeting with me, say next Saturday?" Another thing, as one of my colleagues says, *"The greatest gift a father can leave a child is a mother who can visit but doesn't have to stay."*

16) **"WE NEED TO TALK TO OUR ACCOUNTANT OR ATTORNEY BEFORE WE MAKE ANY MOVE."**

"A good idea—As I said before, we're talking about a lot of money here—yours, and ways to keep it yours. *You also have some tax possibilities here that may be of benefit to you. I would love to explain to your attorney/accountant some of the latest events in the tax areas of our industry.* When you discuss this with them, mention that my greatest concern comes in the area of asset preservation. That should be of interest to them, and perhaps you could ask them to call me, or allow me to see them so they can see where I'm coming from. *I would think they would be happy to encourage asset preservation where both you and your children are involved. Another thing, your accountant will see the difference in paying premiums once a year, as opposed to paying a nursing home every month for years."*

17) **"THIS STILL SEEMS LIKE MORE MONEY THAN WE'D LIKE TO PAY, DO YOU HAVE ANY SOLUTIONS TO A LOWER PRICE?"**

"You know, Bill and Mary, I've been successful in the insurance business for several years and one of the reasons for that success is that *I believe in sending as little premium as possible to insurance companies.* Sound strange? Well, it's really not. *I refuse to saddle any of my clients with a payment that they're not comfortable with because if you're not comfortable with the payment, you'll drop the policy and we wouldn't have done anybody any good.* Many people don't know that high *deductibles can really lower* their insurance bill."

"Auto, homeowners and health insurance are all examples of this, and perhaps you've saved money this way over the years. We can do the same thing for you with your LTCI coverage. Let's take a look at it. Your assets are liquid enough that you could pay the first hundred days yourself and that would lower the premiums considerably. We can also *lower the benefit period*, but let's be very careful on this. Let's look at some of the other combinations."

18) **"WE THINK WE'LL JUST WAIT AND TAKE OUR CHANCES."**

"Well, Bill and Mary, would you be very proud of me if *I came back and offered you a policy just like this, but with a premium of $42,000 per year? And that would cover just one of you.* I didn't think so. But could you afford the $42,000 per year for a Long Term Care insurance policy? Or perhaps even one at $130,000? No? Well, that's what you are really doing here, you are doing what's known as self-insuring. Yes, *you are literally self-insuring, writing yourself your own policy, at a cost of at least $42,000 to $72,000 per year for who knows how long. Please remember I can do the same thing for a fraction of that cost."*

**19)** **"WE STILL WANT TO WAIT AND THINK ABOUT IT."**

"Okay, Bill and Mary, but I've found out over the years, that there are really only *two times* people think very much about these coverages. One is right now, when we're discussing it, and the other is when they need it."

**20)** **"MARY MIGHT NEED THIS, BUT I DON'T. IN MY FAMILY THE MEN DIE YOUNG AND QUICKLY, HER FAMILY SEEMS TO LIVE TO A "RIPE OLD AGE."**

**"Again, Bill,** *you've brought up something that neither of us have* any control over. I'll agree that family history may have something to do with longevity, but today things are much different than even *twenty years ago.* **Think about it. Look at all the advances that science and medicine have made in the last decade. Did you know** that according to the American Health Association, (1999 Heart and **Stroke Statistical Update)** *13.9 million people alive today have a* history of heart attack, angina pectoris, or both? In other words, your chances of surviving today are good, compared to the history *of the men in your family.* **And Mary's "ripe old age" relatives point out an even greater need for coverage for the both of you. That's why my company offers a** *spousal discount, for situations just like yours.*

**21)** **(AFTER A DENIAL BY EITHER OF TWO PARTIES IN THE ORIGINAL LTC APPLICATION) "YOUR COMPANY DENIED BILL, SO WE DON'T WANT THE POLICY."**

**Well, Mary, I'm really sorry about the denial, but the underwriters deal with doctor's reports and medical details, so there must have been something important to cause the denial, and they're never going to tell me what it was.** *Let me explain to you now, however, that coverage on you becomes even more important.* **For instance, let's assume that you eventually have to take care of Bill for whatever reason,** *now what do we do if, God forbid, something should happen to you?* **My experience tells me that we should raise your benefits as high as possible, (perhaps even double up with an indemnity policy) so that** *if something happens to you there is enough benefit money payment that could then be used to help pay for Bill's care, as well as your own.* **We really need to look at this alternative, now that this new possibility has surfaced."**

**22)** **"LONG TERM CARE IS JUST FOR OLD PEOPLE, AND IS JUST FOR NURS-ING HOME CARE."**

"**Ah ha! I know you've heard that, but it's simply not true.** *An automobile accident, stroke, heart attack or lingering cancer can happen ANYTIME, TO ANYONE!* **That's where the home care benefits of a policy come in. As for nursing homes, did you know, that according to a government study,** *40% of long term care is utilized by people under 65? Makes you stop and think, doesn't it?*

23) **"WE WANT TO WAIT AND TALK TO SOME OTHER AGENTS AND COMPA- NIES."**

"**Bill and Mary, that's certainly within your right. And I know that one of the things you will be doing is shopping price.** *Please remember that these things can be fairly complicated on the front end with accurate comparisons, but the back side is the most important.* **When it comes claims time, you will want a real live human being in your corner, that's what you pay me for. In addition,** *I can help you analyze the maze of information you will be seeing, and help determine if something is being overlooked or is really in your best interests.*"

"*I respect your feelings in this matter, and don't mind the competition, and I won't knock them, but I am also a good agent. I believe in client education,* **that's why I've taken the time to visit with you and point out a lot of different factors involved. I've seen a lot of companies' policies and have studied a lot of LTCI products.** *Let me refer you to some of my satisfied policyholders.* **When you do talk to somebody else, please do me a favor and** *make sure the other agent shows you an "apples to apples" comparison.* **If another agent is serious about presenting you with his or her best plan, they should be able to do so within a few days.** *Could we do this?—I'll wait a few days and give you a call. If my competition hasn't gotten on the ball to service your request, you've got me, and I want to work for you. Fair enough?*"

24) **"WE'RE WORKING AND JUST TOO YOUNG TO WORRY ABOUT THIS TYPE OF INSURANCE, ANYWAY, WE'VE HEARD THAT IT'S JUST TOO EXPEN- SIVE."**

"**Well, Bill and Mary, let me ask you a question.** *Why are you working? There are really only two answers and they are simple. Number one is to pay the bills, and number two is to prepare for a retirement, a comfortable retirement. That pretty much covers it.* **Work today and build for tomorrow. Build What? Assets. Your assets...and hope that nothing comes along that interferes with your work, your plans, and your building...the building of your assets.**" *Again, let me remind you that young age and good health have a way of keeping premiums low.*

Let's look at this sheet and see how incredibly low the premium is today, as opposed to the costs of care and the amount of premium you would have to pay to cover those costs if you delay your purchase. Waiting to purchase at an older age is what drives premiums up. ***Look at it this way, with today's premiums, including an inflation rider—you can insure your asset base TODAY—including what you are working to build, and haven't accumulated yet—against TOMORROW'S costs. Let's beat the clock on this one!***

(Please see the next page for the sheet.)

# LET'S DO THE MATH !

The "TRIPLE WHAMMY" tells us there are THREE problems involved with DELAYING PURCHASE of LTC Insurance:
  1) *Inflation—Cost of care goes up @ 5% compounded per year*
  2) *Increasing age—Delayed age purchase price goes up*
  3) *Insurability—Delay can cause pre-existing denial or rate-up*

Now let's run the numbers to show how severe this problem can become. Remember that as your assets increase, they become more vulnerable. We can "beat the clock." But, here's what happens if you choose to delay:

## *Couple age      Inflation cost of care      Purchase age premium*

| | | | |
|---|---|---|---|
| **50** year old couple today: | need is for **$120** per day | if today's premium is | **$125** per month |
| Delay for ten years: | need is for **$190** per day | the premium will be | **$310** per month |
| Delay for fifteen years: | need is for **$240** per day | the premium will be | **$525** per month |
| Delay for twenty years: | need is for **$300** per day | the premium will be | **$940** per month |
| **55** year old couple today | need is for **$120** per day | if today's premium is | **$150** per month |
| Delay for ten years: | need is for **$190** per day | the premium will be | **$415** per month |
| Delay for fifteen years: | need is for **$240** per day | the premium will be | **$750** per month |
| Delay for twenty years: | need is for **$300** per day | the premium will be | **$1,315** per month |
| **60** year old couple today | need is for **$120** per day | if today's premium is | **$195** per month |
| Delay for ten years: | need is for **$190** per day | the premium will be | **$600** per month |
| Delay for fifteen years: | need is for **$240** per day | the premium will be | **$1,050** per month |
| Delay for twenty years: | need is for **$300** per day | the premium will be | **$1,954** per month |
| **65** year old couple today | need is for **$120** per day | if today's premium is | **$260** per month |
| Delay for ten years: | need is for **$190** per day | the premium will be | **$830** per month |
| Delay for fifteen years: | need is for **$240** per day | the premium will be | **$1,560** per month |
| Delay for twenty years: | need is for **$300** per day | the premium will be | **$2,750** per month |
| **70** year old couple today | need is for **$120** per day | if today's premium is | **$375** per month |
| Delay for ten years: | need is for **$190** per day | the premium will be | **$1,240** per month |
| Delay for fifteen years: | need is for **$240** per day | the premium will be | **$2,200** per month |
| **75** year old couple today | need is for **$120** per day | if today's premium is | **$525** per month |
| Delay for five years: | need is for **$150** per day | the premium will be | **$980** per month |
| Delay for ten years: | need is for **$190** per day | the premium will be | **$1,740** per month |

**Solve tomorrow's LTC problems today with a 5% compound inflation rider!  Remember—when protecting your assets—delay can turn into denial.**

# CHAPTER **20**

# **PERSONAL INVENTORY**

*This chapter is designed to allow you to take a personal inventory of your individual needs regarding Long Term Care, Short Term Nursing Home Care, Home Health care, Home Care and Final Expense Plans. It will help you evaluate your own needs or desire for preservation of your existing or anticipated assets. For your convenience, I have divided the chapter into a number of categories, which will assist you in this effort. Complete the items at your pleasure. Visit with your spouse, children, banker, broker, LTC insurance agent, financial consultant, attorney or accountant if you desire. Completion will take some work, will be very interesting, and above all, you may uncover a number of previously overlooked items regarding yourself, your family, your health and your assets.*

## **PERSONAL INVENTORY**

Name_____Date of inventory_____
Address_____ City_____State_____Zip___
Birthdate_____ Ages at time of inventory _____    _____

|  | Yes | No |
|---|---|---|
| Do I have a spouse? | _____ | _____ |
| Do I live with my spouse? | _____ | _____ |
| Do I have living children? | _____ | _____ |
| Do I live in the same house as my children? | _____ | _____ |
| Do I live in the same city as my children? | _____ | _____ |
| Do I live in the same county as my children? | _____ | _____ |
| Do I live in the same state as my children? | _____ | _____ |
| Are my children in good health? | _____ | _____ |
| Are my parents living? | _____ | _____ |
| Are my spouse's parents living? | _____ | _____ |
| Do either live "on their own?" | _____ | _____ |
| Are my brothers or sisters living? | _____ | _____ |
| *Can my children expect an inheritance?* | _____ | _____ |

# FAMILY INVENTORY

Number of living children _____

|  | | |
|---|---|---|
| Age of child 1_____ married? | _____ | _____ |
| Age of child 2_____ married? | _____ | _____ |
| Age of child 3_____ married? | _____ | _____ |
| Age of child 4_____ married? | _____ | _____ |

| | | |
|---|---|---|
| Do they have children of their own? | _____ | _____ |
| Number of living grandchildren_____ | | |
| Are all my children employed? | _____ | _____ |
| Are all my children in good health? | _____ | _____ |
| Are my children's spouses in good health? | _____ | _____ |
| Would I want to live with my child(ren)? | _____ | _____ |
| Would I want to live with my parents? | _____ | _____ |
| Would I want to live with a brother or sister? | _____ | _____ |
| Would I want to live with an in-law? | _____ | _____ |

# LEGAL INVENTORY

Note: Nobody will have all of the items listed below. The point is to inventory what you do or don't have, and evaluate what is, or is not, beneficial to your own case. Questions denoted by an asterisk (*) are those which are important when considering long term care planning. By no means are we suggesting all of these items, only asking you to inventory them if you have them.

| | Yes | No |
|---|---|---|
| Do I have an updated will? * | _____ | _____ |
| Do I have a Durable Power of Attorney? * | _____ | _____ |
| Do I have "living will?" | _____ | _____ |
| Do I have any form of "Trust?" | _____ | _____ |
| Have I transferred assets to my children? * | _____ | _____ |
| Have I considered transferring assets? | _____ | _____ |
| Do I have an aversion to transferring assets? | _____ | _____ |
| Is qualification for Medicaid Eligibility the only *reason I would consider transferring assets?* | _____ | _____ |
| Do I (we) have an attorney ? * | _____ | _____ |

Readers should be aware that we do not offer or claim to offer legal advice. We do, however, discuss legal terminology which is available to any person, and which pertains to LTC insurance policies and asset preservation through currently available methods. We do recommend seeking legal counsel for legal matters.

# HEALTH INVENTORY

Note: Many times people delay thinking about asset transfer or purchase of LTC insurance because they are in great health. However, that is THE PROPER TIME to make the consideration. Why would a person wait until their health was affected to make decisions of an important nature?

How would I describe my health?
___Perfect ___Great ___Good ___Fair ___Poor

How would I describe my spouse's health?
___Perfect ___Great ___Good ___Fair ___Poor

|  | Yes | No |
|---|---|---|
| Do I have pre-existing conditions which would prevent me from obtaining an LTC policy? | ___ | ___ |
| Does my spouse have pre-existing conditions which would prevent him/ her from obtaining an LTC policy? | ___ | ___ |
| Do I think I will "live forever?" |  |  |
| Do I think I am "going to take it with me?" | ___ | ___ |
| Do I have a sound major medical program? | ___ | ___ |
| Do I have Medicare Part A and Part B | ___ | ___ |
| Does my spouse have Medicare Part A and B? | ___ | ___ |
| Do I have an adequate Medicare Supplement? | ___ | ___ |
| Does my spouse have a Medicare Supplement? | ___ | ___ |

Note: Doctors have been telling us for decades that the key to maintaining good health is related to diet and exercise. Remaining in good health and restoring poor health is an entirely personal matter. Good health is like the weather. When you feel good, its hard to remember what it's like to feel bad. When you feel terrible, it's hard to recall what good health felt like. So, maintenance of good health is a necessity, based on proper diet, nutrition, and use of medication

# PERSONAL ASSET INVENTORY

A complete inventory of **all of your assets** is of great importance when evaluating asset preservation, inheritance considerations, and Long Term Care Insurance. If your assets are even of a "modest" nature, you are a likely candidate for LTC insurance. Please take care to complete the inventory by including and combining all of your assets, whether you are tabulating them as a couple or as an individual. Remember, when your inventory is complete, that we're talking about a lot of money here—yours—and ways to keep it yours.

| ASSETS | VALUE | HELD JOINTLY? |
|---|---|---|
| 1) Principal Residence | $ _____ | _____ |
| 2) Personal effects, h'hold furnishings | _____ | _____ |
| 3) Jewelry, (wedding rings, etc.) | _____ | _____ |
| 4) Autos—RV's, boats, etc. | _____ | _____ |
| 5) Secondary Residences | _____ | _____ |
| 6) Marketable Securities—stocks | _____ | _____ |
| 7) Marketable Bonds | _____ | _____ |
| 8) Notes or money owed to you | _____ | _____ |
| 9) Checking Accounts | _____ | _____ |
| 10) Savings Accounts | _____ | _____ |
| 11) Certificates of Deposit | _____ | _____ |
| 12) Cash Value Life Insurance | _____ | _____ |
| 13) Annuities | _____ | _____ |
| 14) Final Expense Life Insurance | _____ | _____ |
| 15) Trust Funds in your name | _____ | _____ |
| 16) Agricultural Land | _____ | _____ |
| 17) Business Interests | _____ | _____ |
| 18) Agricultural or business equipment | _____ | _____ |
| 19) Agricultural or business inventory | _____ | _____ |
| 20) Fine arts, antiques, collections | _____ | _____ |
| 21) Other real estate or land | _____ | _____ |
| 22) Expected Inheritances | _____ | _____ |
| 23) Other | _____ | _____ |
| *TOTAL* | _____ | _____ |

# INCOME INVENTORY

|  |  | SINGLES OR SPOUSE 1 | SPOUSE 2 |
|---|---|---|---|
| Monthly income from: | Social Security | $ _____ | $ _____ |
|  | Retirement (PERS, Pensions, etc.) |  |  |
|  | Annuities | _____ | _____ |
|  | Life Insurance | _____ | _____ |
|  | Employment | _____ | _____ |
|  | Other | _____ | _____ |
|  | Total Monthly | $ _____ | $ _____ |
|  | Annual Total— (Multiply by 12) | $ _____ | $ _____ |
| Annual income from: (include taxable and non taxable) | IRA's | $ _____ | $ _____ |
|  | Investments (CD's, Stocks, Bonds, etc.) | _____ | _____ |
|  | Rentals | _____ | _____ |
|  | Sale of Business | _____ | _____ |
|  | Other | _____ | _____ |
|  | Total Annual | $ _____ | $ _____ |
|  | Total Yearly Income | $ _____ | $ _____ |

# INSURANCE INVENTORY

For our purposes, Property and Casualty (Homeowners, Auto, etc.) insurance policies need not be inventoried here.  We are concerned with Health, Life, and Final Expense Plans and more particularly, Long Term Care, Short Term Care, Home Health Care and Medicare Supplement Insurance.

|  | Yes | No |
|---|---|---|
| Do I/we have a Long Term Care Policy? | _____ | _____ |
| Does the policy cover these basic questions: | | |
| 1) Does it pay three levels of care equally? | _____ | _____ |
| 2) Is it a "pool of money" policy? | _____ | _____ |
| 3) Are the "elimination periods" satisfactory? | _____ | _____ |
| 4) Is the benefit level at least $120 per day? | _____ | _____ |
| 5) Is the benefit period satisfactory? | _____ | _____ |
| 6) What was the issue age? | _____ | _____ |
| 7) Does it include an inflation rider? | _____ | _____ |
| 8) Does it contain "pre-existing conditions?" | _____ | _____ |
| 9) What are the "triggers" for benefits? | _____ | _____ |
| 10) Is a hospital stay required? | _____ | _____ |
| 11) Is it federally Tax Qualified or Non-Q? | _____ | _____ |
| 12) Is there a Home Health Care provision? | _____ | _____ |
| 13) Does it allow "Alternate forms of Care?" | _____ | _____ |
| 14) Does it include "Waiver of Premium?" | _____ | _____ |
| 15) Does it include "Restoration of Benefits?" | _____ | _____ |
| 16) How does it treat Assisted Living? | _____ | _____ |
| 17) Is the "elimination period" cumulative? | _____ | _____ |
| 18) Can a family member give home care? | _____ | _____ |
| | | |
| Do I/we have a Short Term Care Policy? | _____ | _____ |
| Do I/we have a Home Health Care Policy? | _____ | _____ |
| Do I/we have a Home Health Care Rider? | _____ | _____ |
| Do I/we have a Major Medical Policy (under 65)? | _____ | _____ |
| Do I/we have Medicare Part A and Part B? | _____ | _____ |
| Do I/we have a Medicare Supplement Policy? | _____ | _____ |
| *Do I/we have Final Expense Life Insurance?* | _____ | _____ |

# CHAPTER 21

# THE CASE FOR SHORT TERM CARE

Let's assume that you have visited the Personal Inventory section of this book, compiled your assets, and you found that they totaled less than $80,000 for a married couple or $40,000 for a single person. (There is no "magic" number, I only use these figures to illustrate the case for Short Term Care.)

1) You have found that your assets would not warrant purchase of a Long Term Care policy.

2) You are living on a "fixed income," which you do not see increasing greatly over the rest of your lifetime.

3) You do not expect a large inheritance or "windfall," which would create the need for a LTC policy.

4) You wish to protect what assets you do have, maintain as much of your independence as possible, and not have to depend on your family, for as long as possible.

## WITH THOSE THOUGHTS IN MIND, LET US BEGIN!

**Q 1— "Our assets-countable totaled $58,699. They are held mostly in Bank Certificates of Deposit, some savings, and some Cash Value Life Insurance. Would Long Term Care Insurance seem advisable? We rent, and have one "older" automobile. We are ages 72 and 70."**

A 1— Probably not. With LTC premiums (depending on the combination of coverages) approaching $1,500 to $2,000 apiece per year, you *do not have the base of assets* which requires $100,000+ in asset preservation protection. However, you are *interested in protecting what you have against some nursing home needs.*

**Q 2— "How can we do that?"**

A 2— Short term nursing home policies *can protect you for a shorter period of time, a period running from 80 days to 365 days, and are considerably cheaper (obviously) than Long Term Care.* Some of the insurance industry has recognized this need for shorter term protection, and more companies will "come on board" as this need is publicized.

**Q 3—** **"What are my chances of "getting by" with a Short Term policy?  My recent reading says that a large number of people will need Nursing Home care or at least Home/Home Health Care."**

**A 3—** That's true, the numbers are astonishing, but they also need to be evaluated a little bit.  For instance, "The National Nursing Home Survey" Series 13, No 97, completed by the US Dept. of Health and Human Services, says that ***over 50% of all nursing home patients stay for three months or less.  That study also says that 63% of patients stay in the nursing home six months or less.  So, if it's true that nearly two-thirds of nursing home stays are six months or less,*** (and nobody can determine ahead of time just who that two-thirds will be) ***it makes sense that a short term nursing home policy could suffice.***  Just as in all insurance purchasing, nobody can determine ahead of time whose needs will be different, but this important study says that 63% of the people will not need an LTCI policy, but could use at least six months of protection.

**Q 4—** **"So, you're saying that a Short Term Policy of 80 days, 180 days, nine months, or a year** *may by sufficient* **to protect our $58,699?"**

**A 4—** I'm saying that the US Dept of Health and Human Service ***study seems to bear this out***.  Additional numbers in that study indicate that an another 11% stay from 6 to 12 months.  Now, if you add that up, it comes out to 74%.  The problem is that for those in need of long term care, the stays above six months have an average of about another two and a half years according to other studies.  So, while we are somewhat involved in uncharted waters, a six-month to one-year policy could seem to be the answer to about three-fourths of the people's needs.  Remember, that at a $120 per day charge, even a six-month stay amounts to $21,000.  This would have an impact on your life's "nest egg," should either of you need even a short nursing home stay. ***The premium for a short term policy is much more affordable and is easier to qualify for.***

**Q 5—** **"I am single and my asset total (excluding exempt assets) amounted to $21,400.  Why couldn't I just spend these assets to pay for my Nursing Home care and then just qualify for Medicaid?"**

**A 5—** ***You can***.  Nothing wrong with that, ***but most people would prefer to protect what they can, while they can***.  My guess is that your $21,400 is as important to you as $200,000 would be to a person who has $200,000.  There really seems to be no difference.  Bankers tell me that for every 1,000 accounts in the bank, at least five are spending their own money to pay for Nursing Home costs.  But even more importantly, my banker tells me that no matter what amount of money people retire with, ***they don't want that amount to go DOWN.  They want the amount to at least stay even, and most work at growing it as much as they can.***

**Q 6—** "As you assumed at the beginning, we are living on a fixed income and we cannot afford Long Term Care Insurance. Why would Short Term Nursing Home Insurance do a better job?"

**A 6—** *It won't do a better job, but will do a more affordable job.* With a smaller asset base, a fixed income, and government figures which point out that 63% of the people can "get by" with a six month policy, and 74% will need only one year of nursing home care, all the elements add up to a *limited amount that can be spent on premium. Short term policies (depending on the term selected) can run from one-third to one-half the premium of Long Term Care. For you, this may make economic sense.*

**Q 7—** What do you mean by "economic sense"?

**A 7—** Quite simply, *if the dollars aren't there, and if the need is not there, you should not feel that you need protection beyond your means.* It is far *more important to be able to "put beans on the table", and pay your normal living expenses such as medicine, transportation, utilities, Medicare, etc., than to spend necessary personal moneys for Long Term Care policies. ABOVE ALL, YOU SHOULD NOT BE MADE TO FEEL THE NEED TO PURCHASE BEYOND YOUR MEANS BY ANY INSURANCE AGENT, RELATIVE, OR NEIGHBOR who is not aware of your personal status.*

**Q 8—** "My Medicare Supplement salesman told me that I didn't need to worry about the first 100 days of Nursing Home Care because between Medicare and his policy the first 100 days would be covered!

**A 8—** Oh, Oh!!! Oh, Oh!!! Naughty, Naughty, Naughty!!!

*BE REALLY CAREFUL WITH THAT INTERPRETATION.* It is a shame that so many people have been lead to believe this "quasi", not even "semi" truthful statement. The statement is *SOMEWHAT true, BUT ONLY FOR SKILLED CARE!!!* I cannot repeat this enough, but unfortunately, far too many people are left with a false sense of security for a variety of reasons.

1) The insurance agent does not properly make a point of saying that *Medicare pays for the first 20 days of* SKILLED care, and skilled care ONLY.

2) The agent does not properly make a point of saying that days *21-100 of SKILLED CARE HAVE A $109.50 PER DAY DEDUCTIBLE, in 2004.* In other words, if for some *MEDICALLY NECESSARY reason* (this excludes intermediate or custodial care) you need *SKILLED* CARE, the policy (in some cases, and then, only with certain "standardized" forms) will pay the $109.50 PER DAY deductible. THIS IS A VITALLY IMPORTANT POINT if retirees are to understand the true and proper way this coverage is interpreted.

3) The client simply **refused to hear "the fine print" and just** assumed enough to be dangerously "comfortable." "My agent (or some mail order outfit) will take care of me," seems to be the most blatant part of this misunderstanding.

4) The Federal Government through Medicare plays an important role in this misunderstanding because of the way it prints its "standardized plan" presentations. The "Guide to Health Insurance for People with Medicare" and the illustrations which companies must follow refer to this coverage as... "Medicare pays **all but** $109.50 per day."

Well, big deal! If the cost is $115.00 per day, Medicare pays $5.50! The next column says "You Pay (or your policy pays) **Up to $109.50 per day"** BUT **REMEMBER, ONLY FOR SKILLED CARE**. The Guide and illustrations SHOULD say what the benefit is—**a $109.50 per day DEDUCTIBLE!** Only one Med Supp policy that I know of, sold before 1993, has 100 days of Nursing Home coverage at all levels of care.

**Q 9— What does the phrase "RCR", mean?**

A 9— "RCR"—A new acronym—get used to using it. What are we talking about? Simply stated—**Recovery, Convalescence, and Rehabilitation!** If, according to the Department of Health and Human Services, 74% of Nursing Home stays are for less than one year, we should be talking about the reasons MOST people go to the nursing home—recovery, convalescence, and rehabilitation!!!

With all the emphasis for the last half dozen years being on Long Term Care, which is used to prevent asset erosion, then we have ignored the reason that MOST people go to nursing homes—again, recovery, convalescence, and rehabilitation.

But no longer! **Short Term Care, or by any other name such as Nursing Home Insurance, Nursing Facility Insurance, Convalescent Care, or whatever, we now have products which appeal to many potential Senior clients.**

If potential clients do not have the need for asset protection, or cannot qualify for LTCI, then we have overlooked the needs of the majority of America's seniors—that being Short Term Care. Let's take a look at why "RCR" has to have a place in our thinking, according to one company.

**"For the past few years, people have really become aware of the expense connected with confinement to nursing home facilities. The cost of the average nursing facility can wipe out the bulk of most retiree's saving in just ninety to one hundred and eighty days."**

REMEMBER, RECOVERY, CONVALESCENCE, AND REHABILITATION ARE THE KEY TO **MOST SHORT TERM NURSING HOME PATIENT STAYS**. And, also remember, **the cost is far less, and the underwriting, is much easier.**

# CHAPTER 22

# THE CASE FOR HOME CARE/COMMUNITY CARE AND HOME HEALTH CARE

Let us assume that you have studied the issue of Long Term Care and how it would relate to your personal needs. Having dealt with retired people for several years on this issue, two remarks have continually been brought to my attention.

### 1) "I'M NEVER GOING TO A NURSING HOME!!!", AND

### 2) "I'D RATHER STAY AT HOME FOR MY CARE!!!"

Both statements are commonplace, and with the exception of those who have no choice, I would like to remind my readers that 100% of the people in nursing homes were "never going to a nursing home". **Fortunately, there are alternatives!** Let's talk about the alternatives. But I caution you, keep in mind "there is no such thing as a free lunch." While Home Health Care, Home Care, and Community Care are alternatives—**on a twenty-four hour basis they are MORE costly than a nursing home, but on an eight or six hour basis they can be decidedly LESS than nursing home costs. Therefore, your premium should be less.**

Fortunately, again, most people do not require twenty-four hour care, they **simply need help with SOME health care and/or the activities of daily living—eating, bathing, dressing, continence, toileting, and maybe mobility.**

Another statement which seems to be commonplace is a very genuine issue. "ALL THIS TERMINOLOGY AND ALL THESE DEFINITIONS ARE TOO CONFUSING TO ME."

A VERY VALID ITEM. SO LET'S USE THAT AS A STARTING POINT.

**Q 1— What is the difference between Home Health Care, Home Care and Community Care?**

**A 1—** Simply stated, **HOME HEALTH CARE is care which requires the services of a LICENSED PROFESSIONAL,** such as a Doctor, Registered Nurse, or Physical Therapist. You can **regard Home Health Care as PROFESSIONAL CARE.**

However, the certification of the person providing care does not seem to be the point of confusion. The confusing part comes when **people want to know WHO PAYS for the professional care.**

First of all, you should be aware that if you are on MEDICARE, **Medicare will pay for SOME Home HEALTH Care. However, there are restrictions.** So to clear up the confusion of what Medicare WILL PAY for home health care, let's quote directly from the "Guide to Health Insurance for People with Medicare."

"Home Health Care" -- "Medicare pays the FULL cost of MEDICALLY NECESSARY home health visits by a *MEDICARE-APPROVED HOME HEALTH AGENCY*. A home health agency is a public or private agency that provides *SKILLED NURSING CARE, physical therapy, speech therapy and other therapeutic services in the patient's home.* These services are usually provided on a periodic basis by a visiting nurse and/or home health aide."

"To QUALIFY for coverage, you *HAVE TO NEED INTERMITTENT SKILLED NURSING CARE,* physical therapy, or speech therapy, *BE CONFINED TO YOUR HOME, and BE UNDER A PHYSICIAN'S CARE,* you do not have to pay a deductible or coinsurance (except for durable medical equipment), and *no prior hospitalization is required for home health care benefits.* Coverage is also provided for a portion of the cost of wheelchairs, hospital beds and other durable medical equipment (DME) *provided under A PLAN-OF-CARE SET UP AND PERIODICALLY REVIEWED BY A PHYSICIAN."*

However, there are *"Gaps in Home Health Coverage" of Medicare.* **YOU PAY:**
1) For *FULL-TIME NURSING CARE.*
2) For *Meals delivered to your home and for drugs*.
3) *Twenty percent of the Medicare-approved amount for durable medical equipment,* plus charges in excess of the approved amount on unassigned claims.
4) For HOMEMAKER SERVICES *that are primarily to* ASSIST YOU IN MEETING PERSONAL CARE OR HOUSEKEEPING NEEDS."

Now, all this seems and sounds simple enough, but there are strict definitions of these items, which must be adhered to. People on Medicare and their families should be thankful that SOME home HEALTH care is paid for by Medicare, but *keep in mind that it MUST be HEALTH related, and that most cases of need for nursing home care or transferring that need to the person's residence (home care) do not relate to HEALTH needs.*

So that is where *HOME CARE* comes in. Simple home care is really a case of a person hired through a home care agency to provide care of a PERSONAL nature. Remember when we said that HOME HEALTH Care should be considered PROFESSIONAL CARE? Well, now with HOME Care, we see *a form of care, which is provided by a caregiver for PERSONAL NEEDS.*

These needs are the same needs that we call *CUSTODIAL* care in a Nursing Home. In other words, the needs of a person for help in accomplishing what we call *Activities of Daily Living, or ADL's*. They are more commonly known as the need for help with *dressing, bathing, eating, continence (being able to hold the bladder or bowels), toileting, and transferring (mobility, or being able to get into, or out of, a bed or a chair).*

Now, if we recognize that at any one time, 95% of the people in a Nursing Home are there for Custodial Care, (help with personal care, rather than medical care) then we can assume somewhat the same proportion stay at home for "in home" Custodial care rather than for medical reasons. That is where Home (Personal) Care is utilized. *Personal Care means providing help with ADL's.*

*COMMUNITY CARE OR COMMUNITY BASED CARE is the same as Home Care,* with the exception that it can be given in an Assisted Living Facility, an Adult Day Care Facility, your home, the home of a friend or relative, a community based residential facility, a hospice care provider, or a Christian Science home health care provider. *It can be given by a personal care assistant, not a professional care provider.*

To summarize:
      HOME HEALTH CARE = PROFESSIONAL CARE.
      HOME CARE AND COMMUNITY CARE = PERSONAL
         CARE.
*HHC Policies will cover both personal and professional care.*

**Q 2— So, it looks like Home Health Care from Medicare is very limited. Are the policies for Home and Community care offered by insurance companies more liberal in their benefits?**

A 2— Yes. That is the reason for Home and Community Care policies. In addition to providing coverage for ADL's, the policies cover Medically necessary care, which wouldn't be covered by the limits of Medicare Home Health. For instance, most policies will cover *BOTH PROFESSIONAL AND PERSONAL care, as well as Alzheimer's, Parkinson's and other cognitive losses.*

**Q 3— Why has this Home Health Care and Home Care thing become such a** big item in the last few years?

A 3— Very simply, hospitals are releasing patients much earlier than they were previous to 1983. In 1983, Medicare changed the way it paid for patient hospital stays. Payments to hospitals are now made on a "Prospective Payment System" through the Use of Diagnostic Related Groups, or DRG's. Since this method of hospital payment came into being, patients are being released "quicker and sicker" (This phrase was coined by the Mayo Clinic in its study of post-1983 hospital stays.) Under the DRG system, hospitals are only paid by Medicare for a fixed number of hospital days for a particular diagnosis and treatment. This gives hospitals an incentive to move patients out once they reach this arbitrary number of days' stay, regardless of the individual patient's actual condition or need for continuing care. If acute care (hospital care) is absolutely not needed, the dismissal date may be even sooner.

Not only is home health care hard to come by under Medicare, but after the Balanced Budget Act of 1997, it is even harder for Home Health agencies to deliver. The new payment system, called the Interim Payments System (IPS) capped the amounts that Medicare would pay Home Health agencies. In reality, the fraud and corruption that was disclosed in 1996 studies indicated that somewhere around $2.3 billion of Medicare paid Home Health care had been fraudulently overpaid. Part of the solution was to cap payments to the agencies, through IPS, much like the Prospective Payment System (DRG's), of payments to hospitals. Then, beginning in 1999, Medicare would actually go to a PPS system. This looks simple enough, except that legitimate Home Health agencies couldn't afford to compete with the fraud of corrupt agencies while their real efforts in the area of expensive home health delivery were capped. **This resulted in restricting abilities to take on new cases, and the dumping of existing expensive cases, under Medicare rules..** The system will right itself eventually, but again, the agencies who play by the rules paid the price for those who don't.

**Q 4— Well, then, where do Medicare patients go to recover ?**

A 4— You have a choice. The **convalescent care facility and the patient's home have become the recovery centers for most people. Also, so have children's homes, relative's homes, and friend's homes. According to studies, most people would rather receive "at home" care** than a long term nursing home stay.

**Q 5— This DRG system is unsettling. Who pays for the home care?**

A 5— Essentially, **unless you qualify for twenty days of Skilled Care in a Nursing Home after a three-day hospital stay, YOU DO.** Or, you look at the possibilities of qualifying for a **Home/Community Care insurance policy, which would pay for medical, personal, AND cognitive care needs.**

**Q 6— I have heard that providing care for a loved one (spouse, father, mother, grandparent) within the home, is not an easy a task as it may seem at first. What do you say about that?**

A 6— Literally thousands of articles have been written in the last few years **about people wanting to receive care in their own homes.** This is admirable, and when a family member or friend is expected to provide the care, it seems to work, but for a short time only. **Being able to solve the problem through a Home Care agency with both professional and personal care paid for by an insurance company is the very best possible solution.** Thus, a **Home Care/Community Care/Home Health Care Insurance policy is the product of choice** for those who can't afford, or don't want a Comprehensive Long Term Care Insurance policy, that would also cover them in an assisted living facility, or in a nursing home.

# CHAPTER 23

# THE CASE FOR GROUP LONG TERM CARE INSURANCE

There is no magic formula for purchasing Long Term Care Insurance. But *there are some real advantages to being employed and working for an employer who offers Group LTCI as part of its benefit package.* The surprising thing is that even with all the different variations of group LTCI, and tax advantages now available to both the employer and employee, very few of the nation's employers have embraced the concept. *But, that picture is rapidly changing. Very rapidly.*

For instance, by the end of 2002, *only 5,000 employers* had actually made some variation of group LTCI, available to employees. Although there are several ways group LTCI can be accomplished, we can understand that the concept had not passed beyond its' infancy by the 21st Century. But insurers have began to offer important reasons as to why workers, *should at least have access to some type of group program,* and the idea is taking on meaningful significance. A LIMRA study presented in July of 2003, indicated that *an estimated 300,000 employers* were considering adding group LTCI to their benefits package, at least as a voluntary benefit program. What's a *"voluntary benefit"?* To explain, let's take the group LTCI effort from it's ultimate—that of true group insurance, on through the variety of group offerings, including voluntary benefits.

*1) TRUE GROUP*—The concept of true group insurance is decades old, and quite well entrenched in American employer-employee relations. The background has traditionally seen true group health insurance for employees, followed by less utilized group life and disability insurance. The key here is twofold. Number one is that the *employer will pay all, a large part of, or at least some part of,* the premium—the employer is the policyholder—the employees are certificate holders of the plan—and all employees have coverage. Understandably, *premium payments* for true group health insurance have to be considered a part of the employer's bottom line, and the ability or inability to stay in business. Number two is that, with a true group situation, *underwriting of all applicants (certificate holders) will likely have a guaranteed issue,* or access to guaranteed issue, with the right to "option out" of the program, for whatever reason.

The same is true of true group LTCI, all of the conditions described above are apropos to true group LTCI. However, with LTCI, the first key element listed above may be rather hard to accomplish—that of getting the employer to contribute all, or a large part of, the premium. Companies, as well as governmental units, must watch their budgets and be totally secure, in making a decision that will affect their ability to do business down the road. For that reason, most employers have not chosen to embrace the true group LTCI concept. A similar hurdle is found in the number of employees that the company finds is necessary to guarantee issue to employees, without regard to underwriting. In most cases, the company will require an enrollment of fifty employees, with some allowing as few as twenty. This requirement *imposes a difficulty for the small employer, and resulted in a new approach—that of Voluntary Group LTCI.*

*2) VOLUNTARY GROUP*—Voluntary group insurance is *one of America's finest health insurance innovations.* In a voluntary group situation, the company or governmental unit *simply makes the product, in this case LTCI, available to the employee.* The employer can, but does not have to, participate in any percentage of premium payment. The employer simply *establishes the voluntary group plan with the LTCI company, and allows the employee to choose their own plan from the company.* Three factors remain however, which distinguish the plan from a true group policy. The *employee will normally enjoy at least a 10% premium discount,* and can have a variety of ways to pay their premiums—either through payroll deduction, automatic personal check withdrawal, or on a semi-annual, or annual basis. *Section 125 Cafeteria plans are not currently allowable,* but legislation has been introduced in Congress, which hopefully will allow such. So, even though the employer does not participate in the premiums, at least *the employee can enjoy the benefits of the premium discount, as a Voluntary Group benefit.*

The second factor is that companies with *incredibly low participation requirements* can be found. Some will require that at least *three employees* apply for the group discount to be effective, but I have seen *as few as one employee* being sufficient.

The third factor is understandable, with the *requirement that full underwriting of all applicants will be necessary.* Makes sense—the *advantages of guaranteed issue, or even simplified issue, within a large group disappear, but basic premium discounts still apply.* Another feature, for those who choose to utilize a voluntary group program, is that the applicant *can include their spouse,* thereby receiving a spousal discount as well. The LTCI company *may also extend the voluntary group features to at least one preceding generation (parents) above the policyholder, and in some cases two, including in-laws (parents of either spouse) and one generation below the employee—children, in other words. Again, full underwriting will be required of all applicants.*

*3) ASSOCIATION GROUP*—Association group LTCI *operates similarly to the Voluntary Group plan described above.* In this case however, the plan may be offered through an *association of employers, independent contractors, association members, or any combination thereof.* It makes *no difference how many association members there are, and whether they are local, state, or national.* One important thing to remember, however, is that all states will have group insurance laws in general, and LTCI group insurance in particular, so *each states' laws will have to be satisfied with the program,* if the association functions in more than one state.

As you can see, voluntary group and association group LTCI, offers great opportunities for employers and employees alike, and the concept is fast on it's way to becoming a very large part of the American employee benefit scene. Studies conducted in 2002-03 indicated that *American workers like this option* as a part of the solution to obtaining LTCI. As an employee, it will be of value to you to seek out your employer and find if this benefit is available, or if it is under consideration. Human resources, or personnel, will have the information for you. *Ask—and encourage—if it is not yet available.*

# CHAPTER 24

# THE GENERAL DEFINITIONS OF LONG TERM CARE

Every industry has definitions of terms, which must be understood by the people working in that industry. The Long Term Care, Home Health Care, and Nursing Home industries, and insurance products designed to pay benefits for the needs of those who utilize care are no different. Below are the most common terms needed to in order to discuss Long Term Care and Long Term Care Insurance intelligently. THEY ARE NOT WEBSTER DEFINITIONS. They are terms which you will find valuable to your understanding of Long Term Care and the various fields related to LTC Insurance. The first six pages of definitions are not in alphabetical order, but are listed as the most common and most consistently used nomenclature in both the LTC and LTCI arena. They are the BASIC FOUNDATIONS, to achieving an understanding of LTC. Let us begin.

LONG TERM CARE— There are definitions and there are definitions. Every entity in the Long Term Care field seems to have a different way of describing just what "long term care" is, but let's just settle on a simple understanding which will cover the issue. Most people in good health take for granted that what they do during the course of a day is pretty simple to do. The basic fundamental life skills of walking, bathing, eating, sleeping and toileting "come natural" for them.

Those functions are seen as "normal." But, in an instant, or even over a period of time, "normal" can change, and what once seemed simple becomes difficult. A stroke, heart attack, accident, a lingering cancer, or simply old age, can turn what were once simple daily routines into difficult hurdles. The physical and mental requirements for "normal" activities may now require—and this is the key word—CARE. Somebody else's help. Another word which needs to be introduced is the word "chronic," which relates to having had an ailment for a long time, or recurring, such as a disease, including perpetual and constant need for help. Federal tax qualified policies include the term "chronically ill individual," which sets them apart from the "acute" care a hospital may administer. A few days of hospital care does not demonstrate what happens to the individual after "the event." Hospital care may not even be needed for certain lingering diseases, or for "aging." So what we are talking about here is the care, or assistance and help, of another person to complete daily routines known as "activities of daily living." Thus, the clinical definition of Long Term Care is: *care given to an individual who can no longer independently complete daily regimens, either because of physical or mental limitations, and requires the help of others to complete "normal" activities, or to keep them from injuring themselves.*

*To be more specific, the care would revolve around the need for assistance with up to seven "Activities of Daily Living"—eating, bathing, dressing, toileting and continence, transferring (moving around), and in some jurisdictions— the word "ambulating." The care would also address mental conditions, or what are known as cognitive impairments—those disabilities brought on by certain diseases or conditions known as Alzheimer's and Parkinson's diseases. In some LTC insurance policies, even the term "medical necessity" will qualify the policyholder to receive Long Term Care benefits.* In short, then, Long Term Care means requiring assistance (care) from someone else to complete normal functions due to the physical or mental inability of the individual to accomplish living skills on their own.

LONG TERM— Again, several entities treat the term "long term" differently. We will use the commonly accepted definition of 90 days or longer. Federal Tax Qualified LTC policies use the 90-day certification as qualification for Long Term Care benefit eligibility. Do not confuse with insurance industry definitions (and in some state jurisdictions) of one year or longer. Some insurance companies offer "Short Term Care" policies of 80 days, 90 days, 180 days and 360 days, thus reserving the "Long Term" definition for periods of no less than 365 days.

SPENDDOWN— A down-to-earth, fact-of-life term, which, indicates what people must do with their assets to qualify for Medicaid (a state administered program, called MediCal in California) Nursing Home assistance. In other words, the county Medicaid technician (ask for the county Dept. of Human Services) will determine if an applicant has "spentdown" his or her assets to the "Resource Limitations" allowed by the county in order to be eligible for Medicaid Nursing Home assistance. Current limits will be around $2,000 per person for a single person, and nearly $80,000 for a married couple. Some assets in addition to the $2,000 will be allowed depending on the marital status of the applicant.

In short, for a single person, Resources and Assets (cash, savings accounts, checking accounts, certificates of deposit, stocks, bonds, real estate, life insurance cash values (excluding burial policies), business or land ownership, etc.,) cannot exceed a value of $2,000 for a single person to be eligible for Medicaid nursing home assistance. These assets MUST be "spentdown" to become eligible. In other words, the patient must pay his or her own nursing home bills until he or she has "spent down" his or her eligible assets to the minimum limits to be eligible to qualify for Medicaid assistance. (*Please remember that this a nationwide general definition and does not relate to the Partnership Programs in the states of California, New York, Connecticut and Indiana.*) This is not a term invented by the insurance industry to encourage people to buy LTC policies, it is generally accepted Medicaid qualification terminology and is very real.

For married people (in which one of the spouses has need of Medicaid nursing home assistance), the Spousal Impoverishment Act (a part of the Social Security Act of 1989) allowed the remaining at-home spouse to retain assets of a much larger amount. For instance, the remaining at-home spouse could retain the residence, a car, and various other personal properties for that spouse's use. Check with the county for these limitations since they vary from time-to-time and place-to-place. In most cases, this amount is currently around $80,000. Also be alerted that Medicaid has in "Income Test" for qualification. Again, contact the state or county Department of Health and Human Services to obtain information in any particular state. Remember when older people were obtaining divorces to avoid the "impoverishment" qualifications of resource limitations? Well, solving that dilemma was the reason for the Spousal Impoverishment Act.

IMPOVERISHMENT -A term applied by Medicaid wherein people MUST "spenddown" their assets in order to qualify for Medicaid nursing home assistance. This is REAL. Remember that Medicaid is a Welfare program, therefore impoverishment is a criteria. Again, it is not a term invented by insurance people to get prospects to buy the LTC product.

LEVELS OF CARE— There are three which apply to Nursing Home care.

SKILLED-Simply stated, skilled care is the care a person receives when he or she is dismissed from a hospital (acute care) and admitted to a Nursing Home, is still under the supervision of a physician, care is provided twenty-four hours a day, and the facility has a transfer arrangement with a hospital or medical center. This is the highest degree of medical care in a nursing home. The nursing home must be licensed and certified by the state as a Skilled Nursing Facility and approved by Medicare. Physical therapy and speech therapy are common examples of skilled care.

INTERMEDIATE- The next level of care. Intermediate care means the patient is still in the nursing home, still under the care of a physician, but still needs medical care which can be administered by a Registered Nurse (usually for the purpose of dispensing prescription drugs.) This refers to care that may, but does not necessarily need to be, delivered by a skilled professional. This level of care is seldom actually used as classified.

CUSTODIAL- The final level of care, commonly described as waiting to recover and return home, or just "living in the nursing home." This is the most common level of care to which we refer when we talk of long term care. See the definition for ADL's, which describes the basic human needs such as eating, bathing, ambulating, transferring (moving about), toileting and continence. which can be provided by nursing home personnel or personal home care aids without professional medical skills. Most cognitive care (Alzheimer's, Parkinson's) needs also come under this classification.

TRANSFER (PERIOD) RULE- The amount of time which must elapse before an applicant for Medicaid nursing home assistance can be eligible. In other words, a simple transfer of assets is an alternative to "spenddown," but MUST BE COMPLETED (BY PROOF) outside of a 36-month (3 year) period, or 60 month (5 year) period if transferring to an Irrevocable trust, before becoming eligible. DO NOT attempt do-it-yourself techniques in this transfer process. That is the realm of attorneys, family members and the state department of Health and Human Services. The alternate objective is to point out the need for LTC policies. Individuals should seek legal help regarding transfer techniques, but should be aware that LTC insurance can provide financial relief for several years, during (and even beyond) the transfer period. DO NOT confuse this 3-year rule with Estate Transfer rules in life insurance cases. They are different. *(Again, you will find these rules and definitions will change for those who participate in the various state Partnership Programs.)*

NURSING HOME— A place where people receive any of the three levels of Nursing Home Care and which is Licensed by the State as a Licensed and Certified Long Term Care Facility. Other names, in popular terminology, may include, "Extended Care Facility," "Swing Unit," "After Care Facility" and usually refer to Skilled or Intermediate Care. Other names may include "Rest Home," "Old Folks Home," "Home for the Aged" or other popular conceptions, but nevertheless, the facility must be licensed by the state as a "Skilled Care Facility." Do not confuse with RETIREMENT HOMES or RETIREMENT COMMUNITY, wherein the resident arrives "under his or her own power" for a more satisfying leisure care lifestyle. Some retirement homes will be licensed as "Skilled Care Facilities" and can have a "Facility" which is licensed to dispense "Skilled or Intermediate" Care, but that unit is reserved for residents who become in need of such care as existing residents of the Retirement Home. Many of them will also have "Assisted Living Units" wherein the resident will be transferred from the "retirement" side of the facility to an "assisted living" unit wherin they can recieve help with the "Activities of Daily Living" described further down. Call the State Licensing and Certification Bureau in your state if you are in question as to the licensing status of a facility.

ASSISTED LIVING FACILITY— A non-medical institution (or unit) providing room, board, laundry, some forms of personal care, help with Activities of Daily Living, and usually offering recreational and social services. Licensed by state departments of social services, these facilities exist under several names including domiciliary care facility, sheltered homes, board and care, community-based residential facility, etc.

HOME HEALTH CARE— Simply stated, Home Health Care is care which requires the services of a LICENSED PROFESSIONAL, such as a Doctor, Registered Nurse, or Physical Therapist. Such care (health services) can be given in the patient's home or an alternative living facility, such as an assisted living facility, or the home of a relative, or a hospice center. In short, you can regard Home Health Care as Professional Care. Please remember that Medicare will pay for some Home Health Care, but the requirements are very strict, and qualification is becoming more difficult. Also, many instances of home health care can be ineligible, as outlined in the Guide to Health Insurance for People with Medicare.

HOME CARE— Also known as Community Care or Community Based Care, Home Care differs from Home *Health* Care in that Home Care can be provided by a non-professional (trained and certified by a Home Health Care agency) to provide basic PERSONAL CARE needs. These would be of the same nature as Custodial Care in a Nursing Home, i.e. help with Activities of Daily Living, such as dressing, bathing, feeding, continence, toileting and transferring. The services again, can be provided in the client's home, the home of a friend or relative, an assisted living facility, Adult Day Care, community based residential facility, a hospice care provider, or a Christian Science

Home. To summarize, Home Health Care equals Professional care and Home Care/ Community Care equals Personal Care. When you take into account that most people would rather receive "at home" care, than be admitted to a Nursing Home, these definitions become important, since current Home Health Care/Home Care policies will pay for coverage under either definition.

BENEFIT TRIGGERS— Benefit triggers are conditions which allow a policy-holder to begin receiving the benefits of an LTC policy. They are the need for assistance (care) with: 1) Activities of Daily Living, 2) Cognitive Impairment, and 3) Possibly Medical Necessity.

ACTIVITIES OF DAILY LIVING-Activities of daily living are those basic functions a person performs for himself or herself each day. Depending on which company's policy you are considering, they will number five, six, or seven, which include bathing, dressing, toileting, transferring, ambulating, continence and eating. If any one or two of these activities require stand-by assistance to accomplish, the client is considered disabled and those conditions are considered to "trigger" the need for a Nursing Home admission, or a personal Home Care aid. If you have seen a policy or have literature from a company which requires three ADL condition satisfactions, divest yourself of that company and replace the policy if possible. Three requirements are totally out-of-line with today's products and quite possibly illegal in most jurisdictions. ADL's then, simply can be referred to as "basic human functions" necessary for independent living.

BATHING- The ability to wash all parts of yourself, whether completed in a tub, shower, sponge bath, or basin, getting into or out of such accommo- dations, including soaping, rinsing and drying.

TOILETING- The ability to travel to and from the toilet, and on and off the toilet, or use of a bedpan or urinal, with a reasonable level of personal hygiene and clothing care.

CONTINENCE- The ability to voluntarily control bowel and bladder functions with consideration given to personal hygiene, and perhaps the need for using diapers or disposable pads.

DRESSING- The ability to put on and take off all garments and medically necessary braces or artificial limbs and fasten and unfasten such.

TRANSFERRING- The ability to move in and out of a chair, wheelchair, or bed, to be able to come to a standing position, and move from place to place in the residence. Moving about.

FEEDING (EATING)- The ability to get nourishment into the body regardless of who prepared it or made it available. Includes ability to use utensils.

AMBULATING—Walking about, or moving inside or outside a residence.

*(Not included as an ADL in Federally Tax Qualified LTC policies. Also* not included as an ADL in California)

MEDICAL NECESSITY- Wherein a medical condition is the "trigger" for qualifying for Nursing Home benefits. It is usually not of long duration, and thankfully no longer the lone rule, but nevertheless a possible trigger. Is not a "trigger" for Federally Tax Qualified Long Term Care Insurance policy benefits, but still considered a "trigger" for Non-Tax Qualified LTC benefits.

COGNITIVE IMPAIRMENT— Another form of "trigger" for eligibility for Nursing Home Benefits, accepted by the industry, but not included as Medically necessary or considered in the list of ADLs. Cognitive Impairment is regarded as a deterioration or loss in intellectual capabilities which requires continual supervision or prompting. Such examples would be loss of short or long term memory, orientation as to person, place and time, and the ability to reason. These conditions are normally brought on by such debilities as Alzheimer's, Parkinson's, Senile Dementia, and other mental conditions of a demonstrable organic nature.

LOOKBACK PERIOD- The "lookback period" is the period of time in which Medicaid is allowed to "look back" at an applicant's assets and see if he or she qualifies for Medicaid assistance. The previous rule had been 2 1/2 years. The rule effective with OBRA '93 changed that period to 3 years in the case of a simple transfer, or 5 years in the case of transfer to an irrevocable trust. Simply stated, Medicaid has the right to determine if an applicant transferred assets during the three years previous to the date of applying for and receiving Medicaid assistance. If, in fact, the applicant has transferred assets within that three year period, Medicaid will not allow the applicant Nursing Home assistance. Also, if assets were not disclosed or were transferred during that period, Medicaid has the right to recover the full market value of those assets. *(Once again, remember that these rules change for those who participate in the various Partnership Programs.)* This is not a "gray area". The rules are very strict and very clear. Medicaid was designed to help the poor. Divesting oneself of assets, or hiding assets to give the appearance of being poor, and hence qualifying for Medicaid, is against the law. Providing advice to people in order to illegally qualify for Medicaid can result in a $10,000 fine and one year in jail.

# CHAPTER 25

# WHERE TO GO...

## TO FIND ADDITIONAL INFORMATION ON ELDER AND LTC ISSUES

## THINK TANKS FOR SENIOR ISSUES and PUBLIC POLICY ISSUES

**Cato Institute**
1000 Massachusetts Avenue, N.W.
Washington, DC  20001-5403
202-842-0200
www.cato.org

**Center for Long-Term Care Financing**
2212 Queen Anne Avenue North #110
Seattle, WA  98109
206-283-7036
www.centerltc.org

**Concord Coalition**
1819 H Street, N.W. Suite 800
Washington, DC 20006
202-467-6222
www.concordcoalition.org

**Family Caregiver Alliance**
690 Market Street, Suite 600
San Francisco, CA  94104
www.caregiver.org

**Gerontological Society of America**
1030 15th St. N.W., Suite 250
Washington, DC  20005
202-842-1275
www.geron.org

**Heritage Foundation**
214 Massachusetts Ave NE
Washington, DC  20002-4999
202-546-4400
www.heritage.org

**National Academy on an Aging Society**
1030 15ᵗʰ Street, N.W., Suite 250
Washington, DC  20005
202-842-1150
www.agingsociety.org

**National Council of Women's Organizations**
733 15th Street, NW Suite 1011
Washington, DC  20005
202-393-7122
www.womensorganizations.org

**National Older Women's League (OWL)**
1750 New York Ave., NW  Suite 350
Washington, DC 20006
1-800-825-3695
www.owl-national.org

**Senior Citizen's League**
909 N. Washington St., #300
Alexandria, VA  22314
1-800-333-8725
www.tscl.org

**The Brookings Institution**
1775 Massachusetts Ave NW
Washington, DC, 20036
202-797-6000
www.brookings.edu

# ORGANIZATIONS

**AARP formerly American Association of Retired Persons**
601 E. Street, N.W.
Washington, DC 20049
**202-434-6480**
www.aarp.org

**Alzheimer's Association**
225 No. Michigan Ave.  17ᵗʰ Floor
Chicago, IL 60601-7633
1-800-272-3900
www.alz.org

**American Association of Homes and Services for the Aging**
2519 Connecticut Ave., NW
Washington, DC  20008
202-783-2242
www.aahsa.org

**American Health Care Association**
1201 L Street, N.W.
Washington, DC 20005
202-842-3860
www.ahca.org

**American Hospital Association—Aging and Long Term**
Care Services Division
1 North Franklin
Chicago, IL 60606
312-422-3302
www.aha.org

**American Society on Aging**
833 Market Street, Suite 511
San Francisco, CA 94103
415-974-9600
www.asaging.org

**Assisted Living Federation of America**
11200 Waples Mill Rd., Suite 150
Fairfax, VA 22030
703-691-8100
www.alfa.org

**Association of Jewish Aging Services**
316 Pennsylvania Ave SE, Suite 40
Washington, DC 20003
202-543-7500
www.ajas@ajas.org

**Center for Medicare Education**
2519 Connecticut Ave. NW
Washington, DC 20008-1520
202-508-1210
www.medicareed.org

**Elder Angels**
P.O. Box 882
Pacifica, CA 94044-0882
415-284-1160
www.elderangels.com

**ElderWeb**
1305 Chadwick Drive
Normal. IL 61761
309-451-3319
www.elderweb.com

**Centers for Medicare and Medicaid Services (formerly—Health Care Financing Administration)**
7500 Security Boulevard
Baltimore, MD 21244-1850
Medicare Hotline
1-800-638-6833
www.medicare.gov

**Health Insurance Association of America**
1201 F Street, N.W, Suite 500
Washington, DC 20004-1204
202-824-1600
www.hiaa.org

**Medicare Rights Center**
1460 Broadway, 11th Floor
New York, NY 10036-7393
1-800-333-4114
www.medicarerights.org

**National Adult Day Services Association**
8201 Greensboro Drive, Suite 300
McLean, VA 22102
866-890-7357
www.nadsa.org

**National Association for Home Care and Hospice**
228 Seventh Street, S.E.
Washington, DC 20003
202-547-7424
www.nahc.org

**National Association of Insurance Commissioners**
2301 McGee Street, Suite 800
Kansas City, MO 64108-8175
816-783-8175
www.naic.org

**National Center on Elder Abuse**
1201 15th Street, N.W., Suite 350
Washington, D.D. 2005-2800
202-898-2586
www.elderabusecenter.org

**National Consumers League**
1701 K Street, N.W. #1200
Washington, DC 20006
202-835-3323
www.nclnet.org

**National Council on The Aging**
300 D Street, SW  Suite 801
Washington, DC 20024
1-800-424-9046
www.ncoa.org

**National Council of Women's Organizations**
733 15th St. NW, Suite 1011
Washington, DC  20005
202-393-7122
www.womensorganizations.org

**National Hospice and Palliative Organization**
1700 Diagonal Road  Suite 625
Alexandria, VA  22314
1-800-658-8898
www.nhpco.org

**National Reverse Mortgage Lenders Association**
1625 Massachusetts Ave., NW, Suite 601
Washington, DC 20036-2244
1-866-264-4466
www.reversemortgage.org

**The Catholic Health Association of the United States**
1875 Eye Street, NW, Suite 1000
Washington, DC  20006-5409
202-296-3993
www.chausa.org

# PUBLICATIONS

**"Guarding Your Gold II"**
Ronald J. Iverson
PO Box 4459
Helena, Mt. 59604
1-406-442-4016
www.guardingyourgold.com

**"A Shopper's Guide to Long-Term Care Insurance"**
National Association of Insurance Commissioners
120 W. 12th Street, Suite 1100
Kansas City, MO  64105-1925
816-842-3600

**"Long Term Care Planning: A Dollar and Sense Guide"**
The National Council on Aging
300 D Street, SW  Suite 801
Washington, DC  20024
202-479-1200

Chapter 25

**"Medicare and You—2003"**
Centers for Medicare and Medicaid Services
7500 Security Boulevard
Baltimore, Maryland 21244-1850
**1-800-633-4227**

## *STATE PARTNERSHIP PROGRAMS*

**California** Partnership for Long-Term Care
Consumer Information: 1-800-434-0222

**Indiana** Long-Term-Care Program
Senior Health Insurance Information Program (SHIIP)
1-800-452-4800

**New York** State Partnership for Long-Term Care
1-888-NYS-PLTC

State of **Connecticut's** Partnership Program
1-800-547-3443

## WEBSITES of related interest

www.guardingyourgold.com

e-mail: RonIverson@guardingyourgold.com

www.longtermcareprovider.com

www.medicare.gov

www.hhs.gov

*www.census.gov*

# INDEX

**(Definitions of LTC and LTCI are not included here. See Definitions of LTC...)**